"Do You Have a Band?"

"DO YOU HAVE A BAND?"

Poetry and Punk Rock in New York City

DANIEL KANE

COLUMBIA UNIVERSITY PRESS *NEW YORK*

Columbia University Press
Publishers Since 1893
New York Chichester, West Sussex
cup.columbia.edu
Copyright © 2017 Columbia University Press
All rights reserved
Library of Congress Cataloging-in-Publication Data
Names: Kane, Daniel, 1968– author.
Title: "Do you have a band?" : poetry and punk rock in New York City / Daniel Kane.
Description: New York : Columbia University Press, [2017] | Includes bibliographical references and index.
Identifiers: LCCN 2016056217 (print) | LCCN 2017021090 (ebook) | ISBN 9780231544603 (e-book) | ISBN 9780231162968 (cloth : alk. paper) | ISBN 9780231162975 (pbk. : alk. paper)
Subjects: LCSH: American poetry—New York (State)—New York—History and criticism. | American poetry—20th century—History and criticism. | Punk rock music—New York (State)—New York—History—20th century. | Punk culture—New York (State)—New York—History—20th century. | New York (N.Y.)—Intellectual life—20th century.
Classification: LCC PS255.N5 (ebook) | LCC PS255.N5 K363 2017 (print) | DDC 811/.540997471—dc23
LC record available at https://lccn.loc.gov/2016056217

Columbia University Press books are printed on permanent and durable acid-free paper.
Printed in the United States of America

Cover design by Julia Kushnirsky
Cover photograph © Roberta Bayley

For Jenny and Bramble

Contents

CONTENTS

Acknowledgments

I am grateful for the many conversations about poetry and punk I've had over the years with friends, family, musicians, poets, and scholars. Thanks are owed to Marina Araujo, James Birmingham, Lee Ann Brown, Lynne Cahill, Howard Cunnell, Anne Dewey, Maggie Dubris, Richard Elliott, Andrew Epstein, Thomas Evans, Peter Gizzi, Doug Haynes, Richard Hell, Lisa Jarnot, Michael Jonik, Gillian Kane, Daniel Katz, Sam Ladkin, Jenny Lund, Pejk Malinovski, Peter Middleton, Thurston Moore, Patricia Morrisroe, Eileen Myles, Elinor Nauen, Peter "The King" Nicholls, Cyrus Patell, Lee Ranaldo, Libbie Rifkin, Jody Rosen, Sasha Kane Rosen, Philip Shaw, Linda Steinman, Michael Szalay, Marvin Taylor, Anne Waldman, Luke Walker, Bryan Waterman, and Lewis Warsh. Diarmuid Hester introduced me to the poetry of Dennis Cooper and taught me about the centrality of Cooper's role in mediating between punk and poetry, popular culture and the avant-garde—my section on Cooper's work owes much to the conversations Diarmuid and I had. A chance to serve as visiting associate professor in the Department of English, New York University, proved a great opportunity to work with the graduate research students Kimberly Adams, Andrew Gorin, David Hobbs, Luke McMullan, and Bérengère Riou. All five proved challenging and inspiring readers and thinkers whose insights helped me shape this book.

I would especially like to thank Lytle Shaw and Simon Warner, who were generous and critical readers of an earlier version of this manuscript.

Similarly, the attention to detail and terrific suggestions for redrafting from my editor, Philip Leventhal, are deeply appreciated.

Many thanks to those of you who gave me permission to quote from or reproduce your poetry, your music, your images, and your correspondence: Bruce Andrews, Roberta Bayley, Bill Berkson, Brigid Berlin, Michael Brownstein, Rhys Chatham, Stephanie Chernikowski, Dennis Cooper, Maggie Dubris, Raymond Foye, John Giorno, Richard Hell, Nathan Kernan, Samara Kupferberg, Gerard Malanga, Bernadette Mayer, Eileen Myles, Elinor Nauen, Alice Notley, Ron Padgett, Jon Savage, Robert Sharrard, John Sinclair, Stacy Szymaszek, Anne Waldman, and Lewis Warsh. I would also like to thank Professor Philip Davies and his team at the Eccles Centre for American Studies at the British Library for awarding me an Eccles Centre Visiting Fellowship in North American Studies, 2012, which helped fund a vital period of research leave. Additional thanks to the School of English at the University of Sussex for its financial support and research-leave scheme and to my colleagues in the Sussex Centre for American Studies for helping create a rich interdisciplinary environment conducive to friendly talk about punk and poetry.

Draft versions of some parts of this book were delivered as talks, and I benefited from feedback received at the University of Kent, the Université Libre de Bruxelles, the University of Nottingham, the University of East Anglia, the University of Greenwich, Cambridge University, Oxford University, and the University of California, Irvine. Thanks to Claire Hurley, Jack Davies, Oliver Harris, Franca Bellarsi, Matthew Pethers, Nick Selby, Jeremy Noel-Tod, Emily Critchley, Fiona Green, Ron Bush, Alexandra Manglis, and Virginia Jackson for making these events possible.

Thanks are owed to librarians who helped me access archival materials: Marvin Taylor and his team at Fales Library and Special Collections, New York University; Mary M. O'Brien, reference archivist, and Sean Molinaro, Syracuse University Archives; Kathleen Dow, archives unit and curator, Special Collections Library, University of Michigan; the staff at the Berg Collection, New York Public Library; and Mary Ellen Budney, Beinecke Rare Book and Manuscript Library, Yale University.

Elements of the introduction and parts of chapter 3 appeared previously in different form as "Angel Hair Magazine, the Second-Generation New York School, and the Poetics of Sociability," *Contemporary Literature* 45, no. 2

(2004): 331–367, copyright © 2004 University of Wisconsin Press; and in *Don't Ever Get Famous: Essays on New York Writing After the New York School*, ed. Daniel Kane (Champaign, Ill.: Dalkey Archive, 2006), 90–129, copyright © 2006 Dalkey Archive Press. Chapter 4 is a revised and extended version of "Richard Hell, Genesis: Grasp, and the Blank Generation: From Poetry to Punk in New York's Lower East Side," *Contemporary Literature* 52, no. 2 (2011): 330–369, copyright © 2011 University of Wisconsin Press. Shorter versions of chapter 5 appeared previously as "'Nor Did I Socialise with Their People': Patti Smith, Rock Heroics, and the Poetics of Sociability," *Popular Music* 31, no. 1 (2012): 105–123, copyright © 2012 Cambridge University Press; and as "I Just Got Different Theories: Patti Smith and the Poetry Project at St. Mark's Church," in *Among Friends: Engendering the Social Site of Poetry*, ed. Anne Dewey and Libby Rifkin (Iowa City: Iowa University Press, 2013), 43–64, copyright © 2013 Iowa University Press.

"Wilson '57" is used by permission from *Collected Poems* (Coffee House Press, 2013). Copyright © 2013 by Ron Padgett.

Selections from "Bean Spasms" and "People Who Died" are used by permission from *The Collected Poems of Ted Berrigan*, by Ted Berrigan, edited by Alice Notley. Copyright © 2013 by the Regents of the University of California.

Selections from "Ave Maria" and "The Day Lady Died" reprinted by permission of City Lights Books. Copyright © 1964 by Frank O'Hara.

Selections from "Why I Am Not a Painter" and "At the Old Place" from *The Collected Poems of Frank O'Hara by Frank O'Hara*, copyright © 1971 by Maureen Granville-Smith, administratrix of the estate of Frank O'Hara, copyright renewed 1999 by Maureen O'Hara Granville-Smith and Donald Allen. Used by permission of Alfred A. Knopf, an imprint of the Knopf Doubleday Publishing Group, a division of Penguin Random House LLC. All rights reserved. Any third-party use of this material, outside of this publication, is prohibited. Interested parties must apply directly to Penguin Random House LLC for permission.

Selections from "The Destruction of America" are from *This Is Our Music* (Detroit: Artists Workshop Press, 1965). Copyright © 1965, 2017 by John Sinclair. All rights reserved.

Selections from "Geography" are from *Strange Days Ahead* (Calais, Vt.: Z Press, 1975). Copyright © 1975, 2017 by Michael Brownstein. All rights reserved.

Selections from "I'm Tired of Being Scared," "Pornographic Poem," and "Grasping at Emptiness" are copyright © John Giorno. All rights reserved.

Selections from "On the Death of Robert Lowell" and "Exploding the Spring Mystique" are used by permission from Eileen Myles. Copyright © Eileen Myles. All rights reserved.

"Do You Have a Band?"

Introduction

IT IS NOW commonplace for music fans and critics to claim that figures such as Lou Reed, Richard Hell, and Patti Smith were "poetic" in their approach to making music, writing lyrics, and developing a punk style.[1] Through close and intertextual readings across poetry, song lyrics, and music, *Do You Have a Band?* reveals what "poetic" actually means in the context of punk rock in New York City. This involves complicating the now-familiar story of the Rimbaud-enchanted and Beat Generation–infatuated rocker. New York punk was to some extent "infected by a Rimbaldian script: live fast, disorder your senses, flame brightly before self-immolation," as Jon Savage put it.[2] *Do You Have a Band?* does not deny that there are resonances between the band Television and French symbolism, the rhetoric of punk rock and Situationist International slogans.[3] But what about the work of the poets who actually shared New York City's Lower East Side streets, mimeographed pages, and stages with the pioneering figures of punk? How did downtown writing and poetics of the 1960s and 1970s make their way into rockers' music and approach to art? Musicians in bands from Ed Sanders and Tuli Kupferberg's Fugs through the Jim Carroll Band were as influenced by and productively critical of the writers living all around them as they were by and of authors from the distant and not-so-distant past.

I focus particularly on the direct and dynamic interactions that musicians had with the poets and poetics of the New York School—from Frank O'Hara to second- and third-generation New York School writers including Anne

Waldman, Ted Berrigan, and Eileen Myles. Not all punks who were in New York were in complete thrall to the myths that had developed around monumental poems such as Rimbaud's *Une saison en enfer* or Allen Ginsberg's "Howl," nor were they entirely swayed by the idea that the production of poetry was the preserve of the visionary romantic soul. The New York School encouraged figures as various as Hell and Smith to revise inherited ideas about the role and function of poetry. This is not to say that exchanges between downtown musicians and writers were always blissfully utopian. In fact, as I show throughout this book, musicians were often as much annoyed as they were swayed by the poetry and poetics of the New York schools.

This complex set of interactions between contemporary writing and music was hugely constructive. By reinstating and analyzing the details of mostly obscured relations between poetic and musical contemporaries, *Do You Have a Band?* defines the significance of poetry—as literature, as lifestyle—for a groundbreaking group of proto-punk and punk musicians. While establishing the ways in which so much major music from the mid-1960s to the early 1980s drew on poetry, *Do You Have a Band?* correspondingly reveals how writers such as Myles, John Giorno, and Dennis Cooper turned to punk to develop fresh ideas for their own poetics and related performance styles. This approach offers new ways to think about a range of poets whose debts to punk music have proved consistently generative and fascinating.

"I Could Be a Good Writer If I Work and Work . . ."

Now celebrated as proto-punk and punk-rock archetypes, Ed Sanders, Lou Reed, Patti Smith, and Richard Hell moved to New York City initially to live the life of poets.[4] At New York University to study rocket science and classics, Sanders admitted that "tugging at me . . . was the lure of poetry."[5] Importantly, though, "poetry" for Sanders was a form one saw and heard in the sort of place that sounds more like a rock 'n' roll club than a drawing room or library. "The poetry at the time was what was happening on Mac-Dougall and Bleecker Streets at the little beatnik cafes. The concept of actually reading poetry aloud amidst a milieu of drinking and smoking and having fun. So that won out, over the Mercury Program."[6] Sanders soon became a major player in the Lower East Side poetry scene, publishing the notorious *Fuck You: A Magazine of the Arts*, which included texts as various as stolen manuscripts by W. H. Auden and Ezra Pound, poems and sketches by Amiri Baraka and William Burroughs, and announcements for suck-ins, smoke-ins, and fuck-ins.

In a letter Lou Reed wrote to the late-modernist writer Delmore Schwartz (Reed's former professor and mentor at Syracuse University, whom Reed practically worshipped),[7] Reed framed his early work with the Velvet Underground as merely a way to build up a nest egg so he could get down to the serious business of being a writer. "I could be a good writer if I work and work," Reed explained, adding, "Hope my latest record's a smash because I'll be needing the money to be sure."[8] Reed never forsook the mantle of poet, reading and featuring in mainstream and "underground" magazines including the *Paris Review*, the *Coldspring Review*, and *Unmuzzled Ox* throughout his career. After leaving the Velvet Underground, Reed read his lyrics at the Poetry Project (a downtown reading series, still going strong, on Second Avenue between Tenth and Eleventh streets), announcing in 1971 that he was retiring from music to devote himself full time to the life of the poet.

Figure I.1 From left to right: Dennis Cooper, Mike DeCapite, Lee Ann Brown, Eileen Myles, Richard Hell, Amanda Uprichard. Poets Banquet, St. Mark's Church, 1988.
Source: Copyright © Richard Hell.

From his perch in Manhattan's East Village during the late 1960s and early 1970s, a teenaged Hell published a magazine he christened *Genesis: Grasp*, for which he solicited (and sometimes rejected) work from poets including Bruce Andrews and Allen Ginsberg, Clark Coolidge and Andrew Wylie. Hell ended up coordinating Monday-night readings for the Poetry Project and editing the magazine and imprint *CUZ* in the 1980s. All the poets Hell loved and published wanted the punks in the parish hall: "We're planning to have a benefit on Tuesday, June 7th, with a group of musicians, poets and poet/musicians who've been involved with the Poetry Project, and possibly some who've not been," the poet Bernadette Mayer wrote to Hell in February 1983, adding, "I'm not sure who'll be appearing yet, but we're inviting you & Jim Carroll, Lou Reed, and many others. I wrote to Patti Smith, thinking it worth a try, but she's remained incommunicado."[9]

And as many of her dedicated fans already know, the Poetry Project was the site for Patti Smith's first public performance with Lenny Kaye on February 10, 1971—Anne Waldman, then director of the Poetry Project, introduced her.[10] Reminiscing about the Poetry Project at St. Mark's Church, Victor Bockris effused, "In those days [the early 1970s] the St Mark's Poetry Project was on a par with Warhol's Factory, Mickey Ruskin's Max's Kansas City and the Gotham Book Mart as a bastion of the influential underground art movements that were the emotional engines of New York."[11] The lure of St. Mark's for Smith (and Sanders, Reed, and Hell, among many others) was based, in large part, on its prominence as an irreverent countercultural social space. At the "Project," as the St. Mark's scene was known to its habitués, attendees had the opportunity to participate in John Giorno's poetry bacchanals, dipping their cups into LSD punch or lighting up one of the hundreds of joints Giorno provided as they negotiated their way through flashing strobe lights and fog machines. They could witness the poet Ted Berrigan read from his sonnets about how he "Fucked til 7 now she's late to work and I'm / 18 so why are my hands shaking I should know better,"[12] then join Ted after the reading for smokes, Pepsi, and pills. They could check out the writer Eileen Myles sneering, "'Tweet,' another fucking bird,"[13] and laugh familiarly and sympathetically at Myles's laying waste to the clichés attendant to poetry, the pastoral, and the pretty.

The old boundary lines between avant-garde art and commercial fluff, sung lyrics and lyric poetry, and club music and concert-hall music were all being merrily redrawn and at times erased entirely. As the downtown musician Peter Gordon understood it, by the mid-1970s

> punk rock was in the nascent stages, and was literally just around the corner, at CBGBs and other clubs. The punk aesthetic (not unrelated to minimalism) extended to the visual artists and writers, as well as composers. I took Rhys Chatham to see The Ramones in 1976, and he never looked back. . . . Talking Heads first appeared as a trio at St. Mark's Church Parish Hall. . . . Rhys Chatham and Glenn Branca began writing ringing guitar pieces, with their influence extending to Sonic Youth.[14]

Members of Sonic Youth were well aware of the legacy bestowed upon them by the minimalist performance-artist pop-poet punk composers. Thurston Moore recalls

> hearing about Vito Acconci, doing his performative pieces in New York like *Seed Bed* where he would lie in a construct under the floor of a gallery masturbating . . . there was something very sort of punk rock about that! He was considered to be this really heroic figure among people like Glenn Branca. The first place that Sonic Youth started rehearsing was in Vito Acconci's studio in Brooklyn, and only because the young woman he was involved with was our keyboard player, this woman Anne DeMarinis . . . our connection to people like Barbara Barg, Susie Timmons, that's all there. . . . Richard Edson, the first drummer on our first record, was doing Poetry Project stuff. . . . He's published in some of the early mimeos, and we knew about it, and I thought, "that's cool."[15]

"Hip Hip Hustle in New York City"

Musicians and composers went to CBGB, took writing workshops at the Poetry Project, and, as the following excerpt from a poem by Rhys Chatham reveals, authored verse in downtown magazines like *Ear* in part to report on the scene:

> either hustle to like or don't
> New York City hustle to,

either hustle New York City hustle too,
New York City to hustle city too too either,
—the people try to make it—
* big music business *
hate hypocritical sincerity,
people on display, New York City hustle, don't . . .
either hustle to live or don't eat,
oh ho so, 3 flowers grow, big music business . . .
* hip hustle him *
him hip hip hustle in New York City[16]

Chatham's poem, serving in part to chronicle the historical moment that Peter Gordon describes, when classically trained musicians, poets, artists, and punks mingled and tried to make a buck in an increasingly desperate and practically bankrupt city, is one of many curios that seem mostly overlooked in the accounts of the period. This is despite the fact that much of what we hold so dear in poetry and punk from the 1960s on owes a debt to models first hashed out on Manhattan's streets and in its clubs, poetry performance spaces, mimeographed magazines, and community newspapers. As Victor Bockris speculated, "It's enough to make one wonder if a rock poetry magazine might have been as influential as *Punk* magazine."[17]

While not a "rock poetry magazine," this book does aim for the focus Bockris suggests. Take Max's Kansas City, a nightclub on Park Avenue South run by Mickey Ruskin. Before opening Max's, Ruskin owned a number of East Village coffee shops, including the Tenth Street Coffeehouse and Les Deux Mégots, which featured poetry readings. Ruskin approached Joel Oppenheimer, one of the poets who performed often at Les Deux Mégots (and who in 1966 was appointed as the first director of the Poetry Project), for ideas about what to name his new venture. Oppenheimer "suggested the Kansas City part because of the general feeling that it would sound more authentic for a place featuring steaks; Max's was either borrowed from the poet Max Finstein or, more probably, added simply because it sounded like a reliable restaurant proprietor's name."[18] Oppenheimer also came up with the slogan "chickpeas, steaks, lobster," which Ruskin included on the restaurant's sign. Max's ended up featuring many of the most iconic proto-punk and punk bands on its stages and served as a home away from home for Andy Warhol's Factory habitués. As eclectic as the Max's crowd was, though, practically all of them took on the poet mantle: "It's all really gone now," Lou Reed mourned in his reminiscences of Max's, "The laser light that shone from the back room with all its red tables. The chickpeas. The bad steak and horrible salad. Warhol, the superstars, the rock-groups-to-be and not-to-be. The poets (and almost everyone was thought to be), the painters—in the front at the bar—and, toward the end, the upstairs where entertainment of a more formal nature resided."[19]

Max's served as a particularly lively model for the hybrid poetry/music scene that was to emerge over the course of the 1970s. CBGB is another example. Located on the Bowery between Bleecker and Second Streets just down the street from the Poetry Project, CBGB, as all punk aficionados know, was home to bands including Television, the Talking Heads, and the Ramones. What is perhaps not so well known is that CBGB also took a cue from the Poetry Project—following the Poetry Project tradition of reserving Wednesday nights for readings by relatively well-known national and international avant-garde poets, CBGB initiated its own regular Wednesday-night poetry readings. By the mid-1970s, "CB's crackled with electricity. . . . A whole bohemian genealogy now materialized on the Bowery like ghosts inhabiting descendants' homes: Ginsberg and Burroughs could be seen at tables near the stage. Lou Reed now regularly hung out. 'All those types of people,' one regular would recall . . . 'lent an underground poet-beat sort of feeling to [CBGB].'"[20]

This poetry-inflected punk scene was, at least from the mid-1960s through the mid-1970s, demonstrably different from any other arts community in the United States at the time. It was not until the late 1970s and early 1980s that West Coast bands amenable to spoken-word poetry, such as Black Flag, emerged, and even then these bands generally put up a brash front. As Kaya Oakes put it in her discussion of West Coast indie bands like the Minutemen and Black Flag, "In contrast to LA's gritty, working-class, get-in-the-van style of punk, many East Coast indie bands played an artier, brainier sort of music."[21] West Coast poetry/punk recordings like Harvey Kubernik's *English as a Second Language* (1983) and *Neighborhood Rhythms* (1984) had New York–based John Giorno's *Dial-a-Poem* recordings from the 1960s and '70s as precursors.[22] Yes, there were obviously important music/literary hybrids taking place in the 1970s and 1980s in places like Los Angeles, San Francisco,[23] Cleveland, and, of course, the United Kingdom.[24] Yet much of it was indebted to earlier models hashed out on the Lower East Side. This dynamic certainly had its effect among West Coast–based poets such as Dennis Cooper, who couldn't wait to get out of LA and go to New York so he could be closer to his New York School heroes. Cooper "distinguished himself by . . . championing (and often publishing) writers associated with the 'New York School': Joe Brainard, Tim Dlugos, Peter Schjeldahl, Donald Britten, Brad Gooch, and others" when he was still living in Los Angeles and editing his magazine *Little Caesar*. Cooper "was vitriolic in his description of the Los Angeles poetry milieu in general: 'A small-minded, lax, windbag poetry scene.'"[25] Cooper soon moved to New York's Lower East Side, where he lived for a number of years and became part of the "hip hip" scene almost immediately.[26]

"Underground Autonomous Zones"

The writers and musicians considered throughout this book went far in terms of negotiating the spaces between the underground and the purported mainstream. Poets of the 1960s and '70s valued and romanticized an underground economy based in part on decentralized production and distribution. Recalling the mimeograph revolution that found writers including Amiri Baraka, Diane di Prima, and Ed Sanders publishing their and their friends' work in any number of cheaply produced, hand-stapled journals, Anne Waldman (herself an editor of a number of mimeos, including *The World*, a journal attached to the Poetry Project) enthused, "We were already drawn to underground 'autonomous zones,' tender beauties of small press production."[27] Waldman highlights the "modest" production values of the magazine and points more generally to values attendant to the mimeograph revolution, such as autonomy, low cost, marginalization in the underground, and independence from the constraints of the traditional publishing and bookstore industries. Comments like Waldman's suggest the poetry scene at the time was at least attempting to inscribe itself as a self-consciously avant-garde project, a quasi-Marxist utopia where the cultural workers were in control of the forms of production.[28]

Thus, any number of poets not willing to wait around to be published by the likes of the *Kenyon Review* or the *New Yorker* simply started their own presses using cheap and widely available mimeograph and tabletop offset-printing machines. Mailing lists of friends, friends of friends, and favored artists made up these poets' audiences, supplemented by the multitude of poetry performances taking place in coffee shops such as Les Deux Mégots, Le Metro, and the Poetry Project at St. Mark's Church. Describing his mimeo magazine, *C*, and his efforts to publish the poets John Ashbery, Kenneth Koch, James Schuyler, and Kenneth Koch in it, Ted Berrigan explained:

> There were these four people, and when I first came to New York . . . from Oklahoma . . . I was very interested in these four people. . . . There weren't many people that were interested in those four people. . . . So I got very interested in them. They seemed to me to open up a lot of possibilities. Then someone asked me if I wanted to edit a magazine. So I said, "Sure!" My plan for that magazine was to publish these four people in conjunction with four or five younger people, myself and people that I knew. . . . And I put them in, too. And then I realized that there was such a thing as New York School, because there was a second generation.[29]

The forms of distribution for New York's proto-punk culture mirrored Berrigan's do-it-yourself publishing schemes. Patti Smith's version of Jimi Hendrix's "Hey Joe" and her performance poem "Piss Factory" were first released as a single in 1974 by Mer Records, an independent label set up by Smith and her friend the photographer Robert Mapplethorpe. Distribution, such as it was, was predicated on a network of sympathetic record stores contacted directly by Smith and her peers, then supplemented by word of mouth and sales of the single at shows. Richard Hell's punk anthem "Blank Generation" alongside his "Another World" and "You Gotta Lose" were released as a single in 1976 on Ork Records. Ork Records, run by Television's manager Terry Ork, committed itself, like Mer Records did, to a localized network of musicians, friends, and fans for funding and distribution. Independent record stores like Bleecker Bob's and Colony Records became the new go-to places for the latest manifestation of New York's avant-garde. The writer Colin Murray fondly recalls:

> Behind that counter [at Colony Records] in the back they had pinned to the wall lots of picture sleeve 45s and mixed in with a bunch of crud was a growing number of records that you simply *didn't find* in any other record store that you knew about. You were like, "What *is* that stuff? Are those real records?" You'd squint at them across the counter and try to figure out what the deal was. "Ork Records?" What the heck was that?[30]

Participating in a self-styled "underground" for both poets and musicians did not preclude involvement in the mainstream publishing and recording industries, though. In 1969 and 1970, for example, Harper and Row published the poets Tom Clark, Clark Coolidge, Dick Gallup, and Lewis MacAdams. But this was in no way a harbinger of the downtown scene's being folded discreetly and safely into a publishing industry divorced from the intimate ties to locality and community so important to the New York poets. Ron Padgett, accustomed at the time to being published in mimeograph magazines, removed a manuscript accepted by Harper and Row because he was not pleased with the terms of the contract on offer, and Coolidge, Clark, Gallup, and MacAdams adhered merrily to their original values of small-scale publication by continuing to release work through the tiny imprints they and their friends had set up.

For musicians, it was perhaps a bit trickier to administer the boundaries between mainstream culture and the underground. Lenny Kaye, guitarist for the Patti Smith Group, anticipated the paradox of antiestablishment performers simultaneously blurring the boundaries between poetry and pop and signing on to major labels by insisting on the music's ability to transcend traditional binaries.

> Rock could be Art (as opposed to "craft"), but that didn't mean it had to take on the trappings of moral responsibility. Actually, quite the opposite was true. Art-rat: the more contradictions the better. . . . The bands weren't really alike. There was a self-awareness to their work that spoke of some knowledge of conceptual art—these weren't culturati babes-in-the-woods, despite Johnny's and Joey's and Dee Dee's and Tommy's matching leather jackets. Tom Verlaine once said that each grouping was like a separate idea, inhabiting their own world and reference points.[31]

The story of Seymour Stein's Sire Records label illustrates punk's shifting place within the spectrum of privileged art form and mass culture and, correspondingly, punk's negotiation of "independent" and major labels. Stein signed the Ramones to his fledgling label, and their debut album became a critical success if not an all-out commercial smash. When Warner Records approached Stein for a distribution deal, Stein ensured that his roster of bands—including the Ramones, Talking Heads, and others—retained a great deal of creative control over what they produced. What followed was the unlikely scenario of some challenging records gaining mass-market circulation. The year 1977 alone saw albums including the Talking Heads' '77, Richard Hell and the Voidoids' *Blank Generation*, the Ramones' *Rocket to Russia*, the Dead Boys' *Young Loud and Snotty*, and a reissued seven-inch single of Patti Smith's performance poem "Piss Factory" and "Hey Joe" released to the public. That songs like the Dead Boys' "Caught with the Meat in Your Mouth" and the Ramones' "Cretin Hop" and "Teenage Lobotomy" were distributed suggests Stein was committed to disseminating an aggressive and, at the time, relatively "obscene" music to middle America. Combined with that effort to push the boundaries of taste was the promotion of the quirky, spare, and self-consciously "arty" music and poetry typical of Patti Smith, the Talking Heads, and their ilk. Stein was essentially staging a three-pronged attack using relatively foul content (Ramones, Dead Boys), outré sounds (Talking Heads), and texts that threatened the generic boundaries dividing poetry from music (Patti Smith) to intervene in an increasingly AOR-oriented, soft-rock, pop-music culture.

Again, just because corporations were distributing some of the new sounds, this did not automatically translate into punks "selling out." In a 1978 *Billboard* article Roman Kozak suggested that, far from being domesticated, punk bands actually altered the function and power of the major labels. Pointing out that "just about every record company now has its new wave band," Kozak nevertheless insisted: "Let it be said right from the beginning that punk rock is not a plot by the record companies to foist shoddily recorded, inept and crude rock 'n' roll upon an unsuspecting public. The kids are doing it all by themselves. Slowly, surely and inexorably punk rock . . . is growing like a disease."[32] Stein insisted that the new sounds were going to alter the industry, not the other way around. "With greater exposure will come acceptance of the new wave for what it truly is, a renewal of the freshness, audience involvement and awareness of roots that have always been among rock 'n' roll's greatest virtues."[33]

While the DIY spirit among the first wave of New York punks and second and third waves of New York School poets was certainly part of the culture, it was never an orthodoxy as it would prove to be for more politically oriented punks like the Minutemen (on the independent SST Records label) or the Washington, D.C.–based Fugazi in the 1980s and '90s (on the independent Dischord Records label). Downtown poets and punks were in this sense more in tune with certain strands of the historical avant-garde than was the case for righteous 1980s and '90s punks outside New York, who thought nothing of bringing charges of apostasy on any musician daring to breach the independent-commercial divide.[34] The French poet Guillaume Apollinaire—translated by the Poetry Project habitué Ron Padgett and referred to regularly by the downtown set[35]—"declared that poetic activity could indeed be pursued in more overtly commercial and industrial realms."[36] Apollinaire, as Carrie Noland reminds us, showed future writers how to move beyond the page.

> Apollinaire openly encouraged poets to abandon the page in favour of modern transmission technologies. . . . Apollinaire had good reason to feel that the future of poetry lay increasingly in its collaboration with other arts and other domains. He zealously envisioned a new wing of the avant-garde prepared to realize hybrid poetic forms "unimaginable until now."[37]

Using commercial recording technologies and distribution systems for their own ends, New York poets and musicians developed hybrid poetic forms in the 1960s that would in turn inform punk rock. The sung (and hilarious) version of Allen Ginsberg's "Howl" by the Fugs and the spectacular poetry events that Giorno arranged are just two examples of poets looking to mass-media forms and distribution networks to realize their genre-defying works. Giorno, the Fugs, and other artists showed that being commodified, particularly if such commodification involved the electronic transmission of their work to new audiences, would enable poets finally to get their work read—heard and sung even—by masses of youth traditionally turned off by or uninterested in coterie-based poetry and poetics.

Simon Frith argues that lyric poetry, at least in terms of its impact after romanticism, has generally been understood "as individual expression and as private property. 'High' art was thus institutionalized by the bourgeoisie as a transcendent, asocial experience (in the contemplative bank-like setting of the gallery and the concert hall, the museum and the library)."[38] Downtown punks and poets were committed to overturning such conventions. "I am the master of no art,"[39] Ted Berrigan insisted, taking equal pleasure in canonical literature, television, pop music, and tabloid journalism. Many New York artists, directly or indirectly, took their cue from Ted and company. Recognizing that the lyric poem was no longer sanctified, Jim Carroll customized Berrigan's poem "People Who Died" into a new-wave chant. Poets including Eileen Myles and Bruce Andrews adapted the pejorative-laced lyrics and confrontational style typical of many New York–based punk bands for their own brand of poetry. Influence went gaily around and around.

These efforts marked a new avant-garde at work and play. It is also important to recall that Andreas Huyssen, following Hans Magnus Enzensberger, claimed that the avant-garde never managed "to deliver what it had always promised: to sever political, social and aesthetic chains, explode cultural reifications, throw off traditional forms of domination, liberate repressed energies."[40] The downtown writers and musicians did not necessarily finish the job the historical avant-garde began, but they certainly attempted to "explode cultural reifications" through a complex mixture of engagement with the commercial recording industry, DIY production and distribution, and a performative refusal to differentiate poetry from caterwaul. Their successes and failures on this score are analyzed throughout this book.

Romantic Punks Meet the Second-Generation New York School

One should be careful here, however, not simply to reiterate the tried and tested formula that situates punk musicians and avant-garde poets within a spectrum of cultural activity geared at eliminating the low art–high art divide.[41] It would be remiss not to acknowledge and evaluate how a number of the most relevant musicians' preconceptions about poets and poetry were, for the most part, predominantly corny. The poet, as far as Lou Reed, Patti Smith, and others were initially concerned, was a vatic individual with an all-access pass to Parnassus. Poets were not playful, collaboratively minded neo-Dadaists but rather tortured heroes to emulate, divine beings who might deign to accept you as their apprentice. Reed wrote to his mentor, Delmore Schwartz, "I . . . hope very much that you are my spiritual godfather, and i mean that quite a bit too."[42] Patti Smith proclaimed, "I'm not interested in meeting poets or a bunch of writers who I don't think are bigger than life. I'm a hero worshipper, I'm not a fame fucker, but I am a hero worshipper."[43] While Dan Graham argued that punk in the mid-1970s "sought to eliminate the notion of the rock star," proto-punk rockers like Reed and Smith in no way "concluded that the '60s 'superstar' was a media myth, whose position—and very existence—was tenuous, and that the superstar failed to realistically perceive his or her own situation."[44] In fact, poetry was to some extent a way actually to *reify* the models of stardom that later punk musicians would reject. Romanticism was by no means dead yet. "What we're moving to language-wise," Lenny Kaye told his *Punk* magazine interviewer sincerely, "is all languages then beyond language. And that place is the pre–Tower of Babel which will form the great time circle. That's it."[45]

Considering that musicians such as Reed and Smith conceived of themselves initially as poets and were determined to embody poetic genius and vision, this book explores what happened when Smith and the rest of this cohort were confronted with second-generation New York School poets such as Anne Waldman, Ted Berrigan, Bernadette Mayer, and Lewis Warsh. These writers were committed to building a performance-oriented downtown scene that actively interrogated the model of the poet as oracular tortured figure. The "first-generation" New York School poet Frank O'Hara had already set the punk stage in his mock manifesto "Personism" by stripping shamanic authority from the poet. "I don't believe in god, so I don't have to make elaborately sounded structures," O'Hara pouted cheekily. "I hate Vachel Lindsay, always have; I don't even like rhythm, assonance, all that stuff. You just go on your nerve. If someone's chasing you down the street with a knife you just run, you don't turn around and shout, 'Give it up! I was a track star for Mineola Prep.'"[46] Trotting after O'Hara, the New York School poets based at the Poetry Project worked hard to look like they weren't working too hard. Much of the poetry published in representative magazines such as *Angel Hair* and *The World* was written and published collaboratively—who cared if no one knew who wrote what line? Friends' names were dropped into poems casually, as if to mirror the ways the poets dropped by one another's apartments during a time in New York's economy when one didn't have to work all day to "make it." Once again, O'Hara was the model for this kind of approach, as we can see in his oft-anthologized poem "Why I Am Not a Painter":

> Well,
> For instance, Mike Goldberg
> is starting a painting. I drop in.
> "Sit down and have a drink" he
> says. I drink; we drink. I look
> up. "You have SARDINES in it."

"Yes, it needed something there."
"Oh." I go and the days go by
and I drop in again. The painting
is going on, and I go, and the days
go by. I drop in.[47]

Poems written by O'Hara-enchanted younger writers—such as Ron Padgett's "Bingo," which begins with the line "I suffer when I sit next to Joe Brainard's painting Bingo,"[48] or Aram Saroyan's untitled poem that asserts, in its entirety, "Ron Padgett / would approve / this idea"[49]—took O'Hara's approach and complicated it in various ways. Poems like these did not point inward toward some semblance of subjectivity and core sentiment ascribed to an individual but rather outward to an implicitly larger social grouping responsible for interpreting and assigning value to texts. They made material the fact that so much of what we respond to in poetry is based on friendship and social affinity as opposed to the depth models of insight, vision, and intensity attached by musicians such as Patti Smith to poets from Rimbaud through Allen Ginsberg. Such texts inevitably contested the very status of lyric poetry, if by "lyric poetry" we attend to the influential critic Helen Vendler's definition as "the performance of the mind in *solitary* speech" that "in its normative form . . . deliberately strips away most social specification (age, regional location, sex, class, even race)."[50]

As images and anecdotes from the mid-1960s throughout the 1980s attest and as I will illustrate further in chapter 3, the second-generation New York School poets had a kind of hipster caché that pop music before the British Invasion lacked. Waldman's elegant affect alone could serve as a synecdoche for sixties cool. Place Waldman's image alongside Warsh's mop top, leather jacket, and shades; Bernadette Mayer's hippie sensuality; and Bill Berkson's all-American good looks, and it is clear why nascent pop stars like Patti Smith would find this crew so irresistible, even if the poets' aesthetics clashed with Smith's own commitment to bard idolatry. St. Mark's stayed cool through the 1970s. Elinor Nauen remembered that on her arrival in New York in 1976 (the year that saw the first Ramones album released), she "immediately went to my first poetry reading ever, the Frank O'Hara memorial in November (at the Poetry Project . . .). I was stunned. Glamour, beauty, wit. That great big party that made poetry the most exciting thing you could possibly do."[51]

Nascent intellectuals looking to make the culture scene, Smith, Reed, and other related writers and musicians simply *had* to engage with the New York School of poets (as they would with Andy Warhol's Factory, Pop painters, and others). "I pretty well hate most of the stuff you guys do cause it seems you not only violate sound but disregard it completely," wrote a young Patti Smith to Anne Waldman, adding, crucially, "I also love you guys cause you keep poetry alive. I think it's real neat what you're doing, I just got different theories."[52] As I argue throughout this book, it is that clash that Smith alludes to between a traditional romanticism and a more playful and at times even silly New York School aesthetic that informed some of the best early New York–based punk music.

"Yeah, I Write a Lot"

Of course, many of the musicians affiliated with New York's early punk scene were not interested in *any* poetry, let alone the poetry of the New York School. There's little in the way of evidence proving that the New York Dolls, the Dictators, the Dead Boys, or the Ramones sat around reading John Ashbery poems to one another. Bill Ogersby pushes back helpfully against critics who frame punk as art, in part by reminding us that punk was steeped in pop. While "there is truth in accounts which cite bohemia and radical art as an influence on the 70s punk milieu, the role of less cerebral cultural forms must also be highlighted—specifically the suburban pop tradition that runs from 60s surf, through garage and fuzz rock, to the bubble-gum ebullience of the early 70s."[53] Though even here, it is complicated. The New York Dolls' frontman David Johansen thought of himself as a poet, as he explained in an interview with John Holmstrum in *Punk* magazine: "Yeah, I write a lot. I write every day. I write poetry, I write verse and I write short stories and stuff. I like to write. Richard Hell was gonna once print some stuff of mine but i don't know what happened."[54] And, while not affiliated with poetry per se, the Ramones were understood

> initially, at least, [by] some observers as theater. The art critic Dave Hickey wrote in the *Voice* in 1977 that as conceptual art the Ramones were "beautiful." They weren't "just a band," he wrote, but "a real good idea . . . poised with mathematical elegance on the line between pop art and popular schlock. From your aesthete's

point of view, the Ramones sound has the ruthless efficiency of a Warhol portrait."[55]

Tommy Ramone insisted in an interview with *Punk* magazine's editor John Holmstrum that the Ramones "was supposed to be an avant-garde thing, right?" While Dee Dee Ramone interjected, "Not really, no!" Tommy continued,

> Well, to them it was just a hobby to me it was an avant-garde thing. Then we started getting really good and I said "This isn't avant-garde this is commercial!" And that's when i started playing drums. When i $aw the dollar ign . . . changed the whole sound of the group into the way it is. Now—you know—hard rock.[56]

So, when I write "punk," I'm referring specifically to New York City–based proto-punk and punk rock that revealed a marked investment in the poetic avant-garde. I am also writing in sympathy with a certain segment of the original punk audience that delighted in identifying their musical heroes with their poetic counterparts. My punk is the kind of punk a kid named Duane Rossignol, from White Plains, New York, identified back in 1977.[57] Rossignol was the proud recipient of a prize awarded to him by *Bomp* magazine for submitting the best response to a prompt asking its readers to list their five top choices for inclusion in a "Punk Rock Hall of Fame." Rossignol's first two choices were Wyndham Lewis and Ezra Pound, followed by Gene Vincent, Little Walter, and Frank Zappa. Regarding Lewis, Rossignol wrote: "Real tough guy. When dying of tumor and blind, doctor asked him about his bowels; his last words were 'Mind your own business!' That's punk!" Regarding Pound, Rossignol enthused:

> You want style? Dig this description of Ez in 1912 . . . : "Futuristic poet with forked red beard, luxuriant chestnut hair, cane, an aggressive lank figure, one long blue single stone earring dangled on his jawbone. He wore a purple top hat, a green shirt, a black velvet coat, vermillion socks, openwork brilliantly tanned sandals, trousers of green billiard cloth . . . in addition to an immense flowing tie that had been handpainted by a Japanese." And that's in the daytime! Made a lot of enemies and was driven out of England. Arrested for treason by the US in 1945 and placed in asylum for 13 years. When finally released in '58, they asked him how it was. Says he, "Oi've had it tougher." That's punk![58]

My punk (and maybe Rossignol's as well) is the one that elicits the sort of skeptical or contradictory response many critics and fans have issued over the years toward music that aspires to the complexity of weird poetry or more broadly aims to connect itself in one way or another to the historical avant-garde. Examples are rife in the reception histories of New York's punk/ poetry hybrid scene. "The first mistake of Art is to assume that it's serious," proclaimed the fabled *Creem* music journalist Lester Bangs, despite his own very serious commitment to reading punk music critically and deeply.[59] Peter Laughner, the rock scribe and guitarist for the Cleveland bands Rocket from the Tombs and Pere Ubu, seemed practically embarrassed by his early music criticism: "All my papers were manic drooling about the parallels between Lou Reed's lyrics and whatever academica we were supposed to be analyzing in preparation for our passage into the halls of higher learning. 'Sweet Jane' I compared with Alexander Pope, 'Some Kinda Love' lined right up with T. S. Eliot's 'The Hollow Men.'"[60] John Holmstrum and Legs McNeil, editors of the New York–based magazine *Punk*, "preferred the straight-forward pummeling of the Ramones or the raw intensity of Richard Hell's bands to Television's more cerebral anthems: 'party punk' over 'arty punk,' in terms [James] Wolcott would later use."[61] From Greg Shaw's measured celebration of Johnny Rotten as embodying "Tom Verlaine's charismatic intensity, though without the avant-garde pretentions that put me off in so much of the New York scene"[62] to Brent DiCrescenzo's assault on Sonic Youth's 2000 album *NYC Ghosts and Flowers* as a work that "retreads the rancid corpses of beat poetry and avant-garde noise,"[63] critics writing for the music press and rock 'n' roll fans have often drawn a line between poetry and punk rock or at the very least approached such genre-bending efforts suspiciously. Not me, not in this book.

ONE

The Fugs Are Coming

IN HIS "COMPLETE HISTORY of Punk Rock and Its Development on the Lower East Side 1950–1975," the singer-songwriter Jeffrey Lewis argues that punk began when a mix of folk music, drugs, film, and poetry were incubated in the Lower East Side. Name-checking Beat Generation figures like Harry Smith, "a beatnik weirdo" who curated the influential *Anthology of American Folk Music*, Lewis cites the Holy Modal Rounders, who "began to make [folk-revival music] more anarchistic with weird voices and drug jokes." Lewis celebrates the moment in 1964 when

> the Rounders met other beatnik intellectual thugs on East Tenth Street who called themselves the Fugs. They were recorded by Harry Smith playing the punkiest songs yet to exist low-fi noisy shit about poetry sex and drugs . . . The Fugs were real poets with real topics to speak out and through the underground scene this weird music could leak out beginning the punk idea that anybody could do it without needing much musical ability to it and this new music was soon labeled "Freak Out."[1]

What makes "real poets" real in Fugsworld? "We're taking poetry, some of which is highly charged with sexual connotations," Ed Sanders, the lead singer for the Fugs, told the TV presenter David Susskind in 1967,

> and we're dropping it into modern music, into pop music, into rock and roll, into chants and religious statements, and social statements. Some of it involves

using the Blip words, the four-letter words, the seven-letter words, and the six-
teen-letter words that are banned on the airwaves, but which we can say in the
context of theater, and we actually say them on albums.[2]

As Sanders explained, this was not a case of musicians writing elliptical lyrics
that were later defined as "poetic." Rather, the Fugs were "dropping" poems
from writers as diverse as Blake, Swinburne, Auden, and Ginsberg into
their mix, creating entirely new forms of reception for texts that had traditionally been consigned to the page. Lewis's iconoclastic history, then, goes
some way in correcting the historical record, which, with some exceptions,[3]
tends to elide the Fugs both as punk precursors and as riotous cultural critics
who reconciled nineteenth- and twentieth-century poetry with rock 'n'
roll before Lou Reed, Patti Smith, or Richard Hell's own invocations of bardic
authority. The Fugs' "low fi noisy shit about poetry sex and drugs" reveals
them to be the first rock band to show how poetry and rock could work
together to promote a visibly confrontational and noisy youth-oriented
sensibility.

The Fugs formed in 1964 (just before the Velvet Underground came together in the same neighborhood). The band, initially just Ed Sanders, Tuli
Kupferberg, and Ken Weaver, was joined soon after by Holy Modal Rounders
members Peter Stampfel and Ken Weaver. The Fugs came together at a time
when the Lower East Side's underground caché had yet to become market-
able enough to be used by landlords to rent hovels at inflated prices. And
while the Fugs might not have inspired a thousand other people to start
their own shaggy, pot-infused poetry-punk groups, they were nevertheless
seen by subsequent innovators as heralds of punk rock. As Richard Hell put
it in his introduction to an Ed Sanders reading at the Poetry Project, "Ed
Sanders, Egyptologist, Investigative Poet, Fug, and immortal auteur of Fuck
You/a magazine of the arts. And an inspiration to anyone who ever won-
dered if ever they could be a rock and roll musician."[4] Pointing ahead to
punk rants like the Feederz' "Jesus Entering from the Rear," the Fugs delighted in writing scandalous songs such as "Coca Cola Douche" and "Group
Grope"; they also published related mimeograph magazines, including
Sanders's *Fuck You: A Magazine of the Arts* and pamphlets such as *Fuck God in
the Ass.*[5] Carnivalesque troubadours who sang songs including "CIA Man"
and "Kill for Peace," the Fugs laid the groundwork for punk-politico satires
like the Dead Kennedys' "Kill the Poor." And like the best punk bands of the
1970s and '80s, Sanders, Weaver, and Kupferberg, at least initially, barely

Figure 1.1 Fugs Are Coming flyer, date and provenance unknown.
Source: Samara Kupferberg Collection.

knew how to play their instruments. "At its best," wrote one reviewer at the time, "Fugsound always had a doleful, amateur-night quality, and this people liked. It belonged with those loony lyrics. And it was one more way of flipping a big Fug finger at technically slick but shallow mass culture sounds."[6]

More than a decade before the slogan "This is a chord. This is another. This is a third. *Now form a band*" became a guiding principle for punk-infatuated wannabe musicians, the Fugs at least initially made a virtue out of renouncing virtuosity.[7]

This chapter will consider punk as it was formed in the Fugs' early recordings and will illustrate and explore the motivations behind the Fugs' efforts to reimagine poems as shambolic rock 'n' roll. From the Velvet Underground's own invocations of tortured poets such as Delmore Schwartz to Patti Smith's summoning Rimbaud, the Talking Heads' adapting Hugo Ball's poem "Gadji Beri Bimba" into their own "I Zimbra," and Thurston Moore's improvisatory rap "Oh yes, the flowers / they will grow and they will show us how to blow / in the wind / Like a Dylan Fug, / like a Fuggy Wug,"[8] the Fugs' mixture of poetry and noise anticipated and influenced much of what was to follow.[9]

When Poetry Was Hipper Than Pop

The Fugs' performance aesthetic was inspired not so much by the rock 'n' roll bands of the late 1950s and early 1960s as it was by the vibrant performance poetry scene in downtown New York.[10] Kupferberg (who holds a hallowed place in the history of 1950s avant-garde poetry and the political and cultural life of the Lower East Side)[11] and Sanders organized and appeared regularly at coffeehouse reading series, including the weekly events at Café Le Metro on Second Avenue in the East Village. "When I read [*The Toe-Queen Poems*] at Le Metro," Sanders remembers, "the response, in applause and overwhelming laughter, was the first I had received for anything I'd ever read in public, and I think it was an impetus to form a satiric proto-folk-rock group called The Fugs a few months later."[12] While Sanders always, as he put it, "followed rock-and-roll and country and western tunes as if they were sacred chants," by 1964 he, like so many of the Beat Generation poets he looked up to, "was more attuned to civil rights songs and jazz." Things started to change for Sanders when he saw writers of his generation boogying along to the Beatles and the Stones. It got him thinking "about fusing poetry and this new generation of pop tunes. I was getting the urge to form a band."[13]

That "urge" was based in large part—at least initially—not so much on the desire to become a serious rock 'n' roll musician as it was to find a form appropriate to the populist promotion of a particularly dissident, even abject style of poetry:

The three charter members [of the Fugs]—Lower East Side poets all—had long been trying to reach young people with their messages urging the ultimate in personal freedom and condemning violence and war. But they'd found out that printed poetry hardly commands a big audience these days. So why not put it to music, the kind of music the new generation listens to most. Blast out those ballads, satires, and bedtime panegyrics as rock and roll . . . "This generation is a rock generation."[14]

In other words, New York's punk rock scene got started, in part, because a group of irreverent poets wanted to transmit as much as possible of their love for avant-garde poetry to as wide an audience as possible. Becoming rock 'n' rollers was simply the fastest and best way forward to "blast out those ballads, satires, and bedtime panegyrics." That Sanders and his confreres understood and promoted poetry both as text and as edgy, rebellious lifestyle is not necessarily that surprising when we consider that it was poetry, *not* rock 'n' roll, that was pushing the boundaries in the late 1950s.

Thanks to the widely publicized 1957 trial in which Lawrence Ferlinghetti and Shigeyosi Murao were accused of obscenity for distributing Allen Ginsberg's "Howl," thousands of Americans were aware of a long poem celebrating a cast of characters "who let themselves be fucked in the ass by saintly motorcyclists, and screamed with joy."[15] Ginsberg's friends were to face similar problems at the dawn of the 1960s. Obscenity charges were leveled against *Floating Bear*'s editors LeRoi Jones and Diane di Prima for publishing William Burroughs's "Roosevelt After Inauguration" and LeRoi Jones's "The System of Dante's Hell" in 1961. The initial public response to the publication of Burroughs's *Naked Lunch* in 1962

was an almost unanimous interdiction. Interests and authorities as diverse as US Customs, the trustees of the University of Chicago, the US Postal Service, the City of Los Angeles, the Commonwealth of Massachusetts, and a host of journalists and literary critics were all in agreement that what Burroughs had to say should not be said.[16]

And it wasn't just poetry and related publications that earned the enmity of the authorities. Throughout the late 1950s and early 1960s, New York's fire inspectors and representatives from the Department of Licenses regularly invaded poetry readings in West and East Village coffeehouses for breaking fire and zoning laws. In 1959, so-called cabaret laws were used to issue summonses against coffeehouses that held regular poetry readings. Cafés in the West Village, including Café Wha?, the Gaslight, and Café Bizarre, had all been padlocked, cited for various infractions, and threatened with closure for minor offences. In 1963 and 1964, poetry readings in East Village coffee shops like Le Metro faced similar pressure, as did any number of related avant-garde theater and film spaces.

Before 1964, poets and their fellow travelers were in the outré vanguard. Rock 'n' roll musicians weren't. What, after all, were people listening to as early as 1957, the year academics and censors were arguing in court about lines in Allen Ginsberg's "Howl"? The *Billboard* year-end charts for 1957 reveal that although Elvis Presley's "All Shook Up" was number 1 and a number of other artists making frantic sounds, such as Jerry Lee Lewis, Little Richard, and Gene Vincent, appear on the list, rock 'n' roll's ambitious amalgam of black R&B, white-boy blues, and pornographic grunts and hollers was making room for rather more anodyne sounds. Most ominously, Pat Boone's unctuous cover version of the tune "Love Letters in the Sand" was at number 2. The unfailingly polite Boone vacuumed out almost any traces of threat latent in earlier rock 'n' roll. Boone, who continued to achieve tremendous success throughout the late 1950s and early 1960s, performed a kind of radical counterattack against the Beat Generation–era narratives of boundless freedom through immersion in jazz, sex, and drugs. Boone "did not embrace or represent the teenage rebellion and bad boy image of the early rock stars; instead he was a 'goody two-shoes' who made no secret of his Christian faith."[17] Given Boone's growing influence in the popular arena, Sanders's work as a poet and publisher can in this context be seen as a recuperation of the more transgressive elements of 1950s rock 'n' roll.

The *Billboard* Top 100 chart for 1958 reveals an ever-increasing banality and escapism that contrasted violently with the radicalism of Ferlinghetti, Kerouac, and other writers. Each passing year found the disconnect between innovative American poetry and American pop music widening—the year 1959 gave us Alfred Leslie's and Robert Frank's seminal Beat film *Pull My Daisy* and the publication of Jack Kerouac's *Mexico City Blues*, but it also put Johnny Horton's "The Battle of New Orleans" at number 1. If 1960 gave us Donald Allen's groundbreaking anthology *The New American Poetry*, which introduced thousands of new readers to poets including Charles Olson, Frank O'Hara, Jack Spicer, and John Wieners, it also gave us Brian Hyland's "Itsy Bitsy Teenie Weenie Yellow Polkadot Bikini."

While critics have gone to great lengths to explain how and why predominantly white bohemians sought out jazz as their soundtrack,[18] a simpler explanation can be found just by tracking the *Billboard* charts from about 1958 to around 1963—the evidence shows that rock 'n' roll was steadily losing its power as an alternative and even dangerous challenge to American traditional values. Postwar American jazz, beyond being technically and musically challenging, was also fundamentally transgressive in terms of the stories of the musicians. The drug culture and unconventional lifestyles associated with Louis Armstrong, Lester Young, Charlie Parker, Billie Holiday, and Thelonious Monk all provided a stark counternarrative to the increasingly wholesome image rock 'n' roll was working hard to attain. Such a counternarrative—beyond the material fact of the music—rhymed elegantly with much of the singular content being developed by Kerouac, Ginsberg, and their friends during early rock 'n' roll's waning years. It was not jazz's sense of exclusivity that was important to these writers—after all, their literature shows a love for popular culture. Kerouac adored radio personalities and shows such as Symphony Sid and *The Shadow*. Ginsberg loved Charlie Chaplin. Burroughs built his career on a derangement of hipster jargon. What the Beats *didn't* love was that part of popular culture that reflected the vapidity of postwar consumer-oriented capitalist society. The Beats would have to wait for the Fugs to redeem rock 'n' roll, and the Fugs had to go back to the Beats for material that would help them reanimate rock 'n' roll's corpse.

The Fugs: Total Assault on the Culture

An early flyer entitled "NOTES ON THE FUGS!" announcing the formation of the band shows where the band was coming from. As far as contemporary rock 'n' roll influences went, the Fugs ignored what was happening around them in favor of a retrospective shout-out to Chuck Berry. Beyond music, the centrality of poetry to the group project is made manifestly clear:

> The FUGS are an emanation or hallucination of the culture of the lower East
> Side. They write all of their own songs, puking them out of a personal history
> that includes the transistor radio, lots of grass, group gropes, 1000s of hours of
> poetry, reading it, writing it, & listening; peace-freaking, Chuck Berry concerts

in heaven, & scholarship in various esoteric fields of knowledge. . . . The Fug-songs seem to spurt in to five areas of concentration:

a) nouveau folk-freak
b) sex rock and roll
c) dope thrill chants
d) horny cunt-hunger blues
e) Total Assault on the Culture
(anti-war/anti-creep/anti-repression)

Only by hearing & *seeing* the FUGS may one get their total eye/ear ejacula-tion. Much of the FUG Body Poetry is the eyeball kicks they afford on stage thru Operation Sex Fiend, Operation Ankle Grab, & operation *livid dick*, which are, as most know, key code terms in the International Zionist Marijuana Conspiracy.

The real meaning of the FUGS lies in the term BODY POETRY, to get at the frenzy of the thing, the grope-thing; that is, to use the enormous technical proficiencies of modern poetry (the revolutions of Ginsberg, Robt Creeley, W. C. Williams, Ez Pound, & the Big O Charles Olson in musical presentation.

The Body Poetry Formula is this:

The Head by the way of the Big Beat to the genitals

The Genitals by way of Operation Brain Thrill to the Body Poetry.[19]

This emphasis on poetry and poetics as realized most intimately and ideally through the body was a further incentive to combine the scabrous content of much avant-garde poetry in the late 1950s and 1960s with a per-formance aesthetic that owed as much to Charles Olson as it did to Lennon and McCartney. Sanders and Kupferberg are, after all, here transforming Olson's seminal 1950 essay "Projective Verse" into a blueprint for proto-punk performance. "The Head by the way of the Big Beat to the genitals / The Genitals by way of Operation Brain Thrill to the Body Poetry" is a creative rewrite of Olson's formula "the HEAD, by way of the EAR, to the SYLLABLE / the HEART, by way of the BREATH, to the LINE."[20] There is not much of a distance to go from Olson's breath-centered poetics, in which "the line comes (I swear it) from the breath, from the breathing of the man who writes, at the moment that he writes," to the Fugs' conflation of poetry with the communal rock 'n' roll body. If, as Olson put it, we have "suffered" from "manuscript, press, the removal of verse from its producer and its repro-ducer, the voice, a removal by one, by two removes from its place of origin *and* its destination,"[21] the Fugs could now take Olson's performance aesthetic one step forward by making it literal. Poems could now be sung, directly, using an amplified "big beat" whose power could effect physiological change on the bodies of the audience members. The Fugs' performed poems aimed for nothing less than transcending the material distance between audience and performers by inducing a mass polyamory genital response among the "Body Poetry."

As popular music regained critical credibility with the arrival of the Rolling Stones, the Beatles, and other bands associated with the British Invasion, Fugs members emphasized—in interviews, in newspaper articles, and most obviously in their songs—that their music was a space in which the boundaries between pop and poetry would be challenged. The Fugs were creating a world and audience in which the reader of innovative poetry would be the same consumer of the latest mass-market and simultaneously radical rock 'n' roll record. In a letter to Barry Miles, the owner of one of London's most progressive hipster meeting spots, the Indica Gallery, Kupferberg details the events and cultural activity swirling around New York City in the mid-sixties. It shows how proto-punks inscribed stardom and popular music as part of the cultural capital generally accorded to poetry:

> Ed Sanders first book of poems out. Burroughs APO book soon out. New *Fuck You* coming. New *Yeah* 2 weeks away from printer: 108pages108. New *C* readying. Allen de Loach preparing Metro poets anthol. New School Arts Festival approaching. Fugs play the Bridge Theater Sat midnights. Traveling peace-show on truck w Bob Nichols & Peter Schumanns puppets (12 foot tall & non-conventputppets: magnificent masks). NY Folk Singing Festival. Stones in NY. Hear Beatles coming.[22]

And, while Fugs songs were often drawn directly from literary sources, the Fugs petitioned poets, including Ted Berrigan, Jack Micheline, and Al Fowler, to write lyrics the Fugs could then perform.[23]

Fugs performances were real-time meeting grounds for writers and pop stars. At one such event, the Fugs performed sets at an Andrei Voznesensky reading at the Village Theater in May 1967, an occasion that also featured readings by John Ashbery, Ted Berrigan, Gregory Corso, Paul Blackburn, Robert Creeley, Jerome Rothenberg, and Jackson Mac Low. Yet the Fugs' presence at events such as these was as much an opportunity to celebrate poetry as it was a chance to make fun of it, whether it was poetry written by canonical authors or the Fugs' own friends and contemporaries. It didn't matter who the poets were—if they were self-important and too serious about being "radical," the Fugs were coming after them. Even Amiri Baraka (formerly LeRoi Jones) found himself subject to the Fugs' satire. Baraka, arrested in 1967 for illegal possession of firearms, was the author of the much-maligned poem "Black People!," which was read out as evidence against him during his trial.[24] The poem contained one of Baraka's more notorious lines—"Up against the wall, motherfucker this is a stick up!"[25] A cause célèbre following his arrest, Baraka was the last poet one could imagine making fun of. Sanders recalls a 1968 show in the East Village:

> It was our annual concert in [Tompkins Square Park]. We had a new tune, which we performed with straw hats and canes and delivered in a kind of Al Jolson water-mouthed vocal, "Up Against the Wall, Motherfucker" (borrowed from a famous Amiri Baraka poem). The tune also satirized the group called the Motherfuckers, whose leaflets I'd often printed gratis at Peace Eye, whose logo on their publications was UAW/MF.[26]

The Fugs' refusal to take anything too seriously included both the histrionics of rock stardom and the radical chic of figures like Amiri Baraka and the Motherfuckers. While the Fugs certainly loved poetry and rock 'n' roll, they actively satirized anyone who exploited either form to position him- or herself above the crowd.

Ballads of Contemporary Protest, Point of Views, and General Dissatisfaction

In a letter to Miles, Kupferberg detailed how he and his fellow Fugs were "supposedly cutting first FUG (rock&roll satire) for Folkways tomorrow. How many million do you want? Will send you sample when & if. Absolutely lewd & outrageous. Expect to tour England sumday & meet you then."[27] But how "lewd and outrageous" was *The Fugs First Album*?[28] The album included sung versions of William Blake's poems "Ah Sunflower" and "How Sweet I Roamed from Field to Field" alongside wilfully stupid anthems like "Boobs a Lot." There was a healthy dose of oddly cheerful nihilism on the album, too. Kupferberg's song "Nothing" begins despondently: "Monday nothing,

Tuesday nothing, Wednesday and Thursday nothing, Friday for a change a little more nothing," then moves on to "poetry nothing, music nothing, painting and dancing nothing . . . fucking nothing, sucking nothing flesh and sex nothing," and ends with Sanders shouting: "Nothing! nothing! nothing! NOTHING! NOTHING!" These insistently negative chants reverberate with any number of American and English punk refrains, from Richard Hell's "Blank Generation" to the Sex Pistols' "God Save the Queen" to X-Ray Spex's "I Can't Do Anything" to any number of the Ramones' "I don't" songs ("I Don't Wanna Go Down to the Basement," "I Don't Wanna Walk Around with You," "I Don't Wanna Grow Up," "I Don't Want You," and so on).

The Fugs First Album even *looked* punk. The front cover featured a photograph of the band taken by Dave Gahr on a rubble-strewn lot in the East Village.[29] The image is about as far away from folkie gentility as it could be. With the band members posed against a brick wall, the cover has more in common with Jacob Riis's iconic nineteenth-century image *Bandit's Roost*, featuring a group of Lower East Side criminals posed menacingly in an alley, than it does with album covers associated with the American folk-rock musicians who were then all the rage. Kupferberg was pictured scraping a metal rod against something resembling a metal fire grate, like a demented postapocalyptic fiddler. Sanders, facing away from the camera and holding a guitar with its neck pointed down to the ground, had his hair slicked back 1950s bad-boy greaser style. Compare this look to other, more pastoral folk covers of the same period, such as Peter, Paul, and Mary's 1965 *See What Tomorrow Brings*, which highlighted the folk-rock artists as beach-combing friends gently floating, hand in hand, on a sand dune. Similarly, the cover of the Byrds' 1965 album *Turn! Turn! Turn!* seemed designed to attract not so much members of the nascent counterculture as a more docile audience looking for their slice of Americana. While the musicians model Beatlesesque mop tops and a vaguely stoned demeanor, the monochrome blue background and list of anodyne song titles (including "Oh Susannah," "Turn Turn Turn," and "He Was a Friend of Mine") boldly displayed on the right of the cover serve to domesticate whatever latent danger the Byrds album might otherwise be perceived to contain. Compare the Byrds' song titles with the Fugs' "Boobs a Lot" and "I Couldn't Get High," and one can see the extent to which the Fugs were marking a break with the American pop music of the time. And this is all before one even put the needle on the LP.

The Fugs First Album opens with "Slum Goddess."[30] Written by Ken Weaver, the song is a paean to the sexually liberated bohemian women populating the East Village in the 1960s. "Slum Goddess," with its shout outs to hip chicks living on Avenue B, was very much a neighborhood song in terms of its sound as well. The song begins with a country-western guitar motif that would have immediately resonated with downtown hipsters. As John Gruen noticed in 1966, the Lower East Side uniform of the day was "strictly boots and saddles. New Bohemia likes leather jackets, Levis, western boots, work shirts, long hair, beards moustaches. . . . The whole thing is like a romantic revival of the wild, wild West."[31] It is as if Sanders and company borrowed a riff from Johnny Cash's Tennessee Trio to mark, however parodically, their awareness of downtown fashion.

The raunchy humor of "Slum Goddess" made the next track—William Blake's "Ah, Sunflower, Weary of Time" sung in two-part harmony—seem even stranger than it otherwise might. Any traces of humor or parody seem latent at best, and Blake's poem is sung twice in a row. The second time around, there is an increase in volume and urgency; the drums and guitar come to the foreground more, and the singers' delivery speeds up just a notch. But overall, this song is remarkable for its restraint. Yet it is impossible not to question the serious, gentle affect behind this tune, particularly as it is preceded by "Slum Goddess" and followed immediately with Kupferberg's "Supergirl" (featuring absurdist lyrics such as "I want a girl that can / love like a monkey"). This is not to say that Ed Sanders or any of the other Fugs were hostile to or mocking Blake's work. Rather, it is to ask what purposes were served by Sanders's sandwiching of Blake's poem between two ostensibly silly songs.

Given the efforts of the Fugs to situate their album within the East Village counterculture and the poetry scene, "Ah Sunflower" invites us to think about the influence of Allen Ginsberg and the Fugs' contesting of his authority in the poetry world of the time. Ginsberg from the beginning of his career made much of a vision he had in 1948 in which he claimed to hear William Blake intoning "Ah Sunflower" and "The Sick Rose." As he explained the experience to Tom Clark:

> there I was in my bed in Harlem . . . jacking off. With my pants open, lying around on a bed by the windowsill, looking out into the cornices of Harlem and the sky above. And I had just come. And had perhaps hardly even wiped the come off my

thighs, my trousers or whatever it was . . . So anyway, what I had been doing that week—I'd been in a very lonely solitary state, dark night of the soul sort of, reading St. John of the Cross . . . and suddenly, simultaneously with understanding it, heard a very deep earth graven voice in the room, which I immediately assumed, I didn't think twice, was Blake's voice . . . looking out at the window, through the window at the sky, suddenly it seemed that I saw into the depths of the universe, by looking simply into the ancient sky.[32]

He went on to explain how he heard Blake reciting "Ah Sunflower," and Ginsberg would later record the poem for his 1970 album *Songs of Innocence and Experience, by William Blake, Tuned by Allen Ginsberg.* For the Fugs essentially to preempt Ginsberg by recording "Ah Sunflower"—and further dramatize their one-upmanship by actually singing prettily in tune as opposed to parroting Ginsberg's quasi-Hindi keening—was to show that that "vision" was there for the taking. Ed Sanders's co-opting Ginsberg's Blake was a message to the Fugs' rock 'n' roll audience that its members could take on the role of poet-priest while simultaneously holding on to and celebrating trash culture. Blake's poem—contextualized among the detritus of slum goddesses, boobs, and dope—in the Fugs' hands becomes an oddly populist text. Unlike Ginsberg's Blake, who existed to reify Ginsberg's role as spokesperson for the counterculture, the Fugs' Blake was perfectly content to share the stage with a bunch of crassly singing young punks.

True, Ginsberg was no stranger to the abject, the silly, even the goofy. His poetry was replete with moments of winsome candor, and his poems often served as social documents detailing the most intimate aspects of his and his lovers' and friends' lives. Yet Ginsberg's social text more often than not invoked his friendships in such a way as practically to deify him and his peers—thus, his cries of "Holy Peter holy Allen holy Solomon holy Lucien holy Kerouac" in his "Footnote to Howl."[33] Ginsberg's Blake was in the service of icon and myth building and aligned to figures positioned as touched, visionary, transcendent, those "who passed through universities with radiant cool eyes hallucinating Arkansas and Blake-light tragedy among the scholars of war."[34] The Fugs' Blake was in the service of assaulting the privilege attendant to the very idea of "vision." Ginsberg's Blake was romantic. The Fugs' Blake was punk.

The Fugs' performances of other poems on *The Fugs First Album* ensured that the high-art status of poetry would be compromised further by the album's overall tenor of druggy irreverence. "Swineburn Stomp," for example, begins with a band member repeating the phrase "Swinburne stomp" in a breathless, high-pitched, and mocking manner as other voices chime in. "Ain't nobody stomps like Swinburne stomps" opines one Fug in a faux-amazed drawl, as others shriek *whoop de do*." Then, with stentorian mock authority, Ed Sanders arrives on the scene and calls out the title, "*the Swinburne stomp*," an announcement that Peter Stampfel responds to with a chirpy, drawn-out "*Yaaaay!!!*" Sanders goes on to perform "Before the Beginning of Years," the second choral ode from Swinburne's "Atalanta in Calydon," in its entirety. It is a comically abominable reading. Sanders pronounces some words in a phony English accent, and at other times he enunciates lines in his flat Midwestern twang. He hams up and accentuates lines and phrases that were clearly designed by Swinburne to inspire awe and gravitas. Accompanied by bleating kazoos and slide whistles, Sanders barks out Swinburne's opening lines, every stress in every iamb and trochee emphasized to the point that the poem's sense becomes entirely occluded by Sanders's vandalistic caricature of meter: "B*efore* the be*ginn*ing of *years*! / There *came* to the *making* of *man*! / *Time*, with a *gift* of *tears*! / *Grief*, with a *glass* that *ran*! / *Pleasure*, with *pain* for *leaven*! / *Summer*, with *flowers* that *fell*! / *Remembrance* *fallen* from *heaven*! / And *madness risen* from *hell*!"[35] Sanders *destroys* the poem, emphasizing the arbitrariness of its construction.[36]

Sanders's absurd emphases on the "BOOM-ta-ta" accents in Swinburne's lines foreground the implicit noise of the poem. The Fugs' presentation of Swinburne's poem as disruptive music is highlighted all the more by their inclusion of marginal sounds (maracas, whistles, slide whistles, tom-tom beats, kazoos, etc.) that serve to taunt and interrupt Sanders's own taunting performance. "Swineburn Stomp" materially connects poetic language with the one thing critics most loved to complain about in condemning rock 'n' roll—nonsignifying babble. As Richard Aquila contends, parents' "attacks on rock & roll, calling it trash and senseless noise, contributed to . . . youths' solidarity. A common enemy often serves as a catalyst to bring unity to a community."[37] Given that rock 'n' roll in the first half of the 1950s helped create a youth culture through noise—aligning youth against an older generation determined to stamp out what it perceived to be senseless, even dangerous nonmusic—the Fugs' transformation of poetry into noise can be understood as a way to connect Swinburne to a burgeoning counterculture intent on celebrating sex, drugs, and rock 'n' roll. If the formal metrics of Swinburne's poem are a simulation and enactment of order, then the Fugs' tearing apart that order through literal dissonances can be read metaphorically as taking Swinburne out of the classroom and textbook and onto the streets.

Artistic value, as "Swineburn Stomp" illustrates, depends on what the consumers of the artwork *do* with the given piece. The Fugs' and Sanders's treatment of Swinburne questioned the cultural capital traditionally ascribed to poetry even as it celebrated and reinvigorated the community-oriented possibilities of poetry in performance. During his tenure as the publisher of *Fuck You* and in his work on the Fugs' first album, Sanders consistently created environments in which poetry could be celebrated and mocked. Not taking things too seriously was a way for Sanders to make poetry palatable to those members of the public scared off by the elitist associations associated with the form. Sanders's absurd and funny sonic revelation of Swinburne's wacky meters—his emphasizing rather than obscuring the awkwardness of the poem's music—helped listeners fully understand that poetry could be a form defined by readers, not authors.

In applying Carrie Noland's analysis of Patti Smith's appropriation of Rimbaud to our reading of "Swineburn Stomp," we can see how Sanders revealed "how a nonacademic reading of a canonical text could help produce a musical style disseminating a countercultural message of social deviance through the channels of what Adorno denounced—and perhaps misrepresented—as the culture industry."[38] That "countercultural message" delivered through Swinburne's poem was all the stronger in relationship to its place on the album—"Swineburn Stomp" was followed immediately by Ken Weaver's "Couldn't Get High," a song devoted to confessing a dopehead's frustrated attempts to get stoned. Organizing the songs in such a way helped listeners connect the proverbial dots—Swinburne, known and at times reviled in his own lifetime for employing frank, sexual themes in his writing and being a prodigious drinker, was a Fug.

Virgin Fugs

The Fugs' radical irreverence soon changed, however, as the band gained popularity and started to think of themselves as a serious musicians. They had conquered the Lower East Side with their first album—could their second album help them take over "teen america" next? That was the plan, as an "Ed Sanders Newsletter" made clear:

> The second FUGS album, on the ESP Disk label, will be out March 15. Carefully done, with impeccable musical presentation, this second album is headed straight for the top of the charts. Hindering its rise to moneyville may be the fact that we have seriously recorded for teen america Group Grope, Dirty Old Man, & Skin Flowers, plus Ken Weaver having an orgasm with a chimpanzee.[39]

The second Fugs album (simply entitled *The Fugs*)[40] was a more professionally produced LP, complete with its own prog-rock epic (avant la lettre) "Virgin Forest." Clocking in at just over eleven minutes, musically the tune was a curious anticipation of Miles Davis's *Bitches Brew* (1970) jazz fusion, Pink Floyd's and the Doors' psychedelic epics à la *Piper at the Gates of Dawn* (1967) and "The End" (1967), and Frank Zappa's orchestral buffoonery. Sanders's lyrics included quotes from William Burroughs and Anthony Balch's film *Towers Open Fire* (1963), invocations to the goddess Aphrodite, and the like. *The Fugs* also had its fair share of satirical songs. Lionel Goldbart's "Dirty Old Man" was a particularly uproarious standout, with lyrics including "Communist literature in my hands, / Pinchin' all the bosoms I can, / I'm a dirty old man" pointing back to the Fugs' earlier mockery. For the most part, though, satire on *The Fugs* tended toward the somewhat obvious, if consistently funny. Kupferberg's "Kill for Peace," for example, reified a good-versus-bad binary that the first Fugs album had so merrily dispensed with. "If you don't like the people / Or the way that they talk / If you don't like their manners / Or the way that they walk / Kill, kill, kill for peace," the Fugs chanted. The tension between traditionally competing ideologies and registers that the first Fugs album so wonderfully managed to create was here set aside for more accessible, side-taking, and hortatory ends.

Even Allen Ginsberg's liner notes pointed to the Fugs' attempts to entrench themselves within an identifiable counterculture, revealing their efforts to draw on Ginsberg's authority to lend Beat gravitas to their project. "It's war on all fronts," Ginsberg begins. "'Breakthrough in the Grey Room' says Burroughs—he meant the Brain. 'Total Assault on the Culture' says Ed Sanders. The United States is split down the middle. On one side are everybody who make love with their eyes open, maybe smoke pot & take LSD . . . Who's on the other side? People who think we are *bad*." While Ginsberg immediately qualified this black-and-white model ("Other side? No, let's not make it a war, we'll all be destroyed, we'll go on suffering till we die if we take the War Door"), it was clear that there was very much an "us" and "them" in Fugsworld and that "we," for the most part, saw the light.

While *The Fugs* shifted the band's aesthetics and cultural and political positions away from their wildly satirical beginnings in *The Fugs First Album*, the 1967 release of the album *Virgin Fugs*, composed of outtakes from *The Fugs First Album* sessions, reminded listeners that the Fugs were best at their worst. This is notwithstanding the fact that Sanders insisted as recently as 2012 that *Virgin Fugs* shouldn't even be considered part of the official Fugs canon. Ironically in light of the fact that Sanders had made a name for himself publishing poems such as Auden's "The Platonic Blow" and Pound's final Cantos without the authors' permission, Sanders's antipathy toward *Virgin Fugs* was based in large part on the fact that ESP had released the album without consulting the artists. "When the owner of ESP-Disk basically bootlegged a sequence of tunes from the first two Fugs sessions and called it *Virgin Fugs*," Sanders complains,

> it went against my principles of Apt Artistic Flow—that an artist should be able to select what created items get to be placed before the world. Allen Ginsberg didn't like the use of "Howl" lines in the song "The I Saw the Best Minds of My Generation Rock." I didn't like it. And the bootlegger stole all the income derived. Stole Stole Stole. Because of our being dumped by Atlantic Records, *Virgin Fugs* became the only Fugs album to appear during the crucial Year of Love.[41]

Despite Sanders's own take on *Virgin Fugs* and his retrospective embarrassment over his use and abuse of Ginsberg's "Howl," "I Saw the Best Minds of My Generation Rot" is one of the most fascinating punk-poetry hybrid songs the Fugs—or indeed any other poetry-infatuated punk band—produced.

The song opens with a jaunty motif that recalls Americana jug-band classics like "Feather Bed" or "Sandy River Belle." Sanders then comes in and sings "I saw the best minds of my generation destroyed by madness, starving hysterical naked" (the first line of Allen Ginsberg's seminal poem "Howl") while guitar and bass jangle in the background cheerfully. After four iterations, the rest of the Fugs take up the line and repeat it as a kind of ostinato as Sanders reads from the succeeding lines of the poem, maintaining a breathless pace throughout.

The status of the poem as impassioned utterance from an oracular bard was immediately undermined. Ginsberg insisted throughout his life that the lines in "Howl" were predicated on a "Hebraic-Melvillian bardic *breath*"[42] that was intimately, even organically connected to his own privileged body. "Bardic breath" as Ginsberg expresses it in "Howl" becomes bad breath as generated by the Fugs. Sung in unison by a number of Fugs, the visionary status of the poem as tied to a specific vatic individual is entirely compromised. Steve Weber and Peter Stampfel applied exaggerated falsetto harmonies, adenoidal vocals, and skiffle rhythms to the performance. These sounds, circling around and at times overwhelming Sanders's own delivery, went far not just in making a predominantly serious long poem sound silly but in actively questioning the eminence "Howl" and Ginsberg had attained by the mid-1960s.

The Fugs' treatment of "Howl" jarred radically with the rhetoric characterizing the reception of the poem, rhetoric encouraged by Ginsberg, who proclaimed that "Howl" belonged to "the secret or hermetic tradition of art,"[43] that it was an "homage to art," an "emotional time bomb that would continue exploding . . . the military-industrial-nationalistic complex."[44] In his book-length study of the poem, Jonah Raskin thematizes the poem simply by stating: "It was . . . the death of so many members of his own generation and the spiritual death of a mechanized world—that inspired him to create his best work."[45] Far from using the poem to extend the theme of "the spiritual death of a mechanized world," the Fugs' version of "Howl" adapted the text for mainly comic effect. Even the sanctity of the order of the poem was transgressed: Sanders only bothered to sing out the first five lines (ending "staggering on tenement roofs illuminated") before leaping forward seventeen lines to recite "who lit cigarettes in boxcars boxcars boxcars racketing through snow toward lonesome farms in grandfather night," only then to *return* to the sixth line, beginning "who cowered in unshaven rooms in underwear." This infidelity to the text as it originally stood characterized Sanders's approach throughout, as he jumped gleefully from section to section, line to line, regardless of the poem's intended organization.

One of the most curious moments in the song comes when Sanders and company focus on the phrase "eli eli lamma lamma sabacthani" (traditionally ascribed to Christ as he was dying on the cross and translated as "My God, why have you forsaken me"). They repeat the phrase multiple times. They slur it. They enunciate it in a peculiar nasal twang. The phrase "eli eli lamma

lamma sabacthani" as it appeared initially in Ginsberg's "Howl" was used to raise the "holy" status of Ginsberg's "best minds" all the more. Ginsberg's brothers-in-arms "rose reincarnate in the ghostly clothes of jazz in the goldhorn shadow of the band and blew the suffering of America's naked mind for love into an eli eli lamma lamma sabacthani saxophone cry that shivered the cities down to the last radio / with the absolute heart of the poem of life butchered out of their own bodies good to eat a thousand years."[46] These lines are, as Bob Perelman recognizes, "suffused with Christian vocabulary . . . and it quotes Christ's last words on the cross. . . . And while the last line seems most directly a reference to Aztec sacrifice, isn't a heart that's good to eat for a millennium awfully close to the Eucharist?"[47] The dividing lines between body and soul, Jewish and Christian, the sacred and the secular are in "Howl" interrogated steadfastly, the poem building and building throughout its three sections to end in a metaphysical state of grace in which "Everything is holy! everybody's holy! Everywhere is holy!"[48] While acknowledging how Ginsberg's evocative and surrealistic juxtapositions and jump cuts might at first suggest the poet is interested in language as a kind of materialist game, Perelman illustrates how Ginsberg's imaginative aim in the poem is to leave the world for the realm of the spirit, "past language":

> For thinkers such as Augustine and Origen, language was ultimately a barrier to the presence of Christ, the one and only Word. The advent of Christ's Embodiment provided access to the spirit, superseding the letter. The desire to "escape from textuality," [Susan Handelman] writes, "permeates Christian thought." . . . Would Ginsberg . . . be Jewish? We'd have to say no, since the body and the embodied voice are so clearly the origin, locus, and telos of his work. Even what at first look like his "language-centered" moments are directed, ultimately, past language.[49]

With Perelman's analysis in mind, we can now see the extent to which the Fugs were assaulting not only the authority invested in Ginsberg by a fawning counterculture but more specifically the authority Ginsberg aimed to establish in the kind of metaphysically oriented quasi-religious practices whose power he insisted lay beyond language—in Buddhist-inspired meditation, say, or in psychedelics. The Fugs' literal *interruption* of Ginsberg's text, realized most amusingly in the musicians' stretching of the phrase "eli eli lamma lamma sabacthani," parodies the very concept of breath-based vatic insight by disrupting and spoiling the cadences of the original poem for humorous effect. "Howl," Ginsberg the Poet, and religious conviction itself all become Fugs targets.

By 1965, "Howl" had become firmly entrenched in the public imagination as one of *the* crucial documents informing the New Left and the counterculture more broadly speaking. Ginsberg was a celebrity. The year that the Fugs recorded their spoof, 1965, was the same year Ginsberg was crowned the King of May in Prague, Czechoslovakia, and was promptly deported by Czech authorities for sexual peccadilloes and drunken transgressions. It was the same year Ginsberg got kicked out of Cuba by authorities horrified at Ginsberg's public criticism of the government's harassment of homosexuals. It was also the same year Ginsberg was to play a starring role in the "International Poetry Incarnation," a mass poetry reading in London's Royal Albert Hall that was widely cited as marking the birth of the British counterculture. "I Saw the Best Minds of My Generation Rot" pushed back on all that, arguing (if implicitly) that doubt, mockery, and teasing were appropriate responses to any figure claiming or acquiring central authority for himself. *The Fugs First Album* and *The Virgin Fugs*—essentially one glorious album—was a punk hint of things to come. The prophecy was not just in the music. The Fugs, making fun of 1960s icons from Ginsberg to Barry Goldwater, predicted later punks' dismissals or arguments with the psychedelic sixties. From Johnny Rotten's "I hate Pink Floyd" T-shirt to Husker Dü's rageful cover of the Byrds' ecstatic, psychedelic "8 Miles High," punk's assault on the excesses and naiveté of the counterculture had a basis in the Fugs' riotous sound.

*   *   *

The Fugs continued recording through the 1960s, and various solo albums by Sanders and Kupferberg were released in the 1970s, but they ended up abandoning punk irreverence and simplicity in favor of a more professional sound. Sanders now highlights and celebrates the proficient arrangements evident in his subsequent albums *Tenderness Junction*, *It Crawled Into My Hand, Honest*, and *Belle of Avenue A* and insists that they influenced the Beatles, among others. Yet an album like *It Crawled Into My Hand, Honest* finds the Fugs reflecting rather than parodying the dominant psychedelic sounds of the day (their "Crystal Liaison," for example, bears a strong resemblance to Jefferson Airplane's shimmering anthemic harmonies and loony-tunes antics on their 1967 album *After Bathing at Baxters*). Sanders complains about getting rejected by Atlantic Records after playing them a demo of their never-to-be released album *The Fugs Eat It*. As far as he is concerned, this dismissal "prevented The Fugs from putting out an album in the Glory year of 1967 to join *Sgt. Pepper, Big Brother and the Holding Company, Alice's Restaurant, Procol Harum,* Jimi Hendrix's *Are You Experienced,* and 'All You Need is Love.'"[50] Sanders also laments not being recognized for the Fugs' influence on punk:

> I provided the first-known use of the term "punk rock" in an interview in the *Chicago Tribune*. "Self-honesty entails an admission," wrote Robb Baker in that article, published on March 22, 1970: "even if that heritage has been rejected. Sanders does this particularly well in his first solo album for Reprise records, 'Sanders' Truckstop,' which he describes as 'punk rock—redneck sentimentality—my own past updated to present day reality.'"
>
> No one sent a check for coming up with the term.[51]

Yet despite Sanders's grievances, *The Fugs First Album* and *Virgin Fugs* opened up the possibility of making passionate, literary, and simultaneously hilariously stupid music to any number of unskilled, intellectually minded, and deeply irreverent kids. Sanders's belief that he and the Fugs never got their due for achieving things "for the first time in the history of Western Civilization"[52] is unfortunate. The sixties megabands Sanders regularly compares the Fugs to were for the most part always and forever on stage, high above the crowd, impressing us with skills most of us could only dream of having. The Fugs' streetwise proto-punk poetry filth offered another model entirely, one that was demotic, dangerous, strange, vibrant. For that they should be adored and valued, even if they never got the check.

TWO

Lou Reed: "In the Beginning Was the Word"

FOR A BRIEF PERIOD in the mid-1960s the Fugs and the Velvet Underground were considered peers and musical equals. While the Fugs today are too often overlooked in the histories of rock 'n' roll even as the Velvets are invoked as visionary proto-punk deities, both bands saw the other in part as pop extensions of a radical literary counterculture.[1] Placing the Fugs and the Velvets together has much to teach us about how the avant-garde at the time worked to infiltrate the mainstream and adds to our historical understanding of the complex interplay between poetry, poetics, and music that fed into the development of what we now call punk rock.

The Fugs and the Velvet Underground transcended the limits of any one genre by staging their performances as events incorporating elements of theater, poetry, light shows, and dance. Though the Velvets got their start playing in small clubs, avant-garde cinemas, and Andy Warhol's Factory, it was their participation in Warhol's Exploding Plastic Inevitable (EPI) that drew more and more people's attention to their music.[2] Taking place in the Polsky Dom Narodny (the Polish National Home, referred to by its habitués simply as "the Dom") at 23 St. Mark's Place, the EPI events were just up the street from Lewis Warsh and Anne Waldman's apartment and a couple of blocks south from the Poetry Project. The few critics at the time who were attuned to the Velvet Underground lauded their music as an essential part of a groundbreaking multimedia spectacular. Take, for example, "a fledgling critic by the name of Wayne McGuire," who described the Velvets as "prophets of a new age, of breakthrough on an electronic: intermedia: total scale."[3] Contemporary critics including Brandon Joseph continue to characterize the EPI as "an overwhelming expanded cinema production collaboratively orchestrated from 1966 to 1967":

> At the height of its development, the Exploding Plastic Inevitable included three to five film projectors, often showing different reels of the same film simultaneously; a similar number of slide projectors, movable by hand so that their images swept the auditorium; four variable-speed strobe lights; three moving spots with an assortment of coloured gels; several pistol lights; a mirror ball hung from the ceiling and another on the floor; as many as three loudspeakers blaring different pop records at once; one or two sets by the Velvet Underground and Nico; and the dancing of Gerard Malanga and Mary Woronov or Ingrid Superstar, complete with props and lights that projected their shadows high onto the wall. . . . The cumulative effect was one of disruptive multiplicity and layering, as the Velvet Underground, Nico, and other of Warhol's superstars appeared amidst the barrage of sounds, lights, images, and performance.[4]

The word "poetry" does not appear in Joseph's account, and generally speaking it does not make an appearance in histories of the EPI. This is understandable, as discrete poetry readings were not a feature at EPI events. Yet what if we consider poetry more broadly as a discourse rather than a specific genre? Can we accept how poetry signifies beyond strictly literary fields? Can we apprehend a poetic "moment" in something as basic as the very presence of Gerard Malanga, a tousled, ecstatic poet, dancing wildly in public? If so, we can understand how many attendees at the events would read Malanga's place on the EPI stage as a revelation—the Lower East Side poetry scene fused with Andy Warhol's world.

As a young student at Wagner College in Staten Island in 1962 and 1963, Malanga published writers affiliated with the second-generation New York School (including Joe Brainard, Ted Berrigan, Joseph Ceravolo, and Ron Padgett) in the *Wagner Review*. As Andy Warhol's assistant, Malanga played the midwife in introducing downtown poets to the scene swirling around Warhol's Factory. (John Ashbery, Berrigan, and Padgett would go on to serve as subjects in Warhol's Screen Tests series, and Berrigan and Padgett both referenced Warhol directly in their poetry).

Even before his work with Warhol and his role as editor of the *Wagner Review*, young Malanga was drawn to the then barely read and poorly understood first-generation New York School poets. In a 1961 letter to Kenneth Koch, for example, Malanga wrote:

A few weeks ago I had a luncheon with your mother at Losantiville Country Club, and she suggested I contact you when I am in New York for Spring vacation. . . . I am "a young poet searching for an identification," says Daisy Aldan, who was my high school Creative Writing teacher, now my very dear friend, and who guided me closely in my true vocation. I was born in the Bronx, March 20, 1943, and was a young and sensitive adolescent when the Contemporary Poetry Movement started to climb the ladder, which today has reached the height of its prestige in the mid-most of the century. . . . As editor of *MILKWOOD*, a new magazine of literature, art, and ideas, I am interested in collaborating poetry, articles on creativity, short stories, art, translations, verse plays, photography, music, and dance. I believe these facets of culture can bring about more understanding between peoples.[5]

The sympathies Malanga evokes as a young student between "collaborating poetry," music, and dance foreshadow his own performances on the stages of the Dom. It also augurs how, for some in the downtown audience at the Dom, the EPI was evocative of and drew on the Beat and New York School poets as well as on the aspects of a concert, a happening, a disco. If poets never actually declaimed on the EPI's stages, they certainly flocked to the Velvets' shows regularly.

The Dom was by 1966 the latest go-to place in the East Village. Warhol and Paul Morrissey had that year transformed what had formerly been the Dom Restaurant into a nightclub where they could hold their multimedia extravaganzas. The Velvet Underground played the role of house band. The poet Bill Berkson, the subject of many of Frank O'Hara's best poems, recalls seeing the Velvets for the first time at the Polish National Home "in 1966, I think. I remember walking in and right away seeing Allen Ginsberg and Peter Orlovsky and then turning to see Gerry Malanga gyrating in front of the band. The music was right on time."[6] Berkson's friend, the poet Lewis Warsh, was particularly invested in the Velvets' sound. "I went to see the VU shows all the time. . . . Gerry Malanga doing his whip dance. I once saw the VU in a concert space above Max's Kansas City."[7] For the poet Ron

Padgett, the dominant image at the Velvet Underground show he attended was "Gerard Malanga on stage, dancing in leather and cracking a whip."[8] Even LeRoi Jones, who in 1966 was already making a name for himself as a major jazz critic and was one year away from transforming himself from hip beatnik LeRoi to black nationalist Amiri Baraka, found much to admire in the Velvets' sound. Responding to the sounds of John Cale's bass on the Velvets' "White Light/White Heat," Baraka remarked, "So deep, so satisfying."[9]

Poetry, if not literally read out loud at the Dom, eddied in and around the space. Poetry spun off Ginsberg's and Orlovsky's shamanistic dancing; it shone on the faces of the many New York School–affiliated poets in the crowd; it glanced sharply off the whip cracked by Malanga. Poets were there to show people who didn't know better what to *do* at a Velvets show. As Lou Reed remembers, the Velvets "started playing [at a party at *Paris Review* editor George Plimpton's house] and all [Plimpton's] guests said—How do you dance to it? Ginsberg and Orlovsky started writhing about in the corner and they all looked and said, 'Oh, is that what to do to it?'"[10] Poetry was understood to be so resonant with the EPI that Warhol and his entourage at one stage considered adding poetry readings to the multimedia spectacle. "What makes the [EPI] show a success?" Susan Nelson asked Malanga and Ingrid Superstar. "'The ideas,' [Malanga] said." Nelson continued, "What's next for the troupe? Miss Superstar mentioned something about going to London—and continuing the 'concert element.' They may even make room for readings by famous poets, she posed."[11]

Interestingly, the Fugs, that original band of poets, also hovered in the space of the Dom. Prior to his work with the Velvets, Malanga had danced (if only once) for the Fugs. "It was a very funny situation," Malanga recalls:

> I told Ed what I was going to do and he was all fine with that and while they were performing I got up on stage, it was a small stage, and I started dancing with the whip, and afterwards Tuli got really uptight with me! He said, "This is not really part of our scene," and I said, "Oh, oh, OK!" so that was the one-time performance. . . . Tuli was very conservative! I was shocked, actually, but I didn't want to annoy him, that was it, I didn't go back to dance more.[12]

As outrageous as the Fugs were, it seems they weren't quite ready to align themselves with a sexually ambiguous S&M routine enacted on stage by a gorgeous boy dressed in leather trousers. The Velvets, with their lyrics about heroin abuse and sadomasochism tied to a sound throbbing with intensity and solemnity—in contrast to the Fugs' ludic tooting—were more constitutionally capable of linking their experiments in words and sounds to experiments in life.

That said, Sanders saw no necessary dividing line between the two bands' musical projects, despite the Fugs' clear debt to folk and theater traditions. Ed Sanders took an immediate shine to the group and ended up attending their gigs at the Dom. "I liked that tune that started out real slow—'Heroin,'" Sanders acknowledged, adding:

> I liked the drummer. I always liked Lou Reed's voice. The time was pretty good. Then it was more organic, yet with the organism it had certain time changes that were interesting. My wife Miriam seems to remember that the Dom gigs were crowded out by dopers. They had a kind of Allen Kaprow happening factor. I liked the show because it had a lot of energy. I liked the way everything was wrapped up in a good time-change. What The Fugs were doing wasn't exclusive nor were we competitive. There was plenty of room in the whole world for both The Fugs and The Velvets.[13]

The Velvet Underground's guitarist Sterling Morrison returned the favor. "I agree with Ed completely," he enthused. "We often played together at shows and benefits, and liked and were liked by the same people. The Fugs, The Holy Modal Rounders and The Velvet Underground were the only authentic Lower East Side bands. We were real bands playing for real people in a real scene."[14]

Lonely Woman Quarterly

Working as a musician throughout his undergraduate years at Syracuse University, Lou Reed grew to understand late-modernist and New American writing as capable of transmitting discordant ideas in the face of consensus culture. As a freshman at Syracuse University in 1960, Reed

> wanted to make a point of being a writer more than a rock-and-roller. In those days, before the Beatles arrived, the term *rock-and-roller* was something of a

put-down associated more with Paul Anka and Pat Boone than the Rolling Stones. Lou preferred to be associated with writers like Jack Kerouac. Like the classic beatnik, Lou usually wore black jeans and T-shirts and turtlenecks, but he also kept a tweed jacket with elbow patches in his closet in case he wanted to come on like John Updike.[15]

Poetry for Reed was especially significant in terms of how it was aligned with an open-minded approach to daily life and a cool, sexy *look*. The writers Reed loved gave him this permission. Jack Kerouac provided hipsters with a kind of blueprint on how to be "poetic" without their necessarily having to read or write that much poetry. As the following excerpt from a dialogue between the characters Leo Percepied and Yuri Gligoric (alter egos for Kerouac and Gregory Corso, respectively) in Kerouac's *The Subterraneans* attested, poetry could be understood to refer as much to a state of mind and lifestyle as it did to literature:

> Yuri and I had a long talk that week in a bar, over port wines, he claimed everything was poetry, I tried to make the common old distinction between verse and prose, he said, "Lissen Percepied do you believe in freedom? then say what you want, it's poetry, poetry, all of it is poetry, great prose is poetry, great verse is poetry."—"Yes" I said "but verse is verse and prose is prose."—"No no" he yelled "it's all poetry."—"Okay," I said, "I believe in you believing in freedom and maybe you're right, have another wine."[16]

Though Reed was playing at dances to make cash and develop his musical chops, the poetic persona Reed was developing was predicated on the lives of his favored outlaw writers as described in books like *The Subterraneans*. Drinking hard, having sex, talking all night long, smoking pot, shooting up, all of it poetry! The popular crooners of his day had nothing to do with influencing Lewis Alan Reed as he worked out how to become Lou.

It is revealing, then, to note that it was during his apprenticeship period in college rock bands that Reed participated in the mimeograph revolution. In May 1962 Reed, along with fellow students Lincoln Swados and other Syracuse bohos, began publishing a magazine entitled *Lonely Woman Quarterly*, which Reed named after the Ornette Coleman composition "Lonely Woman."

His choice to call the magazine *Lonely Woman* reveals a specific kind of status the editors were seeking and the kind of company they were developing as much as it was a reflection of Reed's listening habits. Jazz music was, after all, tremendously influential to the poets Reed loved, including Ginsberg and Kerouac. Ginsberg explained the relationship between jazz's improvisatory structure and his long poem "Howl":

> In the dedication of *Howl* I said "spontaneous bop prosody." And the ideal, for Kerouac, and for John Clellon Holmes and for me also, was the legend of Lester Young playing through something like sixty-nine to seventy choruses of "Lady Be Good," you know, mounting and mounting and building and building more and more intelligence into the improvisation as chorus after chorus went on.[17]

Ginsberg's concept was realized perhaps most successfully in Jack Kerouac's *Mexico City Blues* (1959), whose 242 "choruses" were described by the author in specifically jazz-oriented terms. "I want to be considered a jazz poet," Kerouac wrote in the introduction to the book.[18]

Yet by 1962 the links between bebop jazz and Beat literature were so well known that they were used within mainstream culture to parody and mock literary and social outsiders.[19] Reed's use of Ornette Coleman's composition, then, was a move away from the kinds of associations that 1950s bebop and hard bop—so beloved by Kerouac, Ginsberg, and the Beats—had acquired. "Ornette Coleman's 1959 arrival in New York City fissured the jazz world as had nothing since bebop," writes David Rosenthal:

> Coleman was hailed by many . . . as a genius, a true original, a "new Charlie Parker." Others, however, felt that far from moving beyond conventional harmonies and the chromatic scale, he had simply never mastered them. Coleman's music, at once revolutionary and atavistic, charged with the raw cry of the blues . . . left no one indifferent.[20]

Beat poets—excepting Amiri Baraka, who proved a tireless promoter of the new sounds—did not exhibit nearly as much interest in the free jazz of Coleman, Albert Ayler, and others as they had in the relatively more conventional bop musicians like Young, Charlie Parker, and Dizzy Gillespie. Reed, a committed reader of the Beats, a lover of rock 'n' roll, and an aspiring poet, defined himself beyond the clichés that would almost inevitably be attached to collegiate bohemians looking to make a name for themselves in the local literary field. Gracing his and his friends' magazine with a

Coleman title would certainly go far in confounding expectations of beat-nik derivativeness.

There were three issues of *Lonely Woman Quarterly*, dated May 7, 1962, May 23, 1962, and April 1963. Typically for the underground press at the time, the editors of *Lonely Woman Quarterly* promoted their new adventure using oppositional, arrogant, and funny language that clearly demarcated an edgy in-the-know "us" versus a mainstream, milquetoast "them." An article in the student newspaper *The Daily Orange* written by Alan Millstein proved a stage for *Lonely Woman* editors to strut their stuff. Referring to the official campus literary magazine, *The Syracuse 10*, Reed's friend and *Lonely Woman* coeditor Lincoln Swados[21] scoffed that the journal "under [Syracuse student] Terry Hughes seemed like the *Saturday Evening Post*."[22] Describing how he and his friends including Reed had had no luck being published at Syracuse, Swados explains to Millstein how he was one of

> a bunch of guys who got together to turn out on their own an informal collec-
> tion of poetry and fiction that the authors felt should be set in print. . . . The
> people who turned out the "Quarterly" felt that this year's "Syracuse 10" was
> not only less literary but also that the vision of the material in the first issue
> was about two feet in front of its nose.[23]

Millstein described the contents of the first issue as a "collection of short stories and poetry in the avant-garde mode," pointing out that the journal was printed "Monday on a ditto machine loaned to the 'publishers' by Gus Josseph [*sic*] of the Savoy Restaurant." Continuing to emphasize in a vaguely patronizing if appreciative manner the casual, unconventional aspects of the *Quarterly*, Millstein went on to explain that "five sophomores contrib-uted the literary material and art work that was used in the first edition: 'Luis' Reed, liberal arts student and sometime singer with a campus rock 'n' roll band; Joseph McDonald, liberal arts; James T. Tucker, liberal arts, and Swados."[24] Swados advised potential contributors to "just drop by the Savoy and look for those customers who look literate."[25]

Reed's contributions to the magazine find him employing a breezily quo-tidian style that is at odds with his tendency otherwise to pastiche the Beats. Take, for example, Reed's "Prologue," published in the first issue of *Lonely Woman Quarterly*. While Reed's text was marred by some arguably adolescent Kerouacian imitations ("We had talked of the soul and its death, and my death, the last of my supplanting lives, spent and completely wasted, except for the knocking and the constant hurt"),[26] the narrative moved rather quickly into a charmingly direct depiction of present-day Greenwich Village. "Have you ever sat in the Square trying to look angry? That's precisely what Isabell and I do every Thursday from 3 to 4, across from the arch near the fountain where the ducks would be if they were given permits, but who ever heard of a legal duck."[27] These two pithy sentences found Reed attempting to illustrate suburban Washington Square day-trippers' efforts to fit in with and reflect the intensity, quirkiness, and chic rage assumed to be part and parcel of the downtown scene.

Reed continued his story with quotidian reportage on the San Remo bar—the space where Beat and New York School poets rubbed shoulders, bought one another drinks, traded barbs, flirted, and fought.[28] Employing O'Hara's conceit of embodying presence by noting place and time, Reed continued in his "Prologue" to write "at six o'clock when the leaves fall and one or two lights go on the excursion to the San Remo's started, a square box-like structure on the tail end of McDougal Street, complete with big green signs and old barber shop quartet type lights."[29] Echoing O'Hara's practice of naming names and situating characters within a markedly queer culture, Reed added: "At San Remo's we picked up A and De John, and after a preliminary discussion it was decided in due course to merge with our rough trade brethren."[30] Though this is prose, not poetry, there is not much distance here between Reed's urbane sociability and so many of O'Hara's most beloved prosaic "I do this, I do that"–style poems—poems published throughout the late 1950s and early 1960s in fugitive mimeos and magazines like the *Evergreen Review*, which were required reading for aspiring free-spirited intellectuals.

The second issue of *Lonely Woman Quarterly* found Reed honing the wildly barbative skills that were to prove his trademark in such aggressively contemptuous songs as "Dirt." Opening the issue with an editorial entitled "Michael Kogan—Syracuse's Miss Blanding," Reed began the piece by sneering "Michael Kogan, the reptilian treasurer of the Young Democrats, recently asserted his obese shape to the extent of slithering on all fours into the uniting arms of the conservative [sic] bastillion, otherwise modestly titled the Young Americans for Freedom." For good measure, Reed continued by describing Kogan with a "nouveau riche attache case in hand, pleated trousers ala Wolsley flapping in the breeze, [who] can be seen at the most any hour at the Western Union desk of the corner store where, American flag placed neatly up his rectum, he can be heard issuing various ultimatums and platitudes."[31]

Lonely Woman Quarterly was serving as a rehearsal space for Reed to try out a variety of poses that would prove to be so fruitful in his later incarnation as rock 'n' roll animal. In fact, the third issue of *Lonely Woman* found Reed coming out both in terms of the increasingly outrageous content he was including in his work and in his own self-fashioning—no more "Luis Reed" or "Lewis Reed" now, just plain "Lou." While Reed didn't publish any of his poetry in this issue, his prose piece "And What, Little Boy, Will You Trade for Your Horse?" found Reed detailing the demimonde in a way that looked ahead to any number of later lyrics, such as "Walk on the Wild Side" and "Halloween Parade." It also revealed a young Reed fascinated by garish New York culture independently of Warhol's and Paul Morrissey's glamorization of transvestites, hookers, and hustlers in films like *Chelsea Girls* (1966) and *Trash* (1970).

"And What, Little Boy" begins with the protagonist "David" (a dissipated teenager and thinly veiled stand-in for Reed himself) riding the subway and noticing all the varied characters populating the scene—a drunken, two-hundred-pound "Negro" shouting to everyone in the subway car how he loves them; an anxious collegiate and his date, desperately trying to keep their cool and not look nervous; a black businessman glowering at the drunk; and so on. David gets out, naturally, at Times Square, and it is here that the story really takes off. A young hustler tells an old man that it costs "ten a throw"; a gang of fourteen-year-old queer hoodlums are presented "mincing and giggling. But they are dangerous. He remembers seeing one slice another's face with a razor blade he carried in his handkerchief."[32] Reed's "I'm Waiting for the Man," with its tale of a strung-out kid heading up to Lexington, 1-2-5, hovers behind such prose sentences as "He thought for a moment of returning to the subway and going uptown. He wasn't afraid of 125th alone."[33] A wretched barfly named Janey, who flirts outrageously with David, anticipates the characters Candy, Holly, and Sugar Plum Fairy from Reed's "Walk on the Wild Side." Winking at David, Janey's eyelid is described as "coated with a lucent, sticky, blue-green smear." "Do you think I'm old," Janey asks David pathetically. "I think you're beautiful,"[34] David replies flatly—and wholly unconvincingly.

While the subjects in Reed's story may have fit neatly into the catalogue of down-and-outers limned so lovingly in Allen Ginsberg's 1950s poetry, the language Reed used was markedly opposite to the aggrandizing "best minds of my generation" tag Ginsberg attached to the suffering, insane, and buggered demimonde of the Times Square depicted in "Howl." Reed seemed to understand that the heroicizing tendencies of Ginsberg and company had to make way for a new aesthetic if Reed was to emerge from under their shadow.[35] Corny turns of phrase needed to be avoided—even the word "dig" was ripe for punishment: "You still use that?" Janey asks David. "What?" asks David. "Dig?" she responds. "Dig what?" David retorts. "Dig, the word, stupid," she explains brusquely. "'Oh. No.' David shook his head and brought his right arm up to his face, and held it there, rubbing his eyes. 'That went out about four years ago.'"[36]

Reed's works published in *Lonely Woman Quarterly* ultimately fed into Reed's lyrics for the Velvets and his later solo career. What's curious about reading *Lonely Woman Quarterly* is to see how little would change in terms of Reed's style and the characters he was drawn to give voice to. Mixing a world-weary, vernacular tone with bursts of inspired disjunction, or interrupting a straightforward narrative with Joycean free association, Reed used the journal to sketch the personae that were to prove obstinate presences throughout his career. Reed's porn freaks, alcoholics, suburbanite wannabes, drag queens, hustlers, and junkies all got their start at Syracuse University, accompanying Reed on his journey from Lewis to Luis to Lou.

Despite Reed's work in collegiate avant-garde publishing, the lure of music proved irresistible, notwithstanding his mentor Delmore Schwartz's hatred of pop music. But how could the young Reed continue to earn poetry credibility while staying true to his rock 'n' roll heart? Paralleling the Fugs' demotic simplification of Blake and Swinburne, Reed redefined Schwartz and other challenging writers into accessible populist figures. Regarding Schwartz's oft-anthologized short story "In Dreams Begin Responsibilities," for example, Reed enthused:

> To think you could do that with the simplest words available in such a short span of pages and create something so incredibly powerful. You could write something like that and not have the greatest vocabulary in the world. I wanted to write that way, simple words to cause an emotion, and put them with my three chords.[37]

Reed also looked to and learned from the more ambitious pop lyricists emerging from the Greenwich Village folk scene, particularly Bob Dylan.[38] What Reed *didn't* learn from Dylan, however, was a consistently healthy skepticism toward anyone investing rock lyrics with the status of poetry.[39] While often self-deprecating and antielitist, Reed nevertheless played up his high-art status throughout his career by insisting his audience consider the words in his songs as equivalent to poetry. "In the beginning was the word . . . closely followed by a drum and some early version of a guitar," Reed wrote in his introduction to *Between Thought and Expression*, adding: "This is a collection of lyrics that I feel can stand alone from the music for which they were originally written."[40] Reed had clearly not abandoned some basic assumptions about poetry as a higher calling. Rock 'n' roll music and lyrics, the very "medium in which he excelled," as Jeremy Reed rightly put it, "was somehow too superficial for his intellectual type."[41]

Lou Reed, the Velvets, and the New York School

With the Fugs playing a part in the day-to-day listening and touring lives of the Velvets, and keeping in mind Gerard Malanga's role in the Velvet Underground, it is tempting, as Andrew Epstein has already done, to align aspects of Lou Reed's songs and the Velvets' early sound at least partly to O'Hara, Ashbery, and their second-generation New York School friends. As Epstein proposes in his tantalizing article "I'll Be Your Mirror: Lou Reed and the New York School of Poetry," reverberations can be heard between New York School poetry and poetics and Reed's lyrics. "Lou Reed's songs pick up on the New York School's dedication to the everyday and the ordinary rather than the romantic, exotic, or fantastic, and often incorporate casual references to his friend's personal names and remarks, a trademark New York School device."[42] To put it another way, for every "Ashes," "Kenneth," and "Norman" in O'Hara's poems, there's a "Jack," "Jane," and "Lisa" in Reed's lyrics. Epstein goes further.

> Reed and some of the New York School poets (O'Hara and Schuyler, especially) were similarly candid about homosexuality: just as the New York School was one of the first poetic communities to be, at least in part, unabashedly queer

during the hyper-macho 1950s, Reed and the Velvet Underground deliberately cultivated a sexually ambiguous, androgynous image that was almost entirely unique in mid-1960s rock, and, as a result, were sometimes viewed as a "gay band," and were critiqued in homophobic terms.[43]

However, there is little in the way of the archives to illustrate Reed's reading New York School–affiliated writing. Indeed, for an oft-interviewed figure like Reed, we cannot avoid the fact that, apart from references to Beat Generation poets and Delmore Schwartz, Reed rarely mentions his own poetic contemporaries in his accounts of the literary influences on his music and lyrics. Additionally, Gerard Malanga casts doubt on Reed as a committed reader of contemporary verse: "I didn't talk to Lou Reed about New York School poetry, really," claims Malanga. "We never really had a talk about the aesthetics [of the New York School] that much. . . . Lou was not walking around with a copy of Frank O'Hara's *Lunch Poems* in his back pocket! [laughs]. I don't think Lou was that much of a reader of poetry, to tell you the truth."[44] Given Reed's lifelong paeans to Schwartz, Reed's cast of characters—his Andy, his Holly, his Jack, his Jim, his Lisa, his Candy, his Sylvia, and beyond—might be based more on Schwartz's example than on the New York School poets.[45]

That said, Epstein has gone far in opening up a window through which we can understand Reed's music and lyrics vis-à-vis a wider cultural world the Velvets inhabited. Facing Reed's entry into Warhol's Factory was Warhol's past, present, and future in New York School and Beat poetry. There was the aforementioned *C* magazine cover. Warhol's film *Couch* (1964) featured Malanga, Ginsberg, Kerouac, Gregory Corso, and other denizens of the Beat Generation. A number of Warhol's Screen Tests cast their eye on poets including Joe Brainard, Padgett, Berrigan, Ginsberg, and Ashbery. And Reed, after all, looked to Warhol as a model for being an artist in the world. As Reed put it retrospectively in the song "Work," featured on his and John Cale's album *Songs for Drella*: "Andy said a lot of things / I stored them all away in my head / Sometimes when I can't decide what I should do / I think what would Andy have said."[46]

And what Andy said quite often echoed what the New York School poets said, particularly when it came to those writers' refusal of anything resembling seriousness or pretentiousness associated with the artistic process. As Frank O'Hara mocked the self-regarding poet in his manifesto "Personism," so Warhol stated blandly, "Why do people think artists are special? It's just another job.... If you say that artists take 'risks,' it's insulting to the men who landed on D-Day, to stunt men, to baby-sitters, to Evel Knievel, to stepdaughters, to coal miners, and to hitch-hikers, because they're the ones who really know what 'risks' are."[47] Part of this humorous assault on seriousness included questioning the primacy of nature as a subject in art. Determined New Yorkers, both O'Hara and Warhol celebrated urban space to the extent that nature itself was often (if complexly) relegated to the status of ornament.[48] "One need never leave the confines of New York to get all the greenery one wishes—I can't even enjoy a blade of grass unless I know there's a subway handy, or a record store or some other sign that people do not totally regret life" insisted O'Hara famously in his prose poem "Meditations in an Emergency."[49] As if continuing the conversation O'Hara started in his urbane pronouncement, Warhol in a pithy dialogue between an unidentified "A" and "B" offered: "A: *Should we walk? It's really beautiful out.* B: *No.* A: *Okay.*"[50] In these two resonant quotations, conventional art-historical narratives aligning painting and poetry's long-standing associations with the natural world make way for the babble and banter of Gotham.

Reed, often featured in magazines that situated him in the neighborhood of the New York School, took on and complicated the prejudices and playful antiacademicism of the poets as a way to define his persona. Writing in Andy Warhol's and David Dalton's creatively designed magazine *Aspen* in 1966,[51] for example, Reed complained, "Now Robert Lowell, up for a poetry prize without a decent word ever written.... Giving Robert Lowell any kind of poetry prize is obscene. Ditto worrying about Ezra Pound. And the Yale Poetry series. The colleges are meant to kill.... How can they give Robert Lowell a poetry prize. Richard Wilbur. It's a joke."[52] This complaint was broadly typical of the way poets Reed loved attacked mainstream writers and mocked the academy. What Amiri Baraka referred to as "Bullshit school poetry"[53] was constantly and at times riotously under attack by writers affiliated with the literary underground.

Just one year before Reed thundered against Lowell, for example, Frank O'Hara complained in an interview with Edward Lucie Smith about Lowell's poem "Skunk Hour": "I don't think that anyone has to get themselves to go and watch lovers in a parking lot necking in order to write a poem, and I don't see why it's admirable if they feel guilty about it. They should feel guilty. Why are they snooping? What's so wonderful about a Peeping Tom?"[54] Reed was on top of the latest prejudices his fellow writers held against the loathed "academic" poets, and he hitched his wagon to the avant-garde pony accordingly. Beyond just criticizing Lowell et al., Reed insisted that musicians and lyricists should now join poets on the avant-garde Parnassus:

> What about the EXCELLENTS, Martha and the Vandellas (Holland, Dozier, Holland; Jeff Barry, Ellie Greenwich, Bachrach [sic] and David, Carol [sic] King and Gerry Goffin, the best songwriting teams in America). Will none of the powers that be realize what Brian Wilson did with THE CHORDS. . . . The only decent poetry of this century was that recorded on rock-and-roll records. Everybody knew that. Who you going to rap with. Little Bobby Lowell or Richard Penniman alias Little Richard, our thrice-retired preacher . . . The only poetry of the last 20 years was and is in the music on the radio. The colleges have to be destroyed.[55]

Reed's insistence on not just aligning pop with poetry but on valorizing it through comparison to purportedly crummy poets compared interestingly to what was happening down at St. Mark's. As Reed attempted to ascribe poetic cultural capital to Martha and the Vandellas, writers including Ted Berrigan and Ron Padgett were citing 1960s pop musicians such as the Kinks and the Velvet Underground in their work in ways that did not necessarily distinguish between purportedly heightened poetic diction and rock 'n' roll lyrics. The distance between the Poetry Project at St. Mark's Church and Andy Warhol's Factory on Park Avenue South was not too far either in terms of actual geography or in a shared, playfully experimental, pop-inflected poetics.

It is true that Reed spoke far more about wanting to achieve in his lyrics what his beloved mentor Delmore Schwartz and other writers, including Ginsberg, had achieved in poetry than he did about O'Hara, Berrigan, or Padgett. Yet, while it might seem counterintuitive, there are affinities among Schwartz, Warhol, and the New York School of poets. Andrew Epstein points out that fifteen years before Reed met him, Schwartz was a brilliant young professor at Harvard at the same moment the original New York School poets were studying there; among his students was Kenneth Koch. As poetry editor of the *Partisan Review*, Schwartz published important early works by John Ashbery and O'Hara in the 1950s. . . . Delmore Schwartz—a writer from the decidedly less avant-garde precincts of mid-century literature—is one of the rather surprising, hidden links between the New York School and the Velvet Underground.[56]

And it wasn't just the old guard of the New York School that Schwartz had a link to. Ted Berrigan made sure to send Schwartz a first-edition copy of his *Sonnets*. "Forgive this invasion of your privacy," Berrigan petitioned in his letter to Schwartz, "but I have always admired your poems. . . . I'd like you to have this copy of my 'Sonnets'. At least one of them, LXVI, owes something to your book."[57] Schwartz's poetry at times also echoed themes that characterized Warhol's durational films, such as *Sleep* and *Empire*, both of which used a fixed camera to focus on, respectively, John Giorno sleeping for around five and a half hours and the Empire State Building over an eight-hour period. In his "Seurat's Sunday Afternoon Along the Seine," for example, Schwartz wrote: "If you look long enough at anything / It will become extremely interesting; / If you look very long at anything / It will become rich, manifold, fascinating."[58] Monomaniacal attention to quotidian details, the use of one's friends and family as material and subject for art, and inno-cent enthusiasm characterized much of the work that Schwartz and War-hol, O'Hara and Berrigan produced. Lou Reed was listening, watching, and learning.

Lou Reed, the *Paris Review*, and "The Murder Mystery"

Given Reed's roles as frontman for the Velvet Underground and as fellow traveler of the New York School of poetry, it made sense that the poet and publisher Tom Clark would include his "The Murder Mystery" in the *Paris Review*, even if the work had appeared initially as a song on *The Velvet Under-ground* (1969), the band's third full-length album. Lou Reed's presence fed into Tom Clark's efforts as editor to interrogate the refined if vaguely roué internationalist qualities the *Paris Review* expressed by publishing work by and interviews with writers including Ezra Pound, Truman Capote, Jean Genet, and Vladimir Nabokov. Clark's inclusion of downtown poets like Larry Fagin, Berrigan, and Alice Notley marked a radical departure in the *Paris Review* from the choices made by "the magazine's upper-crust editorial responsibles."[59]

Describing his decision to bring Berrigan et al. into the *Paris Review*'s staid pages even as he was producing his own small-press mimeograph magazine series *Once*, Clark proposed the St. Mark's crowd as an invasive species "who in turn were soon also popping up like strange weeds in the swank uptown gardens of George Plimpton's journal."[60] Clark went far in showing how a downtown poetics could—indeed, *should*—participate actively in uptown publishing ventures. Previously limited to coterie distribution networks, second-generation New York School poetry could now, thanks to Clark, access a wider audience and, by implication, cause trouble on an even grander scale.

As Geoffrey Canon described the process of recording the Velvet Underground song "The Murder Mystery,"

> Lou's idea, with "Murder Mystery," was to use words one way on one channel, another way on the other, synch them, so that listeners would find their way to listening first on one channel, then on the other, and afterwards on both. The first dialectical rock 'n' roll track. Left hand speaker equals thesis, right hand speaker equals antithesis. And the synthesis is in the listener's own head. So that there is no such thing as the meaning, objectively, of "Murder Mystery." Its meaning, for any listener, depends where his head is at.[61]

Wrenching the song out of vinyl and onto the pages of the *Paris Review* number 53, Clark proved that "The Murder Mystery," given the right literary context and framing, could fit effortlessly alongside the formally ambitious texts of Reed's Poetry Project peers. Transforming the lyrics into a static text for the purposes of publication in a poetry magazine, Reed simply placed two columns on each page to replicate the stereo effect achieved on the album. Leaving its life as avant-garde rock song behind, "The Murder Mystery" in the *Paris Review* became a conceptually elaborate poem. The first two double-columned stanzas evoked nothing so much as a poet working hard to write syllabic and accentual verse:

denigrate obtuse and active verb
    pronouns
skewer the sieve of the optical sewer
release the handle that holds all the
    gates up
puncture the eyeballs that seep all
    the muck up
read all the books and the people
    worth reading
and still see the muck on the sky of
    the ceiling

candy screen wrappers of silkscreen
    fantastic
lurid and lovely with twilight of ages
laconic giggles ennui for the
    passions
rectify moments most serious and
    urgent
requiring replies most facile and
    vacuous
on a subject of great concern, noble
    origin[62]

The rhythms of Reed's lines here are fascinating when read in the context of the pop/poetry divide he struggled so hard to transgress. A psychedelic-heavy phrase like "Candy screen wrappers of silkscreen fantastic" echoes the poetic meter of lines in the Beatles' "Lucy in the Sky with Diamonds"[63] as much as it does to works by any number of more traditional nineteenth-century British poets beloved by Delmore Schwartz. (Lines from Lord Byron's *Don Juan*, for example, comically predict the abstraction Reed exploits through disjunction, in some cases simply by organizing proper names to fit the same rhythmic stress pattern Reed would later follow: "Barnave, Brissot, Condorcet, Mirabeau").[64] While there is little in "The Murder Mystery" that approaches narrative à la Byron, the rhythms defining Reed's stanzas nevertheless work to create a kind of ironic tension between meter and content. The stability of meter is—somewhat humorously—at odds with the *instability* of meaning performed so insistently through Reed's word-salad juxtapositions.

Reading Reed's text in the *Paris Review* was, of course, a completely different experience to hearing it on *The Velvet Underground*. Reed's voice on the LP was engineered to transmit through the right speaker and Sterling Morrison's on the left. The section of the song that one might call the chorus was similarly divided. Maureen Tucker sang lines including "please raise the flag" in her winsome fashion; Doug Yule matched her with phrases like "mister moonlight." The stanzas allotted to Morrison that were aligned to the left speaker were twice as long as they appear in the *Paris Review*. As Reed rapped "denigrate obtuse and active verb pronouns / skewer the sieve of the optical sewer" and so on, Morrison's voice featured on the left channel practically swallowing the following words in a rush to match Reed's timing: "candy screen wrappers of silkscreen fantastic / requiring memories both lovely and guilt-free / lurid and lovely with twilight of ages / luscious and lovely and filthy with laughter," etc. Publication in the *Paris Review* meant, for Reed, that "The Murder Mystery" had to be tamed. Reed's poem in the *Paris Review* was foregrounded as an inherently composed *rule-bound* text—one could say that it was Reed's own version of a Swineburn Stomp.

Reed's sustainment of a monolithic rhythm in the print version of "The Murder Mystery" was foregrounded so aggressively that it unavoidably proved the highlight of the reader's experience. That rhythm was shattered gloriously in the recorded version of the text. "The Murder Mystery" as listeners heard it on the LP *The Velvet Underground* worked actively to undermine and frustrate the listener's expectations of a rhythm one could tap one's toe to. Morrison's logorrhea overwhelmed and interrupted Reed's own carefully patterned vocalization. Reed's work with the Velvets danced along the precipice of incomprehensibility and challenged listeners to alter their conceptions about what a rock 'n' roll song could and should do, while Reed's work as a published poet was of a piece with the games being played by Ted Berrigan, Alice Notley, and others.

In fact, while Reed's "The Murder Mystery" tested and teased out the relationship between meter and content, Berrigan's sonnets published in *Paris Review* 53 reveal a similar tension. The pleasures in reading Berrigan's first of "Three Sonnets for Tom Clark" result almost entirely from recognizing the disconnect between the fragmented, collagist nature of the text itself and the aura of tradition—and expectations of adherence to form—embodied in the very word "sonnet." Beginning "In The Early Morning Rain / To my family & friends 'Hello,'"[65] Berrigan's poem continues almost entirely to resist paraphrase as it flouts all the rules of the traditional sonnet. Yet, guided by the word "sonnet," we nevertheless aim to make some kind of sense out of these fragments. Does the poem have fourteen lines? Well, no, it seems to have more, but perhaps some of the indented lines can be read as part of the lines preceding them, so that we can say, albeit tentatively, that there are fourteen lines. Given that it is unclear as to whether there are fourteen lines in Berrigan's sonnet, can we say with any certainty that there is a "volta" or turn at the ninth line, as there would be in a Petrarchan sonnet? Well, yes, but it is not self-evident—it is there entirely because the informed reader is trained to see one there. Like Reed's "The Murder Mystery," patterns associated with genre poetry are used ironically to emphasize the inherently artificial and even arbitrary ways in which form determines content.

Heroin

If "Heroin" had been a piece of literature, then no one would have batted an eyelid. But as it was, because rock music was seen to be the young person's art form, people couldn't accept that rock music could tackle adult themes, which is what Lou Reed always does. And that's the first thing about this man that has to be accepted. He takes rock music seriously, accepts it as an art form, with real integrity and real purpose.

—Waldemar Januszczak, quoted in Lou Reed et al., *Rock and Roll Heart*

In "Heroin" Reed initially sing-talks the lyrics, the music and overall tempo "played slowly and gently." Reed then segues into "an agitated and noisy part in which the tempo is double-timed and there is wild soloing from the instrumentalists."[66] The band alternates between the slow and gentle and the "agitated and noisy" throughout the song. Reed claimed he was interested in subject matter that hadn't been covered in pop and rock, but the song is in many ways a rock 'n' roll extension of an urban blues tradition whose singers bemoan and/or celebrate their addictions, such as Charley Patton's "Spoonful Blues." "Spoonful Blues" is an interesting tune in large part because of its curious use of elision. "Don't make me mad, baby!" Patton implores, "'cause I want my . . . / Hey baby, I'm a fool 'bout that . . . ."[67] The tendency of the drug's users to make a series of rapid associations— often losing focus on any one thing in the rush—is in Patton's song performed by using the fragment as a unit of composition. Though Reed insists the Velvets "used to have a rule. Anyone who plays a blues riff gets fined five dollars,"[68] the blank spaces in Patton's and related blues lyricists' songs find a counterpart in Reed's great disaffected refrain "And I guess, but I just don't know."

Yet it would be a disservice to the song's lyrics to characterize them merely as an updated version of a familiar theme in blues music. Reed's lyrics for "Heroin" encapsulate and condense some of the more advanced writing of Beat Generation writers into a bizarrely catchy—and sonically unusual— rock song. As Daniel Morris recognizes, "the violence against the body through the needle is the method Reed discovered to destroy one version of the self in order to create the possibility of his connection to a higher con- sciousness, what Ginsberg, in 'Howl,' called 'the starry dynamo.'"[69] In light of Reed's oft-stated love of Ginsberg's "Howl," we can understand "Heroin" in part as a critical conversation with Ginsberg's text, one that questions and complicates Ginsberg's own at-times stentorian tenor.[70]

While it's a cliché at this point to suggest a natural sympathy between alienated adolescent or late-adolescent males and Allen Ginsberg's "Howl," the biographical details in Ginsberg's poem must have proved irresistible to Lou Reed. Like Ginsberg, Reed was an aspiring poet who came from a subur- ban middle-class Jewish family. Reed also suffered at the hands of the psy- chiatric industry when he underwent electroshock therapy to "cure" him of his same-sex attractions. Lines from "Howl," for example, "who were given instead the concrete void of insulin Metrazol electricity hydrotherapy psy- chotherapy occupational therapy pingpong & amnesia,"[71] resonated partic- ularly strongly with Reed as he developed his artistic persona. As the "best minds" in Ginsberg's poem are celebrated in the "Footnote to 'Howl'" as "holy," Reed promises in the first stanza that "I'm going to try for the king- dom if I can," adding later in the second stanza, "And I feel just like Jesus's son." "Howl" begins with the "best minds" searching for an "angry fix" of heroin—it is that quest that serves as the trigger for the series of looping epiphanies that build up to a crescendo in the "Footnote" section of "Howl." Similarly, in Reed's song the protagonist's desire for a practically metaphysi- cal bliss is effected by the plunge of the needle, which results in his becoming "better off than dead." Even Reed's elision of "a" in "I have made big decision" echoes Ginsberg's habit of omitting prepositions and articles. It is "Starving hysterical naked," after all, not "starving, hysterical, and naked."

But Reed's insistence on irresolution and indifference stands as a proto- punk counterargument to Ginsberg's efforts toward transcendence as it is expressed so beautifully in the "Footnote to 'Howl.'" What makes Reed's song remarkable to this day is his refusal to take his protagonist's narcissism too seriously. Every affirmation is countered with a playful ambivalence: "I don't know just where I'm goin'"; "I'm goin' to try for the kingdom if I can"; "Then I really don't care anymore"; "Ooohhh, thank your God that I'm not aware"; and, of course, that epic statement of ennui, "And I guess that I just don't know." Reed's adamantly playful refusal to align heroin use with *either* blissful visionary states *or* wretched down-and-outism shows a refreshing skepticism to truth claims considered generally. Even as it nods to "Howl" and related works, "Heroin" is both an ominous evocation of drug addiction and a joke on self-important dropouts ascribing deep meaning to their habit. Reed would in fact manifest the parodic aspect of "Heroin" in the mid-1970s, when he took to pretending to shoot up on stage while performing the song. In some ways akin to proto-punk songs like the Fugs' "The I Saw the Best Minds of My Generation Rot," "Heroin" pokes fun at Beat-era theatrics and longings for transformative spiritual experience.

The song's "distanced approach—outrageous in its refusal to be outraged," as Matthew Bannister puts it, is matched on *The Velvet Underground and Nico* in a number of songs that are

> inexpressive in the objectivity of their descriptions, in the way that they describe feelings from a second- or third-person perspective, or from the first-person perspective of someone who doesn't seem to have any feelings at all ("Heroin"). [The] stiff, icy majesty of Nico's vocals and Lou Reed's deadpan talk-singing are underscored by the unyielding quality of the musical settings—robotic, unswinging rhythms, the ubiquitous drone, and the dissonance and harshness of the sound, all smacking of an overall indifference.[72]

It's that "indifference" that makes songs like "Heroin" so distinct from the imperative-driven Beat poetics that Reed otherwise loves. Indifference also links Reed to the New York School poets' polymorphously perverse texts. As Mark Silverberg points out, poets like John Ashbery, Frank O'Hara, Kenneth Koch, James Schuyler, and Barbara Guest were, after all, not exactly committed to identifying and overthrowing an established literary/ political order. Not for them the histrionics of a poet like Allen Ginsberg railing against Moloch, nor, by extension, the bearded shenanigans of the Left versus the moralistic militarism of the Right. Rather, the remit of the New York School poets was to develop and sustain a position of *indifference* to oppositional binaries, one that, in the words of John Ashbery, hovered productively "between the extremes of Levittown and Haight-Ashbury."[73] New York School writers, Silverberg argues, opened up "a space beyond 'radical art'—and its favorite gestures of antagonism, individualism, and futurism"[74] that made room for qualifications, skepticism, comicality, and irresolution. This equivocal stance helped the New York poets in their efforts to interrogate the high seriousness ascribed to figures such as Ginsberg.

Also following the New York School's allowance for camp, "Heroin" and related songs find Reed striking a markedly queer pose generated by Reed's intonation of lines that would look serious if considered on the page alone. Take the way Reed articulates "'cuz it makes me feel like I'm a man / when I put a spike into my veins," for example. As it has been recorded on *The Velvet Underground and Nico*, the accent Reed places on *feel* and *spike* sounds like it's coming from a narcotized sensuous adolescent enthusing over a surprise gift. Similarly, what can we make of the section where Reed rather suddenly reveals that "I wish that I'd sailed the darkened seas / On a great big clipper ship / Going from this land here to that / In a sailor's suit and cap"? We are in *Billy Budd* territory here, where our hero chooses not the uniform of a commodore but the vaguely queer "sailor suit," an outfit affiliated practically as much with gay trade as it is with actual sailors.[75] By identifying the sailor suit and cap as his dream getup, Reed inserts a gay subtext into the song. "It's my life / it's my wife" takes on a whole new shade of meaning in this reading—the little sailor boy is as much acknowledging the deep attachment he has to his next fix as he is building an allegory of a trick-turned-longtime companion. In a similar vein, the spike that Reed's protagonist plunges into his body can be read as a heavy-handed metaphor for homosexual sex, even as it is a realist's depiction of shooting up. And it is not just shore leave gone wild that forms part of the imaginary around the sailor suit and cap, an outfit identified as much with actual sailors and queerness as it was a form of "best wear" for children.[76] So, while the sailor suit and cap was worn in drag and vaudeville acts specifically to encourage the audience to make links between naval and homosexual affairs, kids throughout the United States also wore the outfit. Invoking the fantasy of a boy at sea, Reed managed slyly to inject a playground vibe into a song ostensibly about an addictive drug even as he simultaneously made shooting up seem luxuriously, queerly sexy.[77]

Join the Underground

Reed was actively constructing and disassembling seriousness in a way that echoed the writing around him. While critics rightly point to the newness of the Velvets' sound and the strangeness of Reed's lyrics, such moves were consistent with the poetry Reed was so committed to. It is difficult to imagine now, but Beat- and New York School–affiliated poetry in the 1950s and early 1960s—as I hope I have made clear—proved a far more daring forum for the expression of transgressive sounds, feelings, and ideas than rock 'n' roll. And that transgressive poetry was relatively *popular*, in the most literal sense of the word.

Reed, like Patti Smith, read Ginsberg, Kerouac, Burroughs, O'Hara, and related "underground" writers in outlets such as Grove Press's books and *Evergreen Review*, a magazine that made a virtue out of its transgressiveness.[78] Formed in 1957 as a forum for groundbreaking writers from Ashbery to Burroughs to Céline, *Evergreen Review* went far in marketing itself as an amalgam of "underground" literature, drugs, and unconventional sexuality as a lifestyle choice for an emerging hipster constituency. As a result, Grove found itself a target for multiple charges of obscenity.[79] Naturally, Grove Press publications and *Evergreen* garnered all the more publicity from these high-minded moralists. Sales increased, and the avant-garde became increasingly visible correspondingly.

To read *Evergreen*'s magazine and affiliated books was to align oneself, however immaterially or evanescently, to ambitious, troublemaking poets. Six months after it published Kerouac's *The Subterraneans* under its Evergreen Original imprint, Grove

ran an ad in the *New York Times Book Review* trumpeting [*The Subterraneans*' sales figures] as "an experiment in book publishing that worked!", listing *The Subterraneans*' "best sellerdom" as proof of success and offering new titles by Samuel Beckett and Alain Robbe-Grillet as the latest additions to the line . . . By 1962, the *New York Times* . . . confirmed that the "quality" paperback revolution had, indeed, been a success: "Created only eight years ago to meet the curricular and extracurricular needs of academic communities, its popularity is now so widespread that it is being sold in virtually all the nation's 1,700 bookshops."[80]

What Grove Press and the *Evergreen Review* showed English majors like Reed was that avant-gardism and popular success were not inimical—in the March 13, 1966, edition of the *New York Times*, an *Evergreen Review* display ad encouraged readers to "Join the Underground."

Grove Press was not the only outlet that, to encourage sales, highlighted the subversive qualities attendant to the New American Poetry and related prose writing. So-called men's magazines in the late 1950s and early 1960s such as *Swank* and *Playboy* included interviews with counterculture icons like Jack Kerouac and Norman Mailer sandwiched between seminaked bunnies, and poetry by writers including Frank O'Hara and Allen Ginsberg were featured in similar outlets: *Swank*, *Man's Wildcat Adventures*, and *Escapade*.[81] William Burroughs's works were published in a range of men's magazines, from the relatively tame *Escapade* to the hardcore *Screw*. New American poets of the postwar era saw no necessary conflict in publishing their lyrics among the nudie shots featured in *Swank* and related publications. In fact, publishers and poets joined forces to challenge uptight mores.

Take Frank O'Hara's poem "Ave Maria," first published in *Swank*. Beginning with the cri de coeur "Mothers of America, let your kids go to the movies!," the poem continued by limning the possibilities of "little tykes" meeting pedophiles at the cinema. Both mass-marketed as safely naughty by *Swank* ("safely" because grounded in a context that celebrated privileged American consumer/bachelor culture unproblematically) and contained soon after within a coterie context by Ted Berrigan's *C* magazine (thus establishing its underground caché), "Ave Maria" was proof that the avant-garde could play easily within a range of formerly discrete literary, visual, and commercial fields.[82] The poem's place in *Swank* showed how poetry could anticipate—foretell, even—both pornographic intergenerational sex (Hustler's *Barely Legal*, for example, or certain strains of Japanese *manga*) as well as the sexualized images of children that would be used to sell everything from American Apparel T-shirts to Abercrombie and Fitch thong underwear in children's sizes with slogans including "eye candy" and "wink wink" printed on the crotch. And "Ave Maria" showed this without repudiating its own avant-garde credentials. Equally at home a short while later in the pages of *C*, the poem's "broken vertical column of caesurae"[83] evokes Charles Olson's open-field poetics, as its lighthearted diction contrasted radically with the tortured confessionals of poetry popular in the early 1960s, poetry by Robert Lowell, John Berryman, Richard Wilbur, and the like.

Reed read "men's magazines" and commented trenchantly on the distinctions between hardcore porn and purportedly more urbane, intellectual publications like *Swank*. In Reed's "And What, Little Boy, Will You Trade for Your Horse?" "David" describes the scene inside a Times Square sex emporium:

Inside the store the propriators are cursing. . . . The clientle ignores three quarters of the store, and at this hour centers around the section labeled For Adults Only—Minors Under Twenty One Not Allowed. The girlie section. Stacks and stacks of old mens magazines, old Playboys, Desire, Flesh, magazines and more magazines . . . the more esoteric ones being wrapped in sealed cellophane, the better to tantilize and tittilate. To the left are the racks, rows and rows of picture packets, slides, regular, color, stero. White girls, colored girls, spanish girls, all in various stages of dress or undress, single, in groups, two, three, four, spanking pictures, wrestling pictures, no pretense made that this is sophistication for the urban male.[84]

It is that identification of the *pretensions* of "sophistication" typical of magazines like *Swank* that Reed, after O'Hara, satirizes here. O'Hara's perverse celebration of child-adult sex sits uncomfortably within the normalized sexuality feted by *Swank* editors. The issue of *Swank* that O'Hara's piece appeared in, after all, was nothing if not aggressively straight. Its cover featured an image of a scantily clad Julie Newmar in a balletic pose. With articles including "Brendan Behan: Uncle Tom with a Brogue?" and "The Girls in the Grey Flannel Undies" advertised prominently in caps, *Swank* was practically urgent in affirming its consumers' heterosexuality even as it appealed to their desire for underground status. While it published the San Francisco poet Bob Kaufman's "Abomunist Manifesto," Lawrence Ferlinghetti's "Loud Prayer," and jazz poetry by Dan Propper, such potentially transgressive texts were tamed by their placement alongside advertisements for luxury items like the "Abacus Cufflinks and Tieclasp Set." The poetry's evocations of marginal sexual practices were countered by a host of images affirming the most vanilla of male desires.[85] O'Hara's poem interrogated—whether the poet and editors intended it to or not—all the significations of white male privilege the magazine was so apparently eager to reflect and extend. "Mothers of America" served to remind readers that their sexuality, celebrated in an entirely airbrushed and sanitized form throughout *Swank*, could veer easily into darkly icky realms.

Following O'Hara, Reed's description of the porn-magazine store's contents in "And What, Little Boy" revealed how uncomfortably close "straight" magazines could be to their more purportedly kinky "esoteric" counterpart publications. And as it would for O'Hara's and related New American poets' writing, particularly as it was contextualized through literary and porn magazines, sexual candor determined the shock value and wondrousness of many of the Velvets' songs included in *The Velvet Underground and Nico*. Consider the "shiny shiny shiny boots of leather" ground into the ecstatic body of the supplicant Severin in "Venus in Furs" or the heroine in "There She Goes Again," who's "down on her knees again." Both O'Hara and Reed foreground what was formerly a latent conversation between marginalized "perverse" practices and mainstream libidinal pleasure, as they participated in the amicable relationship forged between New American poetry and softcore porn, popular culture and the "underground."

"It Must Be Writing"

During the period that found Reed on the cusp of his recording career and being influenced by Warhol, Reed still wanted to align himself more with the serious writer's life than with the rocker's. In a letter to Schwartz written soon after Reed released his single "The Ostrich" (1964) for Pickwick Records,[86] Reed made it clear where his dreams lay:

> I decided that I'm very very good and could be a good writer if i work and work. i know thats what ive got to do, no getting around it, but things had to get established, maybe i will go to school again. maybe i'll teach, maybe europe, who knows. But mainly it must be writing and I think I'm good enough to give it a run for its money.[87]

The son (Reed) beseeches the wise father (Schwartz) to pass on the poetic baton. Reed petitioned for this relationship even as the first inklings of the Velvet Underground were being nurtured in Reed's pick-up band the Primitives and, shortly after, by the Warlocks (featuring Sterling Morrison, Angus MacLise, and John Cale). Commuting between his parents' home in

Long Island and Pickwick International Studios in Long Island City, Reed admittedly wasn't quite yet living the dream. However, he was making a living as a lyricist and musician, was already working closely with avant-garde luminaries, and was on the cusp of forming one of the most important rock 'n' roll bands of all time. Yet, as his letter to Schwartz shows, he craved the life of the writer. Making money from records was good insofar as it could fund Reed's literary aspirations.

Reed's desire to be taken seriously as a poet lingered and inflected his activities throughout the Velvets' tenure and may have influenced his decision to drop his musical career (albeit temporarily) around the time the Velvet Underground was falling apart. In March 1971, one month after Patti Smith's now-legendary reading, Lou Reed gave a poetry reading at the Poetry Project at St. Mark's Church. Auspiciously, Jim Carroll, who a decade later was to find a place in the punk firmament with his song "People Who Died," opened for him. Reed's reading comprised reciting the lyrics to songs such as "Heroin" and "The Black Angel's Death Song." The audience, including poets like Allen Ginsberg, lapped it up. Bockris reports: "Carried away by the audience's response, [Reed] announced he'd never sing again, because he was now a poet. He went on to say that if he ever did anything as silly as returning to rock and roll the ghost of Delmore Schwartz would surely haunt him."[88] Hankering after the gravitas afforded the poet, Reed reframed his rock 'n' roll lyrics. Gone were the words as servants to sound. Instead, the words shone alone, asking to be taken by the audience on their own austere terms. Songs that, by 1971, had already become underground classics were now to be experienced through the minimalist framework of the spoken poetry performance. Music was a distraction from the real work of following in Schwartz's footsteps as a singular Poet.

Reed was so committed to convincing audiences he was a poet that, nearly twenty years after his performance at the Poetry Project, he used his introduction to his *Selected Lyrics* in part to boast that he was a prizewinning bard: "I've also included two poems, one of which won an award from the Literary Council for Small Magazines."[89] Now, by this stage Reed was well established as one of the most influential and preeminent figures in rock 'n' roll history. Clearly, Reed had not quite rid himself of his poetry-centric beliefs. He wanted audiences to appreciate him as a groundbreaking figure in rock 'n' roll, but he also very much wanted to remind them that he fit in just as easily with the culturally sanctioned field of poetry and poetics.

Reed danced a complicated dance between Lou the Poet and Lou the rock 'n' roll animal. Ultimately, though, Reed's lyrics really could not "stand alone." This is not because Reed's lyrics couldn't fit in to the genre of poetry. Take, for example, "Ferryboat Bill": "Ferryboat Bill, won't you please come home? / You know your wife has married a midget's son / And that's the short and long of it."[90] Conceivably, such a text could have been published in one of Aram Saroyan's small-press chapbooks as a charming and slightly perverse throwaway. Saroyan's poem "Lyric," for example, reads in its entirety: "I'm a cardboard poet / I eat rice."[91] Likewise, Ted Berrigan's poetry following *The Sonnets* was often amusingly minimal. Much of Reed's shorter poetry, alongside his more formally ambitious work like the double-columned "The Murder Mystery," is comparable to some of the work of his poetic contemporaries hanging out at St. Mark's.

The problem, of course, is that it is almost impossible to think of Reed as a poet without having the history of his life in rock 'n' roll determining our reception of his lines. As much as many of his lyrics resonate with Beat poetics, New York School antiseriousness, and Schwartzian romanticism, Reed's voice will forever color reader's reception of his words. Reed's *Selected Lyrics* represents not the convergence of two media but their divergence. Poetic text and sung lyric mutually undo the other, with Reed's recorded voice haunting our reception of the published lines. Reed's beloved Beat Generation writers would in the later 1950s and 1960s record their own poems, which informs how some readers "hear" the texts. However, Beat writing entered the world initially as *text* and reached (and continues to reach) its broadest audience via the printed word. For all their emphases on performance, the breath, the *sounding* of a poem, the writers Reed loved were ultimately still what Bob Perelman called "page poets."[92] The vast majority of people engaging with Beat and New York School writing did so and do so as readers—not listeners—of individual authors, while Reed's words were and are first and foremost distributed, received, and *heard* as part of a collectively produced musical experience.

This conundrum between printed poet and performing musician in Reed's case became clearer from the 1980s onward. The casual affect and witty transgressiveness that Reed developed was renounced in favor of the more serious mode expected of a Poet. With occasional exceptions, such as the rightly celebrated 1982 album *The Blue Mask*, Reed's humor and challenging music in works as diverse as *Street Hassle* (1978) and *Metal Machine Music* (1975) were not so evident. Instead, what audiences got were concept albums like *New York* (1989) and multimedia theatrical spectaculars like *Time Rocker*, his 1996 collaboration with the stage director Robert Wilson. Schwartz's haunting of Reed, one suspects, had much to do with Reed's ever-growing sense of himself as a serious artist and writer. Responding to the question "Could you say [*Time Rocker*] is a fulfillment of what Delmore Schwartz did say to you, like, you're a real writer?," Reed mused, "That would be a very pleasant thought. I haven't thought about that actually but I think at this point I could hold my head up to him . . . there you go, Delmore."[93] As recently as 2012, Reed introduced a new edition of Schwartz's *In Dreams Begin Responsibilities* with a series of clichés typical of the romantic vision of the doomed poet: "O Delmore how I miss you. You inspired me to write. You were the greatest man I ever met. You could capture the deepest emotions in the simplest language. Your titles were more than enough to raise the muse of fire on my neck. You were a genius. Doomed."[94]

Lou Reed's post-1970s career is a kind of renouncement of his naughty, faux-naive, and fundamentally non- (or even anti-) academic values. That said, Reed's work from the beginning of his career revealed an important ambivalence about the role poetry should play in rock music. Reed challenged his audiences to consider how earnestly one could and should treat the rock musician as an artist working beyond conventional understandings of what constituted the "popular." Eager from the start to attain the status he felt was implicit in the solemn poet's role, he nevertheless couldn't help but return to and defend, time and time again, that fine fine music—a rock 'n' roll that, in large part thanks to his model, would soon mutate into a poetry-inflected punk rock.

THREE

Proto-Punk and Poetry on St. Mark's Place

SOCIAL LINKS BETWEEN musicians and poets throughout the East Village were formed casually. Apartment buzzers were pressed, visitors welcomed in to talk. According to the poet Lewis Warsh, for example, Lou Reed and fellow members of the Velvet Underground dropped in to Waldman's and Warsh's flat at 33 St. Mark's Place to listen to *The Velvet Underground and Nico* for the first time. "Gerard [Malanga] and René Ricard were very much around," Warsh recalls.

> And we were living on St. Mark's Place, which was like the center of the East Village, and the Electric Circus is up the street, and I have this memory of the Velvet Underground coming to our apartment . . . they were saying "This is the first time we've heard this record," and it was the Banana record.[1]

And where Lou Reed weaved poetic allusions into his song lyrics, the new sounds and words he and his contemporaries were composing found their way into the downtown poets' poems. This cross-fertilization of genres is revealed clearly in Ted Berrigan and Anne Waldman's collaboratively written poem "Memorial Day," in which lines from the Velvet Underground's song "I'm Beginning to See the Light" were adapted into a text that owed as much to Charles Olson's characterization of the manuscript page as a field on which words could dance wildly as it did to Lou Reed and friends:

I met myself
      in a dream
            Everything was just all right
   Here comes two of you
        Which one will be true?
I'm beginning
     to see the light
            How does it feel?
      It feels,
          Out of sight![2]

A poem like this served in part to mark a generational shift away from the cultural world of New York School poets like O'Hara and Ashbery, who were more likely to cite Rachmaninoff's works than they were rock 'n' roll songs. As Anne Waldman points out, rock 'n' roll "was more *our* music."[3] Similarly, Bill Berkson remembers:

A regular itinerary by the time I moved downtown, 1968–70, was to walk from Lewis and Anne's or George and Katie Schneeman's on St. Marks Place, or my apartment on 10th Street, to the Fillmore, to Ratner's and Gem Spa, or in the other direction, up Second Avenue to the Poetry Project. I went to many shows at the Fillmore with Ted Berrigan, Michael Brownstein, Jim Carroll and others. The most amazing was a double bill featuring Neil Young and Miles Davis—more properly, Miles Davis with his *Bitches Brew* contingent *opening* for Neil Young and Crazy Horse! [Rock 'n' roll music . . .] was in the room, on the turntable, everywhere all the time. Lines from songs got into the poems, and the poems, like our conversations, learned to ride on this stream of continuous music.[4]

By the early 1970s, William Burroughs had returned from England and taken up residence at the "Bunker," a basement apartment on the Bowery in a building that was also home to the performance poet John Giorno. Naturally, Burroughs's first reading on home soil was, as Waldman recalls,

at the Church in 1971, '72, one of the first readings when he returned to New York City, and he had a job at City College . . . he was entertaining people like Debbie Harry, who were showing up at the Poetry Project and the Bunker . . . and

I'd already met John Lennon by 1973, for that concert for John Sinclair, and Yoko was always very friendly and I went to see her with Allen after John died, and I'd seen the Stones in England at Panna Grady's parties, Lewis Warsh was there as well . . . there was a lot of hobnobbing with these superstars, but I didn't feel my poverty around them . . . I felt like this was part of my generation.[5]

Waldman's talking about her "generation" reveals a fundamental difference between her poetic contemporaries and first-generation New York School predecessors like Ashbery, O'Hara, Barbara Guest, Kenneth Koch, and James Schuyler. Ashbery was so distanced from the countercultural music scene despite his friendships with younger rock 'n' roll-loving poets that he claims, "I never attended any of those events and have in fact never been to a rock concert."[6] However, as Tony Scherman and David Dalton write, Ashbery *was* in the audience at Andy Warhol's first Exploding Plastic Inevitable event on St. Mark's Place, at which the Velvet Underground were playing. "Few incidents better illustrate the shift from New York's fifties artistic subculture to the new sixties version," they explain,

> than the reaction of . . . poet John Ashbery, recently returned to New York after almost a decade in Paris. Standing in the midst of the strobe lights and guitar feedback and biomorphic slide-projected shapes, Ashbery was traumatized. "I don't understand this at all," he said and burst into tears.[7]

Rock 'n' roll didn't make the younger poets cry. As a 1969 *Newsweek* article on the Lower East Side poetry scene attested, "One common ground for young poets, white and black, is rock. 'My poems are involved with the spoken voice and with melody,' insists Tom Clark, 27. 'My listening to rock—its spirit and gaiety—is bound to affect what I write.'"[8] For Clark, Waldman, and friends rock 'n' roll was accessible, fun, *immediate*. "I was trying to make a poem as immediate as a record or photograph," said Aram Saroyan, adding: "Literature will soon cease to exist, except as an art form. The alphabet won't exist either except as an antique."[9] Saroyan here reframes poetry as a form that ideally elicits an immediate response from the audience. The poem, in Saroyan's hands, eschews the burdens of duration and attention attendant to tracking an unfolding lyric or narrative. One gets it in a flash.

Appealing not only for its spontaneity and its ability to be consumed in an instant, rock 'n' roll was also valued because it was geared toward entertaining an audience and eliciting a collective and joyous response:

> Rock combined lyrics with prosodic soloing, sacrificing much of bebop's conversational dynamic but gaining the opportunity to deliver a verbal message. Second, rock was a music intended for dancing as well as for listening. In bebop, improvisational gestures of the body-mind were available almost exclusively to the musicians; but danceable rock music offered audiences the opportunity to get in on the act.[10]

Propelled by a rock 'n' roll soundtrack, second-generation New York School work introduced a far -more youthful, class-inflected, and populist tenor into a comparatively staid "uptown" high-art scene. Tom Clark and Lewis Warsh's poem "To John Ashbery" seemed especially designed to mark such a break with the first generation. For example, the lines

John

it's

cold out. You are going

uptown[11]

parodically emphasized the uptown, upper-middle-class comfort that Ashbery was headed toward. The cold-water tenement apartments of New York's Lower East Side, where the speakers of the poem were based, take on a fugitive allure and charm. While Ashbery may be on his way to comfort, Clark and Warsh maintained their bohemian status by staying downtown in both word and deed. The next lines continue to differentiate the first and second generations by pointing out the basic class distinctions inherent in the "downtown" versus "uptown" binary. Addressing Ashbery directly, the poets promise, "If you were an Eskimo / we'd invite you / over for a frozen dinner."[12] The fact of the frozen dinner, while vaguely humorous, laid down a gauntlet. References to fancy foods in first-generation New York School work are manifold. James Schuyler, in his poem "Milk," describes "milk-skins" looking "the way dessert plates look after everyone has left the table in the Concord grape season";[13] O'Hara in "Beer for Breakfast" insists he's "happy as a finger / of Vermouth being poured over a slice of veal";[14] and so on. On the other hand, the cheap, accessible, ready-made frozen dinner underscores the economy of the downtown scene.

Freed from the burden of having to sound like sophisticated polymath aesthetes, open to the new sounds of rock 'n' roll, reveling with Warholian delight over cheap, easily reproducible *everything*, whether it be frozen dinner or poem, the hip impertinence on display in second-generation New York School poetry fed directly into what ended up taking place on the CBGB stage in the early to mid-1970s.

Angel Hair Sleeps with a Boy in My Head

Angel Hair magazine, edited by Lewis Warsh and Anne Waldman, was a particularly important publication for second-generation New York School poets.[15] Produced by letterpress, there were six issues in total published between 1966 and 1969. Warsh and Waldman named the magazine after a line in a poem by their friend, the future *Rolling Stone* journalist and music critic Jonathan Cott. Published and edited at the same time as Warsh and Waldman were working on the more freewheeling (and mimeographed) Poetry Project house organ *The World*, *Angel Hair* became a kind of specialist forum for practically every poet affiliated with the second-generation New York School. Seeing how musicians including Patti Smith and Richard Hell were reading second-generation writers' works assiduously (with Hell going so far as to publish a few of them in his own literary journal *Genesis: Grasp*), *Angel Hair* reflects just how proto-punk these poets were. In its issues, *Angel Hair* invited future musicians to revise clichéd notions of the poem as inextricably bound to a monologic lyric voice, proposing the poem as something created *together* with others—the poem as song produced by a band.

Texts in *Angel Hair* 6, for example, made references primarily to the authors featured within the issue. Frank O'Hara's "A Short History of Bill Berkson"[16] would inevitably reecho eight pages later when one reached Bill Berkson's poem "Sheer Strips."[17] Berkson's "Sheer Strips," written in a wide-ranging, open-field form where words scatter and burst all over the page, was engaged in lively colloquy with Anne Waldman's similarly built poem "Sexy Things."[18] Kenward Elmslie's "Easter for Joe"[19] was addressed to Joe Brainard, and Ted Berrigan's "For You" not only was dedicated to James Schuyler, who himself appears as an author in Schuyler's and Padgett's collaboration "Within the Dome," but referred to Joe Brainard in the lines "hand-in-glove and / head-to-head with Joe, I go reeling."[20] The Schuyler-Padgett collaboration also referred to Brainard in the lines "yes, as the great Joe Brainard once said, / 'You can't beat meat, potatoes and a green vegetable.'"[21] The title of Jim Carroll's poem "The Burning of Bustins Island"[22] referred to a Maine island where many of the poets associated with the second-generation New York School spent time together. O'Hara's own poem "To John Ashbery"[23] named the only major male first-generation New York School poet not represented in this particular issue, so it still felt like Ashbery had been invited. Meanwhile, the presence of Schuyler, Koch, and O'Hara in *Angel Hair* 6 lent an authoritative note to the overall party, legitimizing the goings-on. These acts of naming also concretized the relationship between first- and second-generation writers (thus providing a real if casually evoked and willfully nontheorized interpretive framework) and invited readers to consider how second-generation writers were both building on and breaking away from their literary inheritance.

Berrigan's, Carroll's, and their friends' insistent naming borrows from earlier poems like O'Hara's "Adieu to Norman, Bon Jour to Joan and Jean-Paul," which summons figures including Norman Bluhm, Joan Mitchell, and Kenneth Koch in a willfully breezy fashion.[24] Yet where O'Hara's naming tended to fix personages like Berkson, Vincent Warren, LeRoi Jones, Koch, and Ashbery firmly in the reader's imagination, the excessive naming in second-generation work undermined the effort to establish a clear individual presence typical of first-generation work generally and O'Hara's comparatively restrained practice specifically. O'Hara's poems were akin to a dinner party where each individual is distinct, recognizable, and charming. In the world of *Angel Hair*, the party had turned much, much wilder, to the point where it is at times difficult to figure out who's who in all the commotion. As editors of *Angel Hair*, Warsh and Waldman foregrounded process and collaboration within the context of a decentralized community even as they published and promoted individual authors' oeuvres. The magazine manifested more clearly than previous groupings of poets that the place of the solitary and muse-inspired author could productively give way to a poetics of sociability that, at least temporarily and by virtue of the collective, could help create an alternative site of resistance against the literary and political establishment of the era.[25]

Waldman, Warsh, and their fellow poets resisted classification in part by self-consciously rejecting academic jargon and (perhaps inadvertently) their own canonization. Given the poets' propensities for wearing shades, leather jackets, and looking like 1965-era Bob Dylan or Lou Reed, we can at least entertain the idea that downtown writers were learning from popular counterparts how to resist the typical classification of poets. Consider, for example, Dylan's comments in 1965 to a hapless reporter from *Time* that were captured in D. A. Pennebaker's *Don't Look Back*, his documentary on Dylan's tour of England. "Are you gonna see the concert tonight? . . . I won't be able to talk to you afterwards. I've got nothing to say about these things I write, I just write them. I'm not going to say anything about them. I don't write them for any reason. There's no great message."[26] While Dylan was being difficult, if not something of a brat, he was also quite carefully insisting (if obliquely) that his words and music were there to be experienced directly rather than mediated through a critical framework. This attitude—an aggressively blasé pose—was cultivated by the poets who looked to Dylan as one of their own, not least because of Dylan's appropriation of a poetic persona (naming himself after Dylan Thomas) and his widely publicized friendships with contemporary writers including Ginsberg and Michael McClure. As Warsh insisted:

> I wrote a few reviews for *Poetry Magazine*, but to what purpose? I could only reiterate the ongoing decades-long argument between academic and experimental writing and try to draw attention to the work of my friends (though I didn't have much say about what books I could review). Writing poetry criticism during the late sixties was to associate oneself with an academic world, and a tone of voice, which was considered inimical to the life of poetry itself.[27]

Extending his antianalytical position, Warsh (in an interview with Peter Bushyeager) responded to a characterization of his recent work as "impenetrable" with the following conversation stopper: "I like impenetrability. Past a certain point, this book simply exists. What more can you say about it?"[28] Such a message reinforces a familiar binary that values direct, unmediated experience over extended analysis. While Warsh's claims are certainly arguable—after all, impenetrability and mystery can be seen to invite scholarly analysis and canonization precisely thanks to the work's difficult status—they appear to be encouraging us not to talk ad nauseam about second-generation literary work, to consider it somehow part of our daily life. A kind of resistance is being enacted here, one that determines excessive analysis to be detrimental to the spontaneous appreciation of the work.

In her introduction to *The Angel Hair Anthology*, Waldman also positioned second-generation work as necessarily independent of academic discourse: "We weren't thinking about career moves or artistic agendas. We weren't in the business of creating a literary mafia or codifying a poetics. There were no interesting models for that kind of life."[29] According to Waldman, second-generation New York School poets were living and writing in the here and now and were certainly not scheming toward a future life in the archives and syllabi of the academy.

Aspiring poet-musicians hanging around the Poetry Project duly noted the poems and poses associated with *Angel Hair* and related scenes. Richard Hell explained:

> In a way, those [St. Mark's poets] had a big influence on me in music in the sense of their attitudes towards themselves and their relationship to the existing world. . . . The only poets who got any attention or respect from the mainstream world were all conservative and lived their life in universities. Rather than be frustrated and beat their heads against the wall and work their way up that system, the St. Mark's poets just stayed in the streets and did it themselves on mimeo machines and created an alternative. It's just like we ended up doing in music. We made the record companies come to us by making noise for the kids directly rather than trying to impress the record companies to make deals. We brought out records on small labels and started fanzines. We created our own culture until they were forced to acknowledge it and give our records some distribution.[30]

Those St. Mark's poets showed Hell that poetry was available on the most demotic of levels, accessible and celebrated most noisily at least three times a week at often-raucous readings at the Poetry Project. The Lower East Side poem was there both to be read and to promote a dissident, fun, and *live* youth-oriented counterculture. Poems that were proposed as scores to be performed, that were written collaboratively, or that simply contained overt and surprising references to rock's bad boys might have seemed especially pertinent and influential to literary-minded amateur bass players like Hell. The poetry affiliated with St. Mark's assailed high-art status ascribed to the solitary lyric by performing a noisy, revolutionary dialogic poetics propelled in part by a latent rock 'n' roll soundtrack.

In Ted Berrigan's "Bean Spasms," for example, the intertextual references and use of proper names typical of O'Hara's poetry are included alongside a celebration of intoxication and relaxed unemployment that does not, however, preclude an affective transcendence. The following excerpt exhibits some of these characteristics:

THE HOTEL BUCKINGHAM
(façade) is black, and taller than last time
is looming over lunch naked high time   poem & I, equal in
perfection & desire[31]

Berrigan scatters words and phrases across the page in order to evoke the fragmentary, jump-start nature of thought itself. Yet tempering the disjunction is an almost hackneyed lyricism, evident in "poem & I, equal in / perfection & desire." While Berrigan's lyric voice is certainly evident in this poem, overall the text engages the page in such a way as to foreground a polyvocality that generates a sense of immediacy independent of a link to a privileged past. The third-to-last stanza in the fifth and final part of the poem helps us understand further how much of the writing in the second-generation New York School allowed for the lyric "I" while maintaining the poem as a vehicle for establishing a specific community grounded in sixties counterculture:

The rock&roll songs of this earth
    commingling absolute joy AND
incontrovertible joy of intelligence
                    certainly can warm
                    cant they?   YES!
        and they do.
        Keeping eternal whisperings around.
                                Mr. MacAdams writes
                                in the nude: no that's not
(we want to take the underground   me that: then zips in &
    revolution to Harvard!   out of the boring taxis,
                                refusing to join the army

<pre>
and yet this girl has   asleep "on the springs"
        so much grace   of red GENEROSITY
            I wonder!
    Were all their praises simply prophecies
    of this
        the time!   NO GREATER THRILL
my friends[32]
</pre>

Situating us directly within 1960s contemporary tribal youth culture ("The rock&roll songs of this earth"), Berrigan here reminds us that the "first-generation" New York School world has evolved or devolved into a more anarchic community. Ballet makes way for bass, guitar, and drums, and images of a primarily collective experience (think the Monterey Pop Festival, Woodstock, the San Francisco be-ins) work their way into the erudite pep of the New York School.

The stanza then disintegrates into a variety of different voices, beginning with "Mr. MacAdams," Berrigan's friend and fellow poet Lewis MacAdams. By the time we get to the next line, "in the nude: no that's not," we are suddenly confronted with a text that suggests three or more radios being tuned simultaneously to different channels, rather than one lending itself to easy paraphrase. We might be confused: Should we read "no that's not (we want to take the underground" or "no that's not / me that: then zips in & out"? The question becomes even more complicated by the time we get to "and yet this girl has / so much grace / I wonder!"—a private lyric space juxtaposed compellingly next to lines about draft resistance ("re-/fusing to join the army"). Tensions between disengaged hippies and committed politicos (and, metaphorically, between disengaged lyric and socially engaged poetry) are all performed in a wild welter that mirrors the conflicts between the laid-back hippie and anarchist Yippie typical of the Lower East Side scene in the late 1960s. Such disjunctive writing practices provide us with fresh opportunities for creative reading. If we are tempted to read these lines in a "sensible" way, we could organize this section into three distinct parts, each containing a potentially distinct mode. First:

(Mr. MacAdams writes
in the nude: no that's not
me that: then zips in &

out of the boring taxis,
refusing to join the army
asleep "on the springs"
of red GENEROSITY

This part clearly undermines anything resembling a coherent, syntactically sensible theme. Yes, Mr. MacAdams writes, but we immediately leave the purported subject and are pointed toward a variety of other voices and objects. Here, fragment replaces narrative in an effort to represent contemporary experience more fairly. A constantly shifting process of thought mediates a series of cut-up, grafted impressions as they are affected by the rush of life (the taxis, the army). Importantly, an implicit critique of the Vietnam War is encoded into the stanza when we learn that the semantic chaos has as its impulse MacAdams's refusal of the draft. Without resorting to jeremiad, Berrigan captures the absurdities of an urbane poet whose life embodies the O'Haraesque ideal of poetry writing, taxi hopping, and so on even as he is threatened with being drafted.

Second:

(we want to take the underground revolution
to Harvard!

The reader is placed back into "the sixties" via a simple, declarative statement aligned with functional political poetry. The lines here are exuberant, immediate, youthful, naive, and utopian, ushering in the world of the Yippie chant now so ingrained in the North American imagination.

Third:

and yet this girl has
so much grace
I wonder!
Were all their praises simply prophecies
of this
the time!

Here, the poem saves itself from becoming a mere historical artifact of "the sixties" by virtue of Berrigan's employment of a vaguely archaic syntax

("Were all their praises simply prophecies") and a graceful alliteration emphasizing esses: "this," "grace," "praises," "prophecies," "simply," "this." Such sonorities complicate what might otherwise be dismissed as a monologic hippie utterance.

We could divide the stanza in the preceding manner, but the poem certainly encourages a different reading, one toward simultaneity, where all three modes are apprehended concurrently. No one style is privileged over another. The poem invites us to read these lines in a wide variety of permutations. To return to the metaphor of text as party, we might imagine this stanza as representing a variety of voices talking at the same time. Sound replaces sense as the reader allows the din produced by different romantic, good-natured, and youthful voices to characterize the stanza. Berrigan appears to validate such a reading when he ends the stanza with a statement that could serve as a slogan for a poetics of sociability: "NO GREATER THRILL / my friends." Note the plural—the greatest thrill is the number of friends appearing in the poem, and thus the sense we have of the text as social document is further established.

While a group aesthetic is evident in the poems I've discussed, that should not be taken to imply that poets associated with *Angel Hair* were uniform in their approach. Poems in *Angel Hair* 3 introduced a highly conceptual and welcome minimalism into the New York School. These works serve as gentle alternatives to Berrigan's impressive if sometimes exhaustingly all-encompassing cut-ups, lists, and collages. These texts at once resist any attempt to codify what "second-generation New York School" means and defer what would by *Angel Hair* 6 be a perhaps overly familiar aesthetic uniformity that Warsh and Waldman themselves rejected by ceasing production of the magazine and focusing their energies on a series of individual books.

Aram Saroyan, at the time the publisher of the well-received magazine *Lines*, which featured ambitious serial, disjunctive, and resolutely experimental verse, befriended the poets Waldman, Warsh, Berrigan, and Padgett. Not surprisingly, this act of friendship led to his inclusion in *Angel Hair*. Saroyan's poem "Blod" is just that—the word "Blod" placed squarely in the center of the page.[33] Where many of the poets in *Angel Hair* told the reader what they do, what they think, and who their friends are, Saroyan intervenes with a weird blast of a muted tuba, a Blod. "Common sense" demands we treat the word as if it were "blood" or "blot" or "blob," yet the omission of the one letter necessary to make sense leads to playful slippage and a resulting rejection of transparent reference that threatens stable meaning. If "Blod," why not "lobstee" for "lobster," Saroyan seems to ask. The implications of such a deconstructive approach toward socially constituted meaning are now obvious, though still useful, funny, and interesting. Saroyan invests us with interpretive and creative power as we are faced with the misprision of commonsense meaning—a misprision, we should acknowledge, that is a delight, one that leads to laughter (as so much of the work emblematic of sixties conceptualism, minimalism, and performance art aimed to produce) rather than anxiety. It also, importantly, embodies Saroyan's wish to move beyond lyric poetry in favor of a quick hit. The poem happens all at once.

Saroyan's poems were to prove attractive to future punk rockers, including Hell and Patti Smith. In a February 1971 letter to Bruce Andrews, for example, Hell asked the nascent L=A=N=G=U=A=G=E poet, "Met A. Saroyan up there yet? Here's some a what I'm up to (one per page)":

wino
street
dirt
heat
dirt
China
****
thanks for the blood, man
****
I lay down
and really lay into
soft ribbed air
such big white inches[34]

The very shock of seeing a "word" like "Blod" centered on a page, with the attendant silences implicit in the space surrounding the word, might have proved useful for Hell's later work in music. Saroyan's work, for all its humorous qualities, does carry with it a marked violence inherited from earlier sound- and visual-poetry experiments such as Mallarme's *Un Coup de Des* and Italian futurist texts such as Marinetti's "Words in Freedom" (featuring typographically shocking and multiply signifying "words" like "zing").[35] Saroyan, a contemporary of Hell's, was perhaps one of the sources for Hell's own practice of using silences and radical enjambment in song for shock value. Saroyan's work is, in essence, a pop condensation and crystallization of the breaks and fissures on display in modernist durational works by Mallarmé through Stein, Pound, Joyce, Wyndham Lewis, and beyond. A poetics formulated around wordplay and a blurring of borders between visual and verbal genres could be expressed, Saroyan showed us, in an instant. For a young poet like Hell looking to transform himself into a pop star while not forsaking a young lifetime's worth of reading difficult (if often funny) poetry, Saroyan's work must have seemed particularly appealing. The avant-garde did not have to be repudiated in favor of a crass commercialism. Rather, the avant-garde could be *condensed* into a three-minute punk song like Hell's own "Blank Generation." Replete with disorienting silences (the omission of the word "Blank" in "I belong to the _____ Generation")[36] and using fragments as units of composition (Robert Quine's noisily brief, fractured guitar solos substituting for more conventionally expansive and thematically coherent playing), "Blank Generation" in part shows how second-generation New York School poetry might have helped expand the range of 1970s punk lyric and sound.

"We Wear Lipstick"

As Patti Smith, Debbie Harry, Lydia Lunch, Kim Gordon, and any number of other significant female songwriters and performers came to the fore during the punk and post-punk era, so poets including Bernadette Mayer, Alice Notley, Anne Waldman, and Eileen Myles proved central to the poetry scene—editing magazines, organizing readings, running the Poetry Project, and beyond. *Angel Hair* and other second- and third-generation publications including Mayer and Vito Acconci's *0-9* and Myles's *dodgems* rewrote the gender line by engaging women not just as muses but also as public performers and career makers.[37] Waldman's role at the helm of the Poetry Project and on the masthead of *Angel Hair* and Mayer's work as poet and organizer of celebrated poetry workshops at the Poetry Project were to prove particularly inspiring models of women creating and taking charge of a vibrant performance-oriented literary culture.

Patti Smith's transgression of how a female performer was supposed to look, sound, and act—her very toughness and boyishness as a counter to both the Warholian gamine epitomized by Edie Sedgwick and the buxom *Playboy* paradigm—can also be seen in Waldman's and Mayer's writing in the sixties and seventies. Their work articulated a feminist consciousness that anticipated magazines such as Kathleen Fraser's *How(ever)* and today's post-feminism.[38] It also offered a departure from the essentialist feminist poetry of the seventies published in the anthologies *No More Masks! An Anthology of Twentieth-Century American Women Poets* (1973) or *This Bridge Called My Back: Writings by Radical Women of Color* (1981). These anthologies privileged what Kathleen Fraser has identified and critiqued as the feminist "call for the immediately accessible language of personal experience as a binding voice of women's strength."[39] Writing deemed "feminist" tended to be resolutely narrative, accessible, and didactic. Clear moral and political positions were staked out, and previously marginalized stories were told. While sociability was built into such anthologies by virtue of the poets' shared political stances, this was aimed at essentializing identity. What was lost in this mainstream feminist poetics was the tradition of women's innovative writing (Emily Dickinson, Gertrude Stein, H.D., Laura [Riding] Jackson, and so on) as well as the attendant threat to conventional notions of what constituted a gendered identity.

Mayer and Waldman's collaborative prose piece "The Basketball Article," originally commissioned by *Oui* magazine but then rejected and later published as an *Angel Hair* book, promotes a dedicated but festive feminism whose aim is to show the simultaneous ludicrousness and sexiness of stereotypically gendered behavior at odds with the conventional narrative techniques typical of the feminist poetry of that era. In "The Basketball Article," the authors thanked a variety of men for making the publication possible, including a "Mr. Warsh" and a "Mr. Padgett." Such naming troubled (albeit humorously) the assumption of easy participation in an egalitarian scene. That is, referring to Lewis Warsh and Ron Padgett as "Mr." was a distancing move, an acknowledgment that tension between the sexes existed even in such a freewheeling environment.

Lines throughout "The Basketball Article" evoked, as much second-generation work did, O'Hara's "I do this, I do that" mode, but the new feminist and countercultural consciousness enriches the practice. The beginning of the piece at once alluded to O'Hara's famous lines in "The Day Lady Died" (where he asks "for a carton of Gauloises and a carton / of Picayunes, and a NEW YORK POST with her face on it")[40] as it positioned itself firmly within a dissident politics:

> The orange ushers of the Coliseum begin to wonder if smoking Sherman's makes you sexy. Should they smoke them? What magazine? Oui. We begin to dress in red, white and blue, we do not stand up for the national anthem. We always sit next to the opposing team. We distract them. We enter their consciousness. We carry a copy of Shakespeare's sonnets with us. We wear lipstick. We cheer for both teams.[41]

Even as they were rejecting a kind of rote patriotism, Mayer and Waldman don't come across as effete snobs doing anthropology in a sports arena. There is a real sense of play and appreciation for the proceedings. The speakers distract the players with their lipstick, their sonnets, and their nonideological cheers. They describe the movements of the players lovingly—those who "seem desperate running up and down court and the ones who do it like deer."[42] The lipstick displays a feminism more in line with the riot-grrrl and "lipstick lesbian" phenomenon of the nineties than with the radical feminism of the seventies. "There is grace in the men and women who play. A hedonism that turns into a sort of mysticism,"[43] Mayer and Waldman insist in a subsequent line. Pleasure is political, and part of their political vision necessarily included women posing a threat to order, taking over conventionally male spaces, and behaving badly.

Fast Speaking Woman

Increasingly renowned as a performance poet, Waldman was variously being courted by Ed Sanders for a record project he was pitching to Apple Records, joining Bob Dylan on his Rolling Thunder review tour, and inviting rock musicians to play with her on the Poetry Project stage. Waldman saw no rift between pop dreams and a life in poetry. In terms of her work as a recording artist and presence in rock 'n' roll circles, she insists, "I wasn't thinking of it as a path. It felt like a natural extension of what we were doing. I was always involved in concepts of the oral—that was what the Poetry Project was about, to some extent. I enjoyed readings that went a little *further*."[44] The 1975 City Lights edition of her book *Fast Speaking Woman* revealed both verbally and visually the shift Waldman was making from relatively reticent poet to pop shaman. The cover of the book alone was positively electric. Waldman was pictured in profile clad in a full-length short-sleeved glamorous white dress, hand placed provocatively on left hip, right arm curled around her head. Her face was captured in mid-laugh, and she looked *naughty*, perhaps even a tad stoned. Wearing a pair of high-heeled shoes, she toed the ground coyly with her left foot. Drawn around the edges of her body were three shocking pink lines that suggested gaudy 1970s Times Square. Waldman remembers wearing the dress: "Kenward Elmslie and I were performing together in the Palm Casino Review, a beautiful white building on the corner of Bowery and 3rd . . . Jackie Curtis was in [the performance], Candy Darling. . . . I'm so grateful to have been in these worlds, from La Monte Young to Candy Darling . . . that was amazing."[45]

The poetry contained within this markedly pop package emphasized the texts more as musical scores waiting to be sounded than as texts to be read discreetly and silently in private. "Reading aloud as intended," Waldman let her readers know, "I can be more playful improvising new words & sound thus expanding the territory I'm in. The piece began as a travel meditation during a trip to South America, continued back in NYC, then later in India. It keeps growing."[46] While indebted to "Maria Sabina, the Mazatec Indian shamaness in Mexico, guiding persons in magic mushroom ceremony," the chants and repetitions characterizing the work in this book were as much quasi-mystical as they were evocative of what Patti Smith was doing during the same period. Take, for example, the final stanza of Waldman's "Musical Garden":

> Can't give you up, solar energy, speech, and more
> speech & more speech & more energy more
> sunlight more emergency can't give you up
> can't give it up yet won't do it won't do it
> can't give it up yet won't give you up yet
> can't give it up![47]

The poem as a whole, which as extant recordings of Waldman's performances show takes about three and a half minutes to perform, was the perfect length for a pop single. Each line began anaphorically with the phrase "Can't give you up" or "Can't give it up," followed by references to friends,

Figure 3.1 Cover photograph for Anne Waldman's *Fast Speaking Woman*.
Source: Copyright © Sheyla Baykal. Reprinted by permission of City Lights Books.

lovers, writers including Louis Ferdinand Céline and Jack Kerouac, structural linguistics, rum, indulgence, murderous dreams, the color blue, fer-
tility, iridescent dolphins, black magic, Buddy Holly, Jelly Roll Morton, fan
mail, trekking old Inca trails, the Kentucky Derby, the Baltic Sea, and beyond.

A 1976 recording of the poem included in Waldman's and John Giorno's LP *John Giorno & Anne Waldman: A Kulchur Selection* found Waldman acting equal parts rhapsodic Ginsberg and rock star. Increasing tempo and pitch with each line, Waldman by the end of her reading was practically stentorian. Her performance ended dramatically as Waldman enunciated each syllable in the final iteration of "I can't give it up" declaratively: "Can't give you up, solar energy, speech, more sunlight & more speech & more speech & more energy more sunlight more emergency can't give you up yet can't give it up won't do it can't give you up won't do it won't do it can't give it up won't give it up won't give you up yet can't give it up no *I can't give it up*." At the very end, a single voice from the audience is heard saying "Yeah" appreciatively, followed immediately by whoops and applause.[48]

This poem was written and performed around the same time Patti Smith recorded her song "Birdland"—an extended poetic sequence imagining Peter Reich's childhood visions of his father Wilhelm Reich at the helm of a UFO. It is striking how Smith's song resonates with Waldman's hortatory performance of "Musical Garden." Smith's enunciations of the phrases "take them up," "I won't give up," "I'm going up," and so forth in "Birdland" even echo, if unintentionally, Waldman's own "I can't give up." This is not to say that Waldman was indebted to Smith for her own increasingly bardic carriage during the 1970s. Both a serious student of poetry and a practicing writer, Waldman had plenty of models to choose from—Ginsberg and Corso, after all, were included in her social circles, and her increasing engagement with shamanic texts and traditions went far in informing her incantatory turn. Nevertheless, the similarities between the mid-1970s Smith and Waldman are striking, and they reveal how both Waldman's and Smith's work reflected a mode of performance evolving during this period that actively blurred the lines between poetry, performance, and the call-and-response ethos of rock 'n' roll.

Yet despite the fact that Smith started her performance career at the Poetry Project and was in close contact with Waldman and others affiliated with the scene, there is not much in the critical literature to suggest that Smith's actual day-to-day life in poetry affected the composition of "Birdland" and other songs on her first album *Horses* (1975). Smith has been forthcoming on the influence dead titans of poetry like Arthur Rimbaud and rock gods like Jim Morrison and Mick Jagger had on her writing and performing style. James Perone is typical of critics who read Smith's poetic debts primarily in terms set up by Smith herself. For Perone, "Smith's 'Birdland' . . . is a close relative of Jim Morrison's poetics passages performed with the Doors, such as 'The End,' 'When the Music's Over,' and 'Soft Parade' (except that Smith is the better poet, capable of subtlety and range that Morrison never managed)."[49] Philip Shaw offers a fascinating biographical and Oedipal reading of "Birdland," though the song's basis in poetry is passed over.[50]

Much is lost when the very bodies, institutions, and ideas that informed punk's most significant practitioners are elided from historical accounts of the era. To ignore the work of Waldman and the poets attached to the St. Mark's scene more generally in the histories of punk is, after all, to freeze out the tantalizing and complex details showing how some musicians were drawn to the Poetry Project and created music in part as a response to, argument with, and extension of New York School poetics. Indeed, Smith was not the only nascent punk with an ear pitched critically toward the poets. Take, for example, a journal entry a young Richard Hell wrote on February 16, 1971:

> The sense I get of the young NY poets—their writing atmosphere one of simply and totally being children, no attention span, all wonder—all the pure children qualities—which is great BUT I think I'm growing up and it makes me often angry at them—their fearless selflove and babbling it will all be well if we just come together, all highness and continual childlife—Bullshit—that is bullshit to think we could all be one happy family, even *more* to say it—that is a stage to go *through* I think, to reach a real understanding of things.[51]

As we will see in subsequent chapters, second-generation "NY poets" such as Waldman were necessary models for Hell and Smith to emulate *and* to repudiate. The scene around St. Mark's provided them with a necessary apprenticeship as they shifted away from a poetics of sociability toward an abrasive rock 'n' roll.

FOUR

Richard Hell, *Genesis: Grasp*, and the Making of the Blank Generation

RICHARD MEYERS, LIKE Lou Reed, Patti Smith, and Ed Sanders, moved to New York City to be a writer. Dropping out of boarding school in Delaware in 1967, he made it to the Lower East Side, where, with his friend David Giannini, he started publishing the small-press magazine *Genesis: Grasp*. His tastes leaned initially toward nineteenth-century French poetry in translation and toward modernist and late-modernist stalwarts such as William Carlos Williams, James Joyce, and Dylan Thomas. Rock 'n' roll was part of his daily soundtrack, but it wouldn't be until 1972 that Meyers founded the band the Neon Boys with his school chum Tom Miller. But "Tom Miller" and "Richard Meyers" were not exactly catchy stage names. Drawing on their mutual passion for the Rimbaud-Verlaine myth, Miller changed his surname to Verlaine, an appropriation not just of the French symbolist poet Paul Verlaine but also of the whole mystique characterizing Verlaine's transgressive relationship with the *poet maudit* Arthur Rimbaud. Meyers, devoted to Rimbaud's *A Season in Hell*, transformed himself into Hell. In 1973 the Neon Boys changed their name to Television and began playing regularly at CBGB. In 1975 Hell left Television and formed the Heartbreakers with Jerry Nolan and Johnny Thunders, the drummer and guitarist respectively for the proto-punk band the New York Dolls. This venture lasted about a year, when Hell decided to form his own band, Richard Hell and the Voidoids. Their first album, *Blank Generation* (1977), included the by-now classic songs

"Blank Generation" and "Love Comes in Spurts" and is recognized today as one of the most important and influential punk-rock records of the 1970s.

From his early days in the Neon Boys through the Voidoid's *Blank Generation*, Hell seeded references to Nerval, Rimbaud, Artaud, and other writers into his lyrics. "There's something wrong here where the best ones want to go. / Parker, Lautréamont, Monroe they held it just to throw / the world away,"[1] Hell keened in the early Neon Boys song "Don't Die," neatly reconciling bebop, Hollywood, and the avant-garde enfant terrible Lautréamont into one great oppositional sign. Hell the musician

positioned himself on the art/pop boundary. Hell stressed the influence on him "by the twisted French aestheticism of the late 19th century like Rimbaud, Verlaine, Huysmans, Baudelaire." He even gave an artistic spin to his torn shirt and cropped hair look, soon to be imported to England as the emblem of punk. "There were some artists that I admired who looked like that. Rimbaud looked like that. Artaud looked like that. And it also looked like the kid in *400 Blows*, the Truffaut movie."[2]

On the other hand, Hell insisted that in the early to mid-1970s

what I've done isn't about my lyrics—there's never been a rock 'n' roll song that survived on the strength of its lyrics. People give me this same shit about my books, going the opposite direction. That I'm a musician who writes. Fuck that. Also, the way I write songs is to write the music first, and then I listen to the music and see what it makes me think, and write the words to it.[3]

Yet despite his refusal at times to breach ostensibly distinct art forms, Hell can be credited in part for marking out early New York punk as a surprisingly literary affair. From quoting Huysmans in interviews to adapting phrases from avant-garde masters on gig flyers, Hell made his audiences aware of his literary chops. On a flyer promoting performances with the Voidoids, Erasers, and the Ghosts at CBGB (April 20, 21, 22, 1978),[4] for example, Hell included sections from Lautréamont's *Maldoror*. Rewriting Maldoror's "This epithet was *The Vampire!*" as "This epithet was *The Voidoid!*," Hell continued by quoting Maldoror's "I hear in the distance prolonged shrieks of the most poignant agony," a phrase Lautréamont repeated a number of times in the first canto of his book. Hell's alignment of a garland of CBGB bands firmly to the "shrieks" of perhaps the most nihilist of 1890s avant-garde works—a book whose theme was summarized by Anna Balakian as "the recognition of the brutal origin and the biological universality of evil"[5]—provided a latent literary cast to the aggressive, dissonant noise of punk. One could now imagine Maldoror's "shrieks" being translated into material, amplified shrieks projected by Richard Hell and his fellow punk musicians.

The influence of French literature on Hell's musical output is fairly well documented by Bernard Gendron, Jon Savage, and others.[6] What is not investigated sufficiently is how, like a number of the musicians considered here, Hell's love for French romantic, symbolist, and surrealist literature coincided with an increasing attraction to the chirpy poetics of sociability then dominant in New York's literary avant-gardes. In a draft statement for the Poetry Project at St. Mark's anthology *Out of This World*, Hell recalled his arrival in New York. Highlighting the mimeograph and small-journal publications he was drawn to, Hell explained, "I was only 17 when I came to New York to be a writer. I was some kind of hayseed. I wanted to know where the poets were, and I guess I looked in most all the wrong places before finally I found the Poetry Project."[7] Going further, Hell pointed to the Lower East Side poetry community as inspiring him directly in fashioning punk:

> There were really interesting things going on with underground writers, anti-academic poets like Ted Berrigan were writing these amazing things and there was this whole eruption of inspired activity that came with the discovery of how easy it was to produce mimeographed books. This was the original DIY ethic and a huge inspiration for me as a musician.[8]

Part of that huge inspiration the Poetry Project represented for Hell included reassessing his own poetic tastes and inclinations. Hell knew enough about the New York School of poets to understand that it was vaguely uncool to like relatively mainstream writers like Dylan Thomas, especially given that Frank O'Hara and his minions were dismissive of the poet's high oratorical style. Discussing his teen readings, Hell acknowledges,

> I was reading Dylan Thomas. For years, later, I was embarrassed to admit he'd inspired me. He was so overwrought and "poetic," his language all biblical and astronomical and anatomical (saviors, radium, sun, tongues, fountains, nerve,

bone), and concerned with big dramatic subjects, even if the poems didn't really make intellectual sense but were more like music. Whereas the New York poets I eventually came to love were wiseass goofs and collaging phraseologists, adorers of everyday details, never taking themselves too seriously.[9]

Hell was torn. He was attracted to Thomas in part because of his lifestyle. "When I decided at sixteen that I wanted to drop out of school," Hell recalls, "the way that I described it to myself was . . . what my ambition and intention was . . . was to be a poet. To me what represented a poet was Dylan Thomas. It was basically just about living by your wits, being drunk, and being thought of as sexy. Being outside of straight society."[10] However, Hell soon came to realize that Thomas risked being the poetry equivalent of a Led Zeppelin arena show. "When I got tired of that poetry it was because it came to seem like overblown mystification and drama, like fog machines at a rock concert, taking what was probably only a vague little idea or quasi-insight per poem and decorating and declaiming it, Robert Plant style."[11] Hell's suspicion of overblown rhetoric suggests how the St. Mark's poets' critical engagement with seriousness as a mode informed Hell's literary and musical tastes. He would never read poetry or listen, sing and play music in such a way as to presuppose that solemnity, intensity, and passion were prima facie good things.

By the time Hell established himself on the Lower East Side in the late 1960s, other poets deemed questionable by the New York School were soon in Hell's sights. "I disliked the educated, fastidious, grim ones like, say Robert Lowell," Hell recalled.[12] By repudiating Lowell, was Hell, like Lou Reed and so many of the New York School poets he was reading in the late 1960s and '70s, aware of and echoing O'Hara's own distaste for the confessional poet? O'Hara, after all, dismissed Lowell piquantly in a 1965 interview with Edward Lucie-Smith: "I think Lowell has a confessional manner which [lets him] get away with things that are really just plain bad but you're supposed to be interested because he's supposed to be so upset."[13] A 1962 reading at Wagner College featuring, among others, O'Hara and Lowell had become part of second-generation New York School lore.

O'Hara, who read first, introduced his work by saying, "On the ferry coming over here, I wrote a poem," and proceeded to read "Lana Turner has collapsed!" much to the amusement of the audience. When it was Lowell's turn, he said something to the effect: "Well, I'm sorry *I* didn't write a poem on the way over here," the implication being that poetry is a *serious* business and that O'Hara was trivializing it and camping it up.[14]

O'Hara's calculated flippancy, his privileging of spontaneity and improvisation over the more studied and formal approach taken by Lowell, offered a model for those readers suspicious both of the shamanic roles taken on by Beat-generation poets[15] and the metric-heavy formalism of Lowell, W. D. Snodgrass, and related poets collected in such anthologies as Donald Hall, Robert Pack, and Louis Simpson's *New Poets of England and America* (1957). O'Hara taught (if indirectly) young readers like Hell that they didn't have to aspire to the role of Prophet; that mass culture was just as relevant and enjoyable, if not *more* enjoyable, than poetry;[16] that poetry itself could be written on the hoof, at parties, for friends—a seductive model indeed for a young writer and publisher like Hell, suspicious of authorial claims to and performances of grandeur and open to the second-generation New York School shenanigans happening just a couple of blocks away from his apartment at St. Mark's.[17]

Verlaine Versus Chitchat

Hell's distaste for Lowell, his measured and embarrassed appreciation of Thomas, and his embrace of the never-taking-themselves-too-seriously vibe of the New York School poets also suggests a basic difference between him and his Neon Boys and Television bandmate Tom Verlaine. Where Hell's stage presence was madcap frenzied pogoing, Verlaine's persona was often dramatically severe, and it was this difference that in part would lead Verlaine to freeze Hell out of their band Television as the band was gaining increasing attention from New York's music press in 1974 and 1975. Critics were aware of the divergence between the two musicians' styles. Patti Smith, for example, identified Hell affectionately as a "spastic Chuck Berry" whose bass was "total trash." Her paeans were reserved for a practically Zeus-like Verlaine ("the most beautiful neck in rock 'n' roll. Real swan-like—fragile yet strong"), whose playing was "like a thousand bluebirds screaming."[18] Robert Christgau identified in Verlaine's near-virtuosic guitar playing, extended solos, and psychedelically tinged lyrics both a throwback to and expansion of the possibilities offered by bands like the Grateful Dead and the Byrds.[19] As an increasingly professional Verlaine deemed Hell's onstage behavior déclassé, Hell's songs featured less and less in Television's live sets. By 1975, according to Hell, Verlaine was refusing to play Hell's songs at their concerts and even asked Hell not to move onstage so that audience's attention could be focused on the swanlike lead singer. Richard Hell was having too much *fun*, in both his stage persona and his lyrics. As Hell saw it, this is part of what led to the acrimonious split between the two men. Verlaine "heard these crystal-clear crisp sweet-guitar suites of highly arranged series of time and dynamics sections in his head, and they were about specific parts constructed for effects where everything was subordinate to what his guitar would be doing."[20] In other words, while Hell was jumping around, playing his bass gleefully and amateurishly and singing his twisted, funny lyrics about pinheads and love coming in spurts, Verlaine was being far too earnest and self-important.

The New York School poets hovered behind the two men, poking, teasing, daring them to value the quotidian and the lighthearted over and above anything smacking of stardom. Hell recalls:

> [Verlaine and I] also read the new books, mostly mimeographed, stapled pamphlets, from the "second generation New York School" poets linked to the St. Mark's Church Poetry Project, which was a block away from Tom's apartment. I was more interested in those guys than Tom was though. He could never accept the low-key, daily, Frank O'Hara chitchat, "I did this, I did that" style they used a lot.[21]

True, Hell would not become a regular at the Project until the 1980s and 1990s, when he curated reading series there and published and edited the literary journal *Cuz* and Cuz Press (publishing St. Mark's–affiliated writers including Ron Padgett and Maggie Dubris). However, the Project's place in his life during the 1960s and 1970s clearly informed his aesthetics as his attention shifted from mimeos to punk. Behind Hell's work as budding poet, publisher, and musician was that gorgeous mixture of high-toned French surrealism and New York School jesting that, as the remainder of this chapter will show, burbled behind much of Hell's work so curiously.

This is not to say that Hell was uncritical of the St. Mark's scene. In a letter to the poet Bruce Andrews detailing his contempt toward the conglomeration of second-generation New York School and West Coast poets in the small California coastal town of Bolinas, Hell sneered,

> I think "Bolinas" poetry totally sucks. I hate all "styles." With me it's just a big struggle—each poem should be unique and real because it's the mission result-ing from innumerable impossible-to-reproduce conditions—place, state of mind-body-emotions etc, whatever if any experience provoked it, etc etc etc. As far as other peoples poems go it's really a matter of mood—the only ones I actually voluntarily read are my friends' plus Rimbaud and this tiny pamphlet of Nerval's *Chimeras* translated by Andrew Hoyem that I have an unexplainable love for.[22]

Hell, influenced by New York School–affiliated writers despite his hostility to "styles," began in his early roles as poet, editor, and publisher of *Genesis: Grasp* to develop an aesthetic that demanded a new genre entirely. In ana-lyzing Hell's hostility toward the way "beautiful" could so easily become synonymous with product, his emphasizing speed and instantaneity over measured reflection, his placing the visual hierarchically over the verbal, and his desire to communicate not with solitary readers but with a crowd, this chapter will trace how Meyers the poet became Hell the punk-rock icon.

Genesis: Grasp

As we've already seen, Anne Waldman, Ted Berrigan, Ed Sanders, and other downtown poets started magazines in part as a way to make friends and get in on the literary scene. Hell followed their lead. A vibrant little maga-zine often serves as a record of the editors' increasing sense of identity based around shared aesthetics and growing social networks. This iden-tity, of course, is built up in part by the editors' materially reaching out to those authors they are reading and asking them to send in poems. As Hell describes it, the process of editing *Genesis: Grasp* was "like growing up in public!"[23] That's how literary community is formed. Beginning in 1968, Giannini and Hell (still going by his birth name, Richard Meyers) published *Genesis: Grasp* for three years, producing six issues. The journal coincided with Hell's job working as a clerk at the Gotham Book Mart on Forty-Seventh Street between Fifth and Sixth Avenues. It was at the Gotham where Hell developed a love for the small-circulation magazines affiliated with modernism as they stretched into the New American Poetry of the 1950s and 1960s:

> I got assigned to help catalog the hundreds and hundreds of old literary magazines, many in complete runs, that filled a storage room on the second floor. I spent day after day alone up there, crouched at the bottom of the shelves, turning over in my hands such signifying artifacts as T. S. Eliot's august *Criterion* ("it must be said"); Harriet Monroe's *Poetry* when it was publishing Pound's circle in the teens and twenties . . . ; Eugene and Maria Jolas's Paris journal *Transition* [sic], where a lot of early modernists and surrealists appeared (champagne, frottage); Princess Caetani's *Botteghe Oscure* (Renaissance print shop), a gorgeous high-toned bohemian thing from Rome; Wyndham Lewis's British magazine *Blast* (Lewis with his hair on fire); Margaret Anderson's *The Little Review* (grid of tweedy breasts); Charles Henri Ford's *View*, where all the 1940s temporarily New York European Dadaists/surrealists like Breton and Man Ray and Max Ernst published (avid narcissism of bohemian style); Ashbery's and Koch's and Schuyler's and Mathews's *Locus Solus* (swoon of witty word chess); Diane di Prima's and LeRoi Jones's *The Floating Bear* (a bear who can't drown because he's a doodle).[24]

The names Hell cites here represent some of the most vital little magazines devoted to publishing new and experimental work. There is a social element to Hell's list as well. The trajectory from early-modernist magazines like *transition* to something like Charles Henri Ford's *View* and onward to Mathew and Ashbery's *Locus Solus* was based not simply on shared literary affinities but on real personal networks that found "elders" like Henri Ford passing the modernist baton to younger colleagues, who would then publish in a similar avant-gardist spirit that was materially independent from what Hell infers are less desirable and less fun academic, socially detached alternatives. These magazines represented a messy and fascinating world as much as they did an innovative poetics. Indeed, Hell continues in his autobiography to highlight Ted Berrigan's *C* as the zenith of small-press publishing:

> My very favorite literary magazine . . . — the greatest literary magazine of the twentieth century—was a clumsy, cheap, legal-sized, stapled mimeo, published on the Lower East Side, 1963–1967, called simply *C*, edited by Ted Berrigan. You

could extrapolate everything worthwhile in the universe from its thirteen issues, and you'd have a great time, giggling.[25]

Berrigan's *C* and related journals, as some of the more charming examples
of journals that embraced a community-oriented DIY approach to publishing, were for Hell literary-inflected punk signs that could be adapted productively in Richard Meyers's own work as a publisher of *Genesis: Grasp* and
later publishing projects and in Richard Hell's future role as a singer in the
Neon Boys, Television, the Heartbreakers, and the Voidoids. Hell's identifying *C* as the greatest magazine of the twentieth century is interesting given
that Hell's model of value was a magazine that was slapped together, marked
by staples, published on cheap paper, and cranked out of a primitive press.
As his favorite poetry magazine was shoddy so Hell would go on to project
himself through what would soon be known as punk style—torn T-shirts,
spiky hair, and so on. Berrigan's *C* and the scrappy downtown magazine
aesthetic found a walking, talking, and singing corollary in Hell's body.

The first issue of *Genesis: Grasp*, published in 1968 when Hell was just
eighteen years old, featured a fairly motley group of contributors. The issue
included poems by the English novelist and poet Sylvia Townsend Warner;
Hell's associate David Giannini; the Trappist monk, poet, and activist Thomas
Merton; Hell himself (as Richard Meyers); Goerge Wagner; a little-known
New York poet named William Leo Coakley; the Pulitzer Prize–winning American poet Richard Eberhart; and the downtown-affiliated poet Yuki Hartman. The magazine had yet to find its legs. It lacked the coherent house style
typical of the magazines Hell was beginning to love in his job as clerk at the
Gotham. "A lot of the content of those early issues of G:G was pretty random," Hell recalls:

> We took a shotgun approach regarding soliciting work from established writers.
> If we'd seen a single piece we liked by anyone we'd be liable to write them at
> their publisher . . . the only issues of that magazine that I can stand to look at
> are the final two (#s 4 & 5–6) and even they still make me cringe in places.[26]

Despite Hell's retrospective embarrassment, there are signs even within
the early issues of a kind of avant-garde commitment to challenging the
distinctions between art and life that would find full flower in the later
issues and, most spectacularly, in Hell's music career. A manifesto included
in the first number of *Genesis: Grasp* states this challenge clearly: "Of course,

there is no art, only life. In the practical sense that nothing a living being can produce or imagine can transcend his being alive. But, art is entirely impractical, and transcendence is exactly what it attempts."[27]

And, while we might understand why the first two issues of *Genesis: Grasp* (volumes 1.1 [1968] and 1.2 [1969]) now make Hell "cringe," volume 1.3 (1969) is another—and better—story entirely. With its spare cover by the California-based artist Nicol Allan, composed of five delicate lines arranged abstractly around the top of two longer, gently arced lines, the issue coheres around a vibrant blend of symbolist and surrealist poetry, modernist and postmodern art, and the collaborative, mischievous, and pseudonymous writing typical of second-generation New York School poets. This kind of aesthetic was on show most interestingly in the final two issues but began to take shape with *Genesis: Grasp* 1.3.

The magazine included a "Manifesto" by the poet and Bates College professor John Tagliabue, a poem by the surrealist Andre Pieyre De Mandiargues, poems by Yuki Hartman, paintings by Jordan Davies, Charles Baudelaire's "Le Gouffre" (translated by Sylvia Townshend Warner), poems by the British modernist writer Valentine Ackland, a reproduction of a Claes Oldenburg pen-and-ink drawing entitled "Man and Woman Talking" (1960), fiction by Robert Cordier and Henry Roth, and poetry by Hell. Hell also made an early pseudonymous appearance as "Ernest Stomach," in a review of William Saroyan's *I Used to Believe I Had Forever—Now I'm Not So Sure*, which contrasted Saroyan with Gertrude Stein. Included in the issue was the "essay" "Antilove and the Supraconscious" by Hell and Tom Miller (Verlaine).

Baudelaire's appearance in the journal marks an early if vaguely defined affiliation between French symbolist poetry and a nascent punk attitude that valued a complex blend of intensity, innocence, and existential nausea.[28] The inclusion of Warner's translation of Baudelaire's "Le Gouffre" from *Les fleurs du mal*, read in light of Hell's future role as punk icon, is one among a number of crucial signs pointing the way forward to the visual and verbal nihilism and play typical of his group Richard Hell and the Voidoids:

Pascal had his abyss, opening at his feet
Whichever way he turned. Do, think, desire, that pit
Lies under all. Witness my hairs, time and again
Raised on my scalp because the wind of Fear went by.

Above, below, around . . . the fathomless, the stretch
Of barren shore, silence, space that lures and appals [*sic*].
On the dark background of my nights, God with skilled hand
Paints an implacable, ever-changing nightmare.

I dread to fall asleep as one dreads a cavern
Thronged with nameless fears and leading—to what? I see
Only infinity from every window,

And my soul, driven on from one brink to another,
Envies the Uncreate's insensibility.
—Oh! stay within the bounds of number and person![29]

There is a nebulous but interesting correspondence between Baudelaire's "The Abyss" and the future Richard Hell's overall "look" in the various bands he participated in during the 1970s. This is not to say that Hell thought to himself that Baudelaire's poem should in some way determine the name of his own group (that is, the "abyss" as a synonym for "void"). Rather, abstract conceptions of existential despair and emptiness, combined with the latent gloomy visuality (generated by words and phrases like "abyss," "the pit," "fathomless," "dark background of my nights") informing Baudelaire's poem, can be tracked from French symbolist poetry to New York punk. We might dare to go even further here and suggest that Richard Hell's punk haircut resonates with Baudelaire's poem. In "The Abyss" we find the frightened, bitter speaker describing "my hairs, time and again / Raised on my scalp because the wind of Fear went by." The speaker in Baudelaire's abyss, motivated as he is by the realization that there is no transcendent truth, no foundational meaning, no sensate God, is writing to us with his hair literally standing on end. Indeed, alternative translations emphasize the practically cartoonlike image of the speaker's spiky hair. William Aggeler's 1954 version, for example, reads "and over my hair which stands on end / I feel the wind of Fear pass frequently."[30] Similarly, Roy Campbell's 1952 translation shocks with "And often by the wind of terror stirred / I've felt the hair shoot upright on my head."[31] Baudelaire's "The Abyss," along with Rimbaud, Artaud, and the "kid" from Truffaut's *400 Blows*, may have provided a small part of the back story that led to those spiked-hair haircuts and ripped clothes we associate with the look Hell initiated around 1973.[32] The punk look is not just a sign of aggression but a visible acknowledgment that the world one lives in is terrifying and strange. Rereading Hell's spiky shards of hair through the abyss of Baudelaire's poem, we can understand that part of what initiated Hell's style was an effort on his part to signify both aggression and, as Baudelaire would have it, fear and despair.

After all, in the 1960s and '70s the municipal and federal government had essentially given up on New York neighborhoods like the East Village, leaving the area to fester in the hands of drug dealers, absentee landlords, arsonists, and worse. As Alan Vega of the band Suicide characterized it in 1976, "New York is the grandest shit scene of all time. It's like the Titanic a thousand times over; just sinking away but it's beautiful."[33] The rock journalist Lisa Persky described the neighborhood as "loathsome and desperate territory" that nevertheless "harboured great artists and their work."[34] The origins of the punk look, then, are not just emanating out of a vaguely defined "rage" and rough-hewn libertarian/nihilist politics but rather are informed in part by a complex negotiation between the dark, neogothic rhetoric of French symbolism and the material dissolution of the heavily romanticized Lower East Side and East Village.

Given Hell's investment not just in Baudelaire's poetry but in Baudelaire's style, we should consider also how Baudelaire defined the figure of the dandy, particularly in light of punk rock's debts to proto-punk glam-rock bands like the New York Dolls.[35] In his celebrated essay "The Painter of Modern Life," Baudelaire provided a template for critical performative types to come:

> Whether these men are nicknamed exquisites, *incroyables*, beaux, lions or dandies, they all spring from the same womb, they all partake of the same characteristic quality of opposition and revolt; they are all representatives of what is finest in human pride, of that compelling need, alas only too rare today, of combating and destroying triviality. It is from this that the dandies obtain that haughty exclusiveness, provocative in its very coldness.[36]

Baudelaire's dandy displays the self as a performance that significantly includes a publicly acted-out resistance to absorption in normative community. Foucault argues:

> Modernity for Baudelaire is not simply a form of relationship to the present; it is also a mode of relationship that has to be established with oneself. The

deliberate attitude of modernity is tied to an indispensable asceticism. To be modern is not to accept oneself as one is in the flux of the passing moments; it is to take oneself as object of a complex and difficult elaboration: what Baudelaire, in the vocabulary of his day, calls *dandysme*.... Modern man, for Baudelaire, is not the man who goes off to discover himself, his secrets and his hidden truth; he is the man who tries to invent himself. This modernity does not "liberate man in his own being"; it compels him to face the task of producing himself.[37]

Baudelaire is modern precisely through his rejection of the natural, that is, the discourses of depth associated with language like "discover," "secrets," and "hidden truth." The act of self-invention ("producing himself") is, in this sense, a potentially oppositional act. The self-conscious production of the dandy's public display takes as its starting point a rejection of those roles we associate with the purportedly natural heterosexual matrix through which queerness is always and forever deviant. (I use "queerness" here to include non-normative behavior considered broadly—my goal here is not to conflate the dandy with homosexuality strictly defined, particularly as Hell and earlier glam rockers were not "gay" in the traditional sense.) The dandy, like the punk, *sticks out* because of his display of self as one that can be altered, refigured, and reimagined. Tearing a symbolic and material rip in the social fabric initially through radical fashion practice, the dandy/punk uses appearance both in order to draw attention to himself as a subject circulating freely within and outside of dominant social codes and to interrupt, if slightly and evanescently, the flow of public order.

Again, Baudelaire's work might have formed one small part of the story that resulted in the look Hell developed around 1973 when his music career was beginning to take off. Hell's beloved *Maldoror* could be another source, given that the nihilist narrator in the opening pages of Lautréamont's book of prose poetry petitions the reader, "Excuse me: it seemed to me that my hair was standing up on my scalp."[38] To Baudelaire and Lautréamont we should certainly add the images of Artaud and Rimbaud that Meyers included on the cover of the final issue of *Genesis: Grasp* (with both poets' hair styles remarkably like Hell's own in the 1970s).

Baudelaire, Rimbaud, and the whole pantheon of French symbolist writing generally were to play a significant role in Hell's self-fashioning. Hell insists:

The connection between the whole world of values of rock 'n' roll and the world of values of poetry in the Rimbaud/Lautreamont/Baudelaire world . . . there are definitely connections. The thing that made me pick poetry as a way of life when I was at school . . . it could just as easily have been rock 'n' roll and I don't know what else it could have just as easily been because it was the same idea. It was rejecting the values of straight society and looking for this kind of just level of intensity.[39]

Hell emphasizes the almost arbitrary way in which the self is constituted as invention (one can "pick" poetry or art "as a way of life" as opposed to understanding the "self" as some kind of innate, natural phenomenon). The young Richard Meyers, on the cusp of anointing himself "Richard Hell," is visible within the pages of *Genesis: Grasp* as an editor seeking a level of intensity that ultimately transforms life into a kind of performance art.

As Hell grew closer to becoming a full-time musician with the formation of the Neon Boys around 1972 and 1973, and particularly when he became a well-known rock 'n' roll figure in the mid- to late 1970s, Baudelaire, Rimbaud, Lautréamont, and others were in the background. The music press invoked the poets fairly often in the 1970s as it was attempting to define a new movement in music that seemed equal parts abjection and erudition. A 1977 article in the British music magazine *Sounds* characterizes the attempts on journalist's parts to make sense of this apparent breach of the high/low divide:

> But over in NY, NY, people are not ashamed to use the word ART. Richard Hell is an ARTIST, or, more specifically, a poet, from an academic/artistic background. . . . The state of Richard's consciousness as reflected in his room proves that Richard functions on more levels than rock and roll. His heroes are French poets and novelists, Baudelaire, Lautreamont's "Maldoror," Rimbaud and Huysmans.[40]

The music journalist Lester Bangs on the one hand wanted to liberate Hell from anything approaching a debt to symbolist aesthetics and, on the other, made sure to point out how Hell's lyrics in his song "Down at the Rock & Roll Club" echoed Baudelaire's decadent narcissism:

> Hell has found solace in late 19th century French Symbolist poets, in fact he fancies them his muses or mentors. But, though I fantasize on them, too, at length, I must say no, because Lautréamont or even Baudelaire would be incapable of following up "Rip off my shirt / Watch the mirror it flirt" (Baudelairean, admittedly) with "Scotch and soda!"[41]

Bangs here identifies something central to Hell's practice. Hell's music and lyrics are predicated on a consistently ambivalent play between poetry and punk that accepts, even invites, links to be made between relatively obscure lyric practice and punk rock but that simultaneously wants to cleanse punk of any associations with high culture.

This productive struggle was born in part out of Hell's own poetry published in *Genesis: Grasp*. With the benefit of hindsight, we can see in Hell's juvenilia an attempt to forge a new voice that would take in influences as diverse as Baudelaire, James Joyce, Artaud, Rimbaud, and Gerard Manley Hopkins in the service of projecting a huffy, angry, funny speaker—one that would find successful expression in the music to come.

Hell's "Hot Ice, Seed Water, Letterfwesh," included in *Genesis: Grasp* 1.3, shows a young writer wrestling with influence as he remains determined to develop a provocative, sexualized persona:

"HOT ICE, SEED WATER, LETTERFWESH"
(Tasty Ratpich Song)

Broken (ice) eyes water. When
Your eyes break, then I come
In! Through eyes flow.

Sweet salt? Hot ice? Made love?
Vat, sweet slime, co-heat
Lode! Slick tongues in

Venting wetterflesh. Stiff tongue
In toothless mouth (still young)
Sweet salt: comes![42]

Hell's use of idiosyncratic words ("letterfwesh," "ratpich," and "wetterflesh") suggests the influence of James Joyce's *Finnegans Wake*. Hell's Joycean wordplay here is an early indication of the nascent punk's understanding of neologisms as part of an overall strategy—akin to the glam-rock star's and dandy's wardrobes—to confront readers with the artificiality of language and, by extension, the failure of language to represent "reality" or "truth" transparently. The rules of syntax and grammar, the social consensus on the relationship between signifier and signified, are in poems like "Hot Ice" given a rude shove through the disruptive practice of an allusively Joycean language.

This poem can be read in part, then, as a reflection of the poet's developing reading habits and understanding of what constitutes literary heritage.[43] For example, the use of the almost homonymic word pair "ice" and "eyes" shows a marked appreciation for the kinds of poetic practices foregrounding the abstract effects of a denatured language that, in the late 1960s and early 1970s, was increasingly found in the work of poets like Aram Saroyan, Clark Coolidge, and Bruce Andrews. Hell would go on in subsequent issues to publish New York School–affiliated poets including Coolidge and Saroyan as well as Andrews, who had yet to identify himself as a L=A=N=G=U=A=G=E poet. The inclusion of these writers marked a radical, experimental break with the rather standard lyric practices of earlier issues of *Genesis: Grasp* and reveals how Hell's growing knowledge of postmodern poetry was beginning to make him a more mature poet. Correspondence from Hell to Coolidge in early 1970 shows the young poet committed to a linguistically and syntactically disruptive poetics that Hell linked to an anarchist politics and pop sensibility. Poetry, as Hell put it to Coolidge, is "finally the place where the only law is 'ACCEPT NO LAWS.'"[44] Hell soon entered into a regular correspondence with Coolidge, sending Coolidge his own work for commentary, albeit under the pseudonym "Ernie Stomach." Stomach was a character that, as Hell pointed out to Coolidge, was committed to transforming consciousness via language:

> Here's an old revelation of Ernie Stomach's for a snack
>
>   soap opera
>   so a pop era
>
> After that he spent—in fact occasionally still spends—days looking for the key phrase that could prophesize various looks in the next few years. He's convinced that words given the proper care could/can do absolutely anything from permanently alter one's consciousness—throw you into fits of ecstasy—to accurately and precisely predict a specific future. I'm sure you're onto these things—like your friends' description of you as an anarchist I mean alchemist, depends on how you look at it.[45]

Moving firmly away from a model of writing as one that emanates out of a stable, specific subject position, Hell here links a persona-based writing project with a quasi-mystical, quasi-political agenda that half-jokingly calls for an overthrow of order via a disassembling of normative signify-ing practices. Making use of puns and homonyms, Hell—through Ernie Stomach—shows how easy it is to transform "reality" by redistributing the way letters are arranged on the page. The Sturm und Drang of a soap opera is casually manipulated into a casual "pop" era: Cheesy depth and despair bleed into off-handedness and surface cool. Such an alchemical transformation contains within it an "anarchist" affect, one that firmly places these kinds of language games in the service of a vibrant anti-authoritarianism.

In fact, poems like "Hot Ice" point forward toward Hell's more sophisti-cated prose, poetry, and lyrics of the 1970s and augur the cynical Onan at the heart of one of Hell's most accomplished pop-punk tunes, "Love Comes in Spurts," versions of which were recorded as early as 1973.[46] Hell's early texts are practically drenched with evocations of sperm, big penises, and masturbation. In *Genesis: Grasp* 1.3, for example, Hell writes in an untitled poem: "Set forth in myself for the skin of / The universe, galaxy to phallus I / Travel my infinite skin."[47] In *Genesis: Grasp* 1.4 (1970), Hell continued the theme in his poem "IT" (later included in Hell's volume *Hot and Cold*): "I con-tinue manipulating / My self. / It's very demanding. That's why masturba-tors / Also sleep a lot."[48] Uncollected poems in Hell's archives from this period show a poet absorbed in such details: "I pull this girl to me from behind when I see the hair / drip between her legs one hand on each breast my cock / presses the length between her buttocks . . . / sperm mixed with thick salty blood and a little shit: / fuel shelter food and perfume."[49] Beginning his life as a poet under the sway of writers like Dylan Thomas, Hell was clearly moving on from the sort of wordplay we see in "Hot Ice" to more and more aggressive, literal, and cynical depictions of modern love, replete with pro-fanity and surrealistically inflected depictions of sex.

There is not that much distance from a poem like "IT" to "Love Comes in Spurts." True, "Spurts" is a fairly direct, uncomplicated, and funny song that emphasizes how emotion is often bred and extinguished out of an eas-ily expended lust: "cuz love comes in spurts / in dangerous flirts / and it murders your heart / they didn't tell you that part / *Love comes in spurts* . . ."[50] That said, the song's dismal message is grounded in Hell's depictions of love evident in his poems included in the final issues of *Genesis: Grasp* and sub-sequent publications. Once he began performing with the Neon Boys,

Television, and the Voidoids, Hell seemed to appropriate techniques learned in poetry for the purposes of his pop lyrics and stage role. Moving his way increasingly toward the autodidactic, cynical, funny, and aggressive persona of Richard Hell, replete with torn T-shirts, spiky hair, and the like, "Love Comes in Spurts" is of a piece with Hell's development as an antiestablishment, iconoclastic artist.

Richard Hell published the final volume of the *Genesis: Grasp* project in 1971 and remembers the issue positively. "By the last issue I still felt like . . . my co-editor David Giannini had a little bit of influence on that one and we had just completely diverged in our ideas by then . . . but apart from that I really . . . I'm happy with the last issue . . . the magazine was ready to move on."[51] The cover featured a triptych of faces. On the upper far left was a young Rimbaud, to his right was Antonin Artaud, and in the bottom left corner was "Theresa Stern," a person who, at first glance, appeared to be either a very rough-living, gaudy woman or a member of the New York Dolls. In fact, "Theresa" was a composite shot of Tom Miller/Verlaine and Richard Hell, both of whom had applied liberal doses of makeup. The feminized image was rooted in the historical avant-garde, pointing back to the kind of gender play Marcel Duchamp engaged in through his persona Rrose Sélavy. Like Duchamp, Verlaine and Hell created images of themselves as women and then went further by ascribing a number of works to this fictional "Theresa."

Poems in the issue included work by Andrei Codrescu, Simon Schuchat, Bruce Andrews, Toby Sonneman, Richard Meyers (Hell), Ernie Stomach (Hell), Albert Goldbarth, Patty Machine (a pseudonym for Patty Oldenburg, Hell's lover at the time), Tom Miller/Verlaine, Clark Coolidge, and Yuki Hartman. Coolidge's and Andrews's appearances are particularly interesting. Hell saw the poets as part of a new "movement" that he, as publisher, could help form by making the necessary introductions. As he wrote to Coolidge:

> By the way, if you do have any remaining interest in a "Movement" and would like to be in touch with someone who it looks like has interests related to yours, a guy named Bruce Andrews (maybe you already know of him) recently sent some works (we're printing two) with a note asking if we knew of any other poets or magazines who might interested in his work.[52]

Andrews, learning in kind from Hell, would end up shaping an experimental punk poetics in the seventies and eighties in books such as *Give 'Em Enough Rope* (1987), titled after the Clash's second album. As Juliana Spahr points out in her discussion of *Give 'Em Enough Rope*:

> The work in this collection is decisively anti-poetic and avoids any hint of lyricism. It is built around disjunction. The work has an uncensored (some would say unedited) quality. Appearing side by side is intellectual and often politically inflected language ("Intentionally leaderless"; "rewriting the body"; "Camera obscura"), accusations, insults, challenges ("Don't give a shit what you think"), and punk lyrics. Throughout this piece are references to groups like the Pop Group ("How long do we tolerate mass murder" 144), Richard Hell and the Voidoids ("blank generation" 145), the Tubes and Nina Hagen ("white huskies on dope" 147), Velvet Underground ("we don't perform Heroin anymore" 153), Joy Division ("Joy division" 156; "love will tear us" 161), the Buzzcocks ("orgasmaddict" 157), Teenage Jesus and the Jerks ("freud in flop" 161), the Sex Pistols ("NO FUTURE" 166), and the Clash ("radio free europe" 166).[53]

Bruce Andrews's poem "5th Collaboration," included in the final issue of *Genesis: Grasp*, while lacking some of the qualities Spahr identifies above, does nevertheless raise some interesting questions regarding who appropriates what in terms of the purported struggle between "high" and "low" culture that defines our ever-expanding (or circular) arguments about what precisely constitutes postmodernism. "5th Collaboration" is here reproduced in its entirety:

1. Two old priests pristinely traipse the Alabama cup
2. The pale apricot rosebud savors
   the poetry of Robert Lowell
3. leaves in a basket with a broke bottom
4. Old Savannah highway
5. black thorn crystal
6. San Pedro[54]

Now, what makes this work a "poem?" Why call it "5th Collaboration" if readers are unaware of the people Andrews is collaborating with? Why is there a marked resistance to lyric evident in the very form of this work, composed as it is of sentence fragments, non sequiturs, and lightly disguised literary politics that, following O'Hara, Lou Reed, and Gerard Malanga, would relegate an establishment poet like Robert Lowell into the realm of effete farce? Is the reference to "San Pedro" an invitation among in-the-know readers to associate this fragmented work with the hallucinatory effects of the San Pedro cactus, or is the place name merely a random gesture? There is an oppositional poetics in place here that resists even the generic category "poem" that the work's place in *Genesis: Grasp* would purportedly fall under.

In a letter dated February 8, 1971, Hell wrote to Andrews, "We accept for our next issue (#5–6) your *5th Collaboration* and 'Strindour . . .' Looks like you're doing some interesting stuff—too bad we can't take more or even see more right now, but we're overloaded with material for this coming issue."[55] Andrews took this letter as an invitation to begin a series of back-and-forth missives in which Hell took the opportunity to describe a muscular poetics committed to immediacy, visuality, and shock value:

> Current tentative plan—BLAK & WITE Mag, not only a "non"—"linear" as they say but—. If you know what I mean.—. BLAK & WITE. Tentative in sense that I want some enthusiasm from prospective contributors. Are you one? Thin issues out fast of the ink between site since black is so visible on white and blood. What kind of explainer am I? Not good that's why I'll stick to paper that reveals the nerve connected to the hipbone etc. Um . . . Am printing the old time mag. Gotta do it fast because I want to forget about it. Another "beautiful" *thing*—aggh.
>
> Well if any of this conveys anything to you send me some apt wrk & then in response further communication & maybe you'll know of others. I'm also interested in "purely" visual work if intended for the page. In other words I want each page in the mag to be as *direct* as possible. I don't want words from the imagination or intellect. I want them from the muscled energy of a being and/ or more particularly *from the page*. I want to turn people on.[56]

Poems of Hell's included in the final issue of *Genesis: Grasp* included the kind of "'non—'linear'" imagery and directness Hell was increasingly aiming for and pointed ahead to some of his best-known songs. In an untitled poem, for example, Richard Hell's Felliniesque carnie aesthetic came to the fore:

> The cattle are barking
> because it is dark. Why, here's
> one at my fourth floor window. Come in,
> old flame, you are my buddy. Wrap your
> flanks around me. Without looking
> I can distinguish against my cheeks
> the brown patch from the white one each
> made out of hairs out of doors
> in the vinyl grass-black
> heat of the streets, many years ago.
> Sit down, rest that big flesh
> fig against the floor. I rise to shut the window
> and looking out resolve never to turn back.
> Then she told me why the pinhead couldn't stay at the party[57]

This work is obviously a long way away from the modernist pastiche of "Hot Ice." Replete with barking cows, non sequiturs, and spooky pinheads, the poem's surrealism is domesticated curiously by its place in a space evocative of a New York City apartment. The portentousness of Hell's language in the earlier work seems to have been left behind for a much more lighthearted if vaguely aggressive diction that at times verges on a kind of twisted cuddliness. These qualities are evident in much of Hell's published and unpublished work from the early 1970s. One untitled poem written initially for Hell's and Tom Verlaine's *Wanna Go Out?* (discussed below) drew on the figure of the pinhead once again in order to promote an aura of surreality, ugliness, and transgression: "destitute Puerto Ricans and me and the Puerto Ricans don't / want to have anything to do with me! / Actually I forgot about the pinheads and mongoloids / but I could never fuck either. / I'm beginning to understand mystical chastity."[58] These kinds of poems are close in spirit to many of Hell's songs. With its homegrown surrealism, its references to "pinheads" (who make an appearance not just in Hell's song "You Gotta Lose" but in the Ramones' classic song "Pinhead"), and its vaguely hostile relationship to people other than the speaker himself, this untitled poem augurs Hell's more ambitious lyrics. The opening verses of Hell's "You Gotta Lose," for example, follow much the same path as the untitled poems above, albeit tamed by rhyme:

> I hope I don't seem immodest when I tell you that my, my
> mother was a pinhead and my father was a fly.
> That's why I love you darlin' with a love that's so unique:
> Your glistenin' wings they complement your head's exquisite peak.
> They all died by coin toss.
> Love's a form of memory loss.
> I can't forget that triple cross . . .
> You gotta lose, you gotta lose.[59]

This text, created during a period of Hell's life that found him increasingly disenchanted with the limited audience attendant to poetry, ultimately characterized much of Hell's contributions to rock 'n' roll.

The great transitional moments for Hell prior to dedicating himself to music was the publication and subsequent abandonment of the *Genesis: Grasp* project, a last-ditch attempt to market poetry for a mass audience through a new publishing imprint, Dot Books, and the creation with Tom Verlaine of the persona Theresa Stern. A letter from Hell to the poet, filmmaker, and publisher Charlie Plymell announcing the formation of the Dot Books imprint and the publication of Andrew Wylie's book *Yellow Flowers* reads like a swan song to poetry:

> To me "*Genesis: Grasp*" is like the archetypal, back-turned, weepy, self-defeating, poor but noble little literary magazine. Who cares? Publishing a mag like that is like writing off the world. It's like committing suicide. It says oh I'm beautiful but it's no use, goodbye goodbye! It's not tough enough. I don't know . . . it aint all that bad—but it's *nothing* compared to what can be done. It's like the poets give up before they start in terms of making a dent in people's consciousness. Whereas the Beatles for instance changed the world—made people happy and shook em up. I think poets can do the same thing. That's where Dot Books is going to be aimed. It'll be a series of paperbacks in the format of mass market drugstore ups. Same size, flashy glossy covers—blurbs, exclamation points, code numbers, pulpy paper inside—everything as closely as I can approximate it

with incredibly less money than Dell, or Fawcett or Bantam. But the first one is being printed now and it really makes it—hottest looking book since The Godfather with poems in it like these two (on facing pages)

hands up	thighs
your skirt	on my neck
warm wet	I suck
pants	the clit

by Andrew Wylie. So that's what I'm up to.[60]

In a letter to Bruce Andrews relating to the formation of Dot Books, Hell made his plans clear regarding his relationship to poetry and publishing. "It's an experiment, the whole thing. I'm gonna see if I can make money in this racket. If this doesn't, something's wrong that I can't fix, and I'll skip publishing for good. I've been thru the poor but beautiful bag & *that* sure don't make it."[61] As poetry's lack of commercial and popular appeal became ever clearer to Hell, though, his response was to work further toward a much more exciting option—rock 'n' roll. Hell soon discovered, of course, that poets could not "do the same thing" as the Beatles. Poets could not reach a mass audience, nor could they *really* materially threaten consensus culture through shock tactics like Wylie's antipoetry in evidence here.[62] (Hell had additional books by himself, Verlaine, and Patti Smith ready for publication by Dot Books, but these projects did not materialize as Hell left poetry for music.)

Poets who had become friendly with Hell via the *Genesis: Grasp* and Dot Books projects intuited the ways Hell was beginning to shift from poetry to rock 'n' roll. Bruce Andrews, for one, wrote in a letter postmarked 1972:

Ok, I saw your Wylie Dot book & am "familiar with" (i.e., I've read all of them standing up at the bookstore) all the Telegraph books. I think I know what you want: *quick hits*, which is only possible with a short and *lean* (uncomplicated) supercharged poem—EROTIC ROCK N' ROLL DOPE poems. Ok. Also, now, most of my poems aren't like that, *mostly* because they're longer, *and* they're more complicated, because a *"hit"* for me is primarily a *language* hit, not a perception/idea/feel/gut hit à la Saroyan-Wylie-T. Clark-R. Meyer.[63]

By early 1973 Andrews ended his correspondence with Hell with a good-humored bon voyage and best wishes for Hell, who, with Tom Verlaine, had just formed the Neon Boys. Even though Hell had suggested that a Dot Books publication featuring Andrews's poetry was in the works, only to then write Andrews with the news he was abandoning the page for the stage, Andrews was the perfect gentleman:

> hello. thanks for the letter (i got a preview-précis from Simon [Schuchat] at xmas). i knew when i put those poems together that you'd like 'em, but too bad DOT has dots no more. Hope rock & roll takes good care of yr soul—where are you playing w/ Neon Boys? Anyhow, really glad you liked the mss so much _____ _____ maybe Andrew [Wylie] could do somethin' with it _____ thanks for thinking of that & showing it to him.[64]

Goodbye small-press publishing, goodbye St. Mark's, goodbye poetry! Richard Meyers was well on his way to becoming Hell.

Blank Generation

Hell's desire for a larger audience, combined with his continuing experiments in writing practices typical of the poets he loved, resulted in the composition of the song "Blank Generation," Hell's most celebrated work and arguably *the* American punk anthem. Before we consider the verses of the song, we should read the famous chorus. Sung in a voice that is part whine, part howl, part snotty assertion, Richard Hell proclaims, "I belong to the blank generation and." And it stopped there. For a moment. On the "and." The chorus continued in this oddly disruptive way, each line refusing—through the violence of enjambment—to be contained. These lines weren't consumable; this was no singalong. The company implicit in the very word "chorus" was not welcome here. This unsociability was sustained throughout the four lines. "I belong to the blank generation and" was followed by "I can take it or leave it each time well" (the "well" stretched just a touch, aurally italicized, posed as a challenge, "*wehllll*"), which in turn was followed by "I belong to the _____ generation but," the word "blank" itself removed from the equation, replaced with its own omission, a materialization of itself as absence. Then, finally, the chorus ground to a halt with the flippant and entirely ambiguous "but / I can take it or leave it each time." Even in the context of Richard Hell's own New York scene—one that found any number of important proto-punk bands like the New York Dolls and the Dictators assaulting the bloated, pretentious arena rock that was increasingly dominating the airwaves[65]—Hell's use of enjambment, his creative employment of silences, and a style that valued ambiguity over direct statement marked "Blank Generation" as a peculiarly sophisticated and literary-inflected song.

"Blank Generation" curiously enough also extended Hell's critique of Beat Generation histrionics. Hell's "Blank Generation," after all, was in part a reverse parody of a parody. It was modeled after Rod McKuen's 1959 novelty record (recorded under the pseudonym "Bob McFadden") "I Belong to the Beat Generation," a tune that poked fun at North Beach beatnik caricatures. Hell's song matched McKuen's use of "the descending perennial chord pattern from innumerable hit 1950s songs [like 'Hit the Road, Jack'] as the appropriately crass way to satirize an 'alternative' culture."[66] Poking wicked fun at North Beach beatnik caricatures, McKuen applied a clearly sarcastic tone and slurred and extended vowels to the chorus "I belong to the *Beeet* Generation, / I don't let anything trouble my mind / I belong to the *Beeet* Generation / And everything's going *just* fine."[67] Hell similarly extended vowels in the chorus to his "Blank Generation." These similarities, however, did not mean that Hell was merely echoing McKuen's song for fun. Rather, Hell's "Blank Generation" engaged critically with McKuen's message and sound.

In McKuen's "Beat Generation," a character identified on the single as "Dor" tossed off Beat clichés in response to McKuen's acerbic narrative. "I run around in sandals / I never ever shave / And that's the way I wanna be when someone digs my grave," growled McKuen. "Put a Beat in the White House!" responded Dor. "I belong to the *Beeet* Generation / and everything's going just fine," continued McKuen. "Back on the road!"[68] Dor flipped back. Hell was not following this particular lead. Instead, Hell's parody of McKuen's parody worked in part to contest McKuen's contempt toward angel-headed hipsters. Hell's urgent whine simultaneously belied the nihilist message of Hell's "Blank Generation" even as it embodied the adolescent's rage at how quickly Beat Generation heroes could be reduced to stick figures in songs like McKuen's. That said, Hell's song was also an acknowledgment that nostalgia for or reiteration of Beat tropes and styles was futile. As early as 1959, McKuen's "Beat Generation" revealed, as Greil Marcus put it, "the mere showmanship of Jack Kerouac,"[69] thereby teaching America's youth a hard lesson on how easily rebellion could be transformed into entertainment. Hell's response to McKuen's erasure of Kerouac was to invoke and then erase the whole lot of them. Beats, squares, wannabe outsiders, and the patronizing elders looking to domesticate or cash in on seditious energy were all targeted implicitly by Hell. Hell's "Blank Generation" opened up a space where a new rebellious (if cynical) sensibility—grounded outrageously in dissonant seconds-long slashes of guitar squall, screeching, and the stunning silence of the omitted word "Blank"—could be cultivated.

Wanna Go Out?

Where was Hell coming from? His unsettling indifference ("I can take it or leave it each time," he reminded us throughout the song) stemmed in part from the second-generation New York School poetry that Hell was drawn to: writers like Tom Clark, Ted Berrigan, and their peers. This was a scene, as discussed in chapter 3, which published seemingly endless reams of collaborative, anonymously, or pseudonymously produced poetry that contested the idea of writing as self-expression and challenged conventional understandings of the author as stable, solitary subject. In light of this community-oriented literary culture, which Hell was invested in, we should note that aspects of "Blank Generation"—which began with the now-iconic stanza "I was saying lemme out of here before I was / even born. It's such a gamble when you get a face. / It's fascinatin' to observe what the mirror does / but when I dine it's for the wall that I set a place"[70]—were developed initially in the pages of *Wanna Go Out?*, a small-press poetry book dreamed up, edited, and designed by Hell. Hell collaborated on the book's poems with Tom Verlaine under the single pseudonym "Theresa Stern." As Hell recalled, "Theresa for me was definitely the big breakthrough . . . and that almost coincided with leaving poetry for music."[71]

The first line of Hell's "Blank Generation," for example, derived from material Hell wrote for the table of contents in *Wanna Go Out?* The book was issued in 1973 under the Dot Books imprint, a series in which Hell made the announcement "Other books from the Blank Generation available from Dot" on the books' verso pages. Hell explained:

> You want to know what the origin of those lines [from "Blank Generation"] is? They have a really sneaky origin. . . . In this book you'll see it's the first time the phrase "Blank Generation" shows up. The table of contents is a poem itself. "Stars I was / Thinking now I've started a new game / How come no one / As I lounge in my parlor / And the cars wish they had some candy comes / To amplify my eardrums / When I look at the floor foreground / For the scissors on my wrists / And ponder upon that little cut / After all I wasn't even born / When I first said lemme out of here / Marionette mon amour / My . . . oh / The light's too dim in here / I'm getting nervous / But I promise / You stranger I'm tight and juicy."[72]

A number of poems in *Wanna Go Out?* evoked further the efforts Hell made to apply a petulant punk attitude to undermine precious associations accorded to the lyric poem. The poem "To Amplify My Eardrums" points to rock 'n' roll clamor in the lines "They came last night and amplified my eardrums. / It's to glee bay / (TERRIBLE TERRIBLE) / they want to take me away. / Well I don't belong here anyway. I'm the only rock band on earth who's the earth's hernia."[73] Phrases in other poems like "Fuck this whole goddamn apartment,"[74] "Of the cunt that was nailed to the cross,"[75] and "Close this book I scream and come look me up so we can fuck as long / as I don't have to talk"[76] augured Hell's literate rage in his own music's articulation of urban blight and provocative nihilism.

Who was this fictional Theresa Stern? As the introduction to *Wanna Go Out?* reads,

> THERESA STERN was born on October 27, 1949, of a German Jewish father and a Puerto Rican mother in Hoboken, N.J., directly across the Hudson from New York City. She still lives there, alone, where all the poems in this book were written over a four month period in the summer and fall of 1971. She has since devoted that of her time not spent in flipping coins to composing a love story, THIN SKIN. It describes the murder, in ten chapters fired by Theresa, of her closest friend. WANNA GO OUT? is a question often asked on the streets around the cheaper bars in New York and Hoboken.

Stern was widely believed to be a real person. John Holmstrom's *Punk* magazine advertised *Wanna Go Out?* with the sarcastically worded phrase "Poetry? in Punk??" leading off a reproduction of a Stern poem followed by instructions to send five dollars to "R. Meyers." Letters to Hell asking for more information and work from Stern show that many in the poetry community believed Stern was some kind of art brut poet. Ron Silliman, who was publishing the proto-L=A=N=G=U=A=G=E poetry journal *Tottel's* at the time, wrote Hell in praise of Theresa:

> Enclosed please find a check for $0.95. please, send a copy of Theresa Stern's book WANNA GO OUT? right away. Darrell Gray has been turning people onto it out here & it certainly intrigues. . . . As I publish a newsletter of poetry, *Tottel's*, and am always involved in a variety of other publishing conspiracies out here, I'd be interested in obtaining her address or in having this note passed on to her, so that she cld drop me a line, or whatever.[77]

In the fourth issue of *Punk* magazine, the writer Mary Harron, who later directed films including *I Shot Andy Warhol* and *American Psycho*, conducted an interview with "Theresa" by providing Hell with a set of questions, who then went on to write the answers. Harron pretended to have elicited the answers herself through a personal visit to "Theresa" in her purported home in Hoboken. In response to the question, "What are your literary influences . . . how and why did you start writing," "Stern" responded:

> I started writing because it was so easy. I saw all this writing being praised and I knew I could do better with a splitting headache on the subway at rush hour. Most poets are such bullshitters—they have so many vested interests, whereas I hardly have any interests at all (laughter). As for influences—my favorite poet of the century is Breton. Infinitely passionate, profound and incorruptible and what's more he's the smartest guy I ever came across, and his poetry doesn't make any sense.[78]

Even in the guise of Theresa Stern, Hell still drew on and simultaneously rejected an avant-garde tradition to buttress his punk style. Breton was great because he was intelligent, passionate, and senseless—a fitting description of Hell's performance style in the mid-1970s as he leaped and cavorted across the stage, wailing his complex lyrics, at times ending a performance on his knees, head tilted up to the ceiling. Poetry was a part of all that. Hell's notes written in one of Patti Smith's 1974 journals show that the increasingly well-known punk rocker still had one foot firmly planted in the literary world:

> I've gotta figure out something pleasurable to do with a pen on paper that I wouldn't want to see in print. Can always read the preceding pages for inspiration. What could be better. Too bad she [Patti Smith] didn't throw in a few drawings. Maybe I'll write a book. Starting with title for next page.
>   PLEASE KILL ME[79]

So, even in June 1974, when Hell had already begun participating in the downtown music scene and had come up with the punk catchphrase "PLEASE KILL ME," which was to be stenciled onto a T-shirt Television's guitarist Richard Lloyd wore onstage—he could not quite disassociate himself from poetry altogether. "Maybe I'll write a book" he wrote, during the period in which his and Tom Verlaine's band Television was performing live at CBGB and other downtown venues. And editing poetry was still on his mind as well. In an entry dated December 17, Hell wrote in Smith's journal, "start passionate mimeoed fanzine of (French) Symbolist Poetry." Appearing on CBGB's stage wearing his exquisitely ripped T-shirts and sporting a chopped-up shock of hair, Hell still had one eye on Baudelaire, Rimbaud, and other poets.

Hell's work as a publisher, poet, and reader of poetry by the likes of Ted Berrigan, Bernadette Mayer, Aram Saroyan, Clark Coolidge, Andrew Wylie, and Bruce Andrews played a real part in Meyers's transformation into Hell. True, we should be careful not to overstate the case. Music finally lured Hell away (if temporarily) from poetry and publishing. All that said, poetry was never far from Hell's mind. While Hell found a measure of fame following the release of the *Blank Generation* LP, he was still drawn to the St. Mark's poets, and the CBGB crowd itself continued to jostle for space in the church's pews. Remembering an October 1978 "St. Mark's Fire Benefit: 3 days of Poetry and Rock" gig he did at CBGB for St. Mark's Church after it suffered a fire earlier that year that nearly destroyed the building, Hell described how

> there were a lot of poets there, along with the CBGB mob. . . . When we brought Elvis [Costello] on, he said I should be president. Then he sang my song "You

Figure 4.1 Richard Hell and Elvis Costello performing at the Fire Benefit for St. Mark's Church, October 18, 1978, CBGB.

Source: Copyright © Roberta Bayley.

Gotta Lose." For the finale, in honor of the church, we did a surprisingly skillful version of the Stones' "Shattered." Allen Ginsberg and Ted Berrigan were
in the crowd. I secretly kidded them in my patter, with an "om" dropped in for
Allen, and then, to blow Ted's mind, since he had no reason to think I'd ever
heard of him, an unacknowledged paraphrase of a few lines of his—appropriated,
as if they were mine, the way he would do. He was always really nice to me
afterwards.[80]

Hell, a longtime reader of Ginsberg, Berrigan, and Padgett, used the occasion to shout out to the downtown bards he saw were in the audience. As a
recording of his song "The Kid with the Replaceable Head" at the Fire Benefit revealed, Hell began by referencing Berrigan's poem "Ten Things I Do
Everyday," perhaps *the* ultimate distillation of Frank O'Hara's "I do this, I
do that" approach.[81] "We're going to tell you about ten things we did today,
alright?" Hell told the audience, continuing à la Berrigan, "I drank a Pepsi,
and then I took a pill!" Responding to catcalls and applause, Hell intoned sarcastically, "Just a moment, *restrain yourselves*, ladies and gents. This is *poetry*,
don't get carried away!" Having pointed to Berrigan, Hell then set his sights
on Allen Ginsberg. "Meditate meditate!" Hell implored jokingly, making a
reference to Ginsberg's efforts to popularize Buddhist meditation. To ensure his audience got the joke, Hell then ventriloquized Ginsberg's mantra,
chanting, "*om*."

Never poetry or punk—always poetry *and* punk. Hell enacted the Rimbaudian script even as he made sure to let that romantic myth clash with
the joyfully messy scene at St. Mark's taking place down the street from his
apartment. Exploiting the tension between the vatic and the phatic, Hell
cultivated an outlaw, funny, and angry style that went far in breaching the
divides separating poem from song, poetry reading from rock show, art
from life.

FIVE

"I Just Got Different Theories"

Patti Smith and the New York School of Poetry

FROM HER TIME as a young performance poet in New York in the late 1960s to her current position as punk rock's éminence grise, Patti Smith has foregrounded the image of the poet as privileged seer. Simultaneously, Smith rejected stereotypically "feminine" personae emphatically both in terms of the content of her writing and in her on-stage performance style. Critics picked up on this early on, never tiring of comparing Smith to Keith Richards, Bob Dylan, Jim Morrison, Mick Jagger, and other rock 'n' roll bad boys.[1] Unlike Richard Hell's response to the St. Mark's scene, Smith developed vatic postures and made gender trouble within the context of her relationship to the Poetry Project. This is especially important because Smith didn't keep her distance from St. Mark's. Hell's affiliation to the Poetry Project in the 1960s and '70s was one based primarily on reading the poets' works and magazines, publishing some of their writing in his magazine *Genesis: Grasp*, and attending occasional readings. Not so for Smith.

The Poetry Project proved fundamentally important for Smith's career. It was at St. Mark's where Smith gave her first poetry performance. This was an auspicious beginning. Looking back on the event in 2014, Smith recalled how many of the poems she read that evening were adapted into songs that would end up on *Horses*. The first line in her poem "Oath," for example, became the first line in her song "Gloria."[2] Already aware and on the edges of New York's counterculture hotspots like the Warhol-centric

Brownies, Max's Kansas City, and Warhol's Factory, Smith knew that St. Mark's stood shoulder to shoulder with these institutions.

Not surprisingly, Smith's poetry was read consistently in the context of the New York School and the wider New American Poetry worlds Smith cut her teeth in. "The words of Frank O'Hara, the genius of the New York School of Poets," Kate Ballen insisted in 1977, informed the opening lines of Smith's "Rape," as the poem made way for other influences: "O'Hara's amusing sense of conversation is soon joined with apocalyptic-acid 'mushroom-cloud' images and American jukebox crooning."[3] In other words, Smith was actively attempting to synthesize O'Hara's "I do this, I do that" style with Beat Generation–affiliated grandiloquence.[4] The first stanza of "Rape" reveals this wild combination:

> yum yum the stars are out. I'll never forget how you
> smelled that night. like cheddar cheese melting under
> fluorescent light. like a day old rainbow fish. what a
> dish. gotta lick my lips. gotta dream. I daydream.
> thorozine brain cloud. rain rain comes coming down.[5]

Opening with a "yum yum" is practically a friendly nod to other winsome opening lines affiliated with the New York School generally and O'Hara specifically. Think back to, for example, O'Hara's poem "Blocks." "Yippee!" O'Hara begins shockingly and hilariously, followed by a series of surrealist non sequiturs that owe as much to Andre Breton as they do to Bugs Bunny.[6] Tantalizingly, O'Hara's "Blocks" also includes its own "yum yum": "O boy, their childhood was like so many oatmeal cookies. / I need you, you need me, yum, yum. Anon it became suddenly."[7] Smith's "yum yum," read alongside O'Hara's "Blocks," draws on and echoes the antiseriousness that characterized so much of the best writing affiliated with the New York School. True, where O'Hara's flights of fancy are stratospheric, Smith paddles. The addressee's scent is evoked through a simile to artificially lit cheese and a *farshtinkiner* rainbow fish (which, despite being "day old" could not smell *that* bad, given that rainbow fish are small, beautifully colored tropical creatures that would naturally lack the olfactory punch of, say, a day-old mackerel). Smith's juxtapositions offer a somewhat tamer series of paratactic surprises when compared to O'Hara's extravagances. Nevertheless, Smith's O'Haraesque humor, cultivated in the poetry that preceded her 1975 album

Horses, reveals Smith working actively to apprehend and echo the casual, caustic, and dreamlike styles favored by the poets gathering regularly at the Poetry Project.

Smith wants to get her New American poets in there as well. The dramatic enjambment in the line "like a day old rainbow fish. what a / dish" echoes Robert Creeley's halting line breaks as much as it does the use of dramatic pauses in the Andrews Sisters' song about seafood "Hold Tight, Hold Tight." Alongside those echoes of old-time popular music shimmers Smith's phrase "thorozine [*sic*] brain cloud." Is Smith matching syllable for syllable Ginsberg's oft-quoted surrealist catchphrase "hydrogen jukebox" from his poem "Howl"?[8] Beyond the vague slant rhymes that match "thorozine" with "hydrogen," there is possibly an analogous metrics that suggests Smith is pointing to the rhythms Ginsberg generally employed when reading his poem "Howl" aloud—like Ginsberg's, her phrase might be read as comprising an anapest (two unstressed syllables followed by one stressed syllable) and a spondee (a foot consisting of two stressed syllables). All told, Smith's stanza, while not necessarily as moving and powerful as the lyrics to many of Smith's songs on *Horses*, nor as funny and surprising as Smith's free-associational interview raps throughout the 1970s, reveals a recognizable core of influences that Smith the poet was sifting through and processing prior to becoming Smith the rock 'n' roll star.

Smith was ventriloquizing Poetry Project–affiliated writers in other ways. Similar to Richard Hell's efforts to write Aram Saroyan–style minimalist poems, Smith offered works including "amelia earhart 1" to in-the-know readers of her 1972 book *Seventh Heaven*:

Amelia Earhart

earheart

ear

heart

air[9]

Smith in this poem is highlighting a word's malleability. This is something the New American poets—from Robert Duncan's "There is a pun of scents in what makes sense" through Frank O'Hara's "Grace / to be born and live as variously as possible" through Aram Saroyan's "blod" and "lobstee"— delighted in.[10] Joining in by deranging a proper name, Smith's linguistic impropriety is of a piece with the poets on her reading list and in her neighborhood.

Not only does Smith deconstruct and indeed turn into sound Earhart's proper name; she literally disorganizes it into a collection of detached or disembodied organs released into the medium of air. Earhart, in Smith's first cut, becomes earheart in a portmanteau evocative of Paul Celan's compressed poetic diction, a monstrous coupling of separate organs capable of both listening and feeling. In the next move, she cuts the two apart. The ear (which emphasizes the procedure overall as a sonic one) is left hanging on its own, followed by the heart in the next line, similarly suspended, as both a material organ and sentimental trope. Then, to complete the procedure and figuratively redoubling Earhart's own fate, the ear and heart evanesce into the air itself. What we see, even in this ostensibly silly name game, is a movement from the personal to the impersonal, from the definite to the indefinite, from the singularity of the name to the singularity of the air. Earhart, semantically torn asunder, merges with the air that both bore her up and ultimately enveloped her.

Yet *unlike* Saroyan and related writers, Smith relies entirely on basic definitions of words to project something approaching a narrative. Despite surface similarities, Smith's poem is in distinction to Saroyan's language games, which use puns, misspellings, homonyms, and homophones to threaten the stability of conventional signification. Far from working to embody the subject à la Smith, Saroyan et al. tended more toward engaging the reader intimately with the very materiality and sound of text practically independent of reference. Smith, learning from the New York School poets around her, used their disruptive, disjunctive styles for entirely different narrative ends. Despite the elliptical nature of the poem, "amelia earhart 1" points ahead to the heroic language Smith was to employ regularly on her recorded work and public performances throughout the 1970s.

As I make clear throughout this book, the Poetry Project—a site Smith has returned to repeatedly—was and is in many ways temperamentally critical or at the very least questioning of grandstanding. What was Smith to do, given that she was, by her own admission, a "hero worshipper"?[11] Smith had to dance a complicated dance. The Poetry Project was not just the place that Smith first made a public name for herself. It was a site in which she negotiated friendship literally and metaphorically as a way to establish herself in New York's downtown scene, from which she launched herself into the world of corporate record labels and rock 'n' roll concert arenas. Smith's friendship with Project-affiliated poets was equal parts target-based ingratiation and strategic distancing verging at times into overt disrespect. This distantiation, performed fairly consistently in interviews during the early 1970s and reinvoked (if in a much-tempered version) in her memoir *Just Kids* (2010), successfully kept Smith from becoming fully absorbed into the Poetry Project scene.

Why this ambivalent approach to becoming friends with Project-affiliated poets? Friendship, as Libbie Rifkin and Anne Dewey rightly insist, can for women poets prove a site for "intersubjective becoming" that serves as a buffer against and wedge into masculinist avant-garde poetic communities.[12] Friendship can also be used in wholly opposite terms. Smith's achieving stardom was predicated partly on an invocation of the authority of poetry generally and her associations with downtown poets specifically to burnish her spectacular aura further. Intuiting the cultural capital to be gained from an alignment with avant-garde poetic communities with street cred, Smith engaged with the Poetry Project scene in part to wedge herself not into a localized, collaborative poetics community but into the hypermasculine world of rock 'n' roll. "I wasn't content to just stand there and read poetry," Smith explained. "I wanted to, you know, *perform* my poetry in the way that I was learning from Jim Morrison or Jimi Hendrix or the great Beat poets."[13] Drawing on Morrison and Hendrix, Ginsberg and Corso, Smith became that heroic divinity whose authority she consistently celebrated both on and off the page before and during her big breakout.

Making a Mark at St. Mark's

Making a beeline for St. Mark's in the late 1960s, Smith cultivated friendships with writers including Waldman, Michael Brownstein, and Bernadette Mayer as well as Beat figures committed to the Project such as Ginsberg and Corso. Yet, in recollecting her debut 1971 reading, Smith discloses what seem to be her ambivalent feelings about being absorbed into that scene:

> The Poetry Project, shepherded by Anne Waldman, was a desirable forum for even the most accomplished poets. Everyone from Robert Creeley to Allen Ginsberg to Ted Berrigan had read there. If I was ever going to perform my poems,

this was the place to do it. My goal was not simply to do well, or hold my own. It was to make a mark at St. Mark's. I did it for Poetry. I did it for Rimbaud, and I did it for Gregory. I wanted to infuse the written word with the immediacy and frontal attack of rock and roll.[14]

While Smith acknowledges here that the Poetry Project was *the* place for exciting poetry during this period, we might pause on that word *even*. "Even" as it is written here connotes improbability, a kind of latent "can you believe it!" that subtly but firmly positions anything resembling a group effort (as embodied in words like "Project" and "forum") as secondary to individual accomplishment. That Smith then goes on to assert her desire to "make a mark at St. Mark's" emphasizes her desire to transcend absorption into community by metaphorically scoring or wounding the very edifice that houses the "Project"—to make one's mark on a place, after all, is to alter it, not fit into it. Smith was in effect getting ready to stage a reactionary, romantically inflected intervention in a dominant postmodern institution whose members would in all probability question anyone using the word poetry with a capital "P."

And what better way to return to a heroic vision of the Poet than by ensuring the Word was heard by living deities or, to put it more prosaically, rock 'n' roll legends? Smith's audience for her debut was composed not just of poets but also of the musicians who haunted Max's and who were gaining increasing prominence in the downtown scene. In an April 1975 interview with the music journalist and punk fellow traveler Lisa Robinson, Smith highlighted the reading as a star-packed happening rather than a *soirée intime*, noting the presence of Lou Reed, Bob Neuwirth, the fashion photographer Francesco Scavullo, and related members of the international jet set.[15] To have one's first reading at St. Mark's was not enough. The reading as Smith understood it should be performed within the more glamorous context of fame, old money, and rock 'n' roll.

Smith's efforts were in real contrast to the writers running the show at the Poetry Project. The house style there, far from being predicated on the kind of heroizing gestures favored by Smith, were instead based on more casual effects. We might look to the lines "Don't be a horrible sourpuss / Moon! Have a drink! / Have an entire issue!"[16] included in Ted Berrigan and Ron Padgett's collaboratively produced "Waterloo Sunset" as a kind of synecdoche for the overall ambiance of Project-related poetry—lines like these point to the way in which the agency for the creation of meaning and pleasure

Figure 5.1 Patti Smith flyer, date and provenance unknown.
Source: Peter Dougherty Collection, Box 13, Folder 36, Fales Collection, Bobst Library, New York University.

in the text is offered metaphorically to the potentially cranky and overly serious Moon/reader as opposed to being linked materially to a site of privileged authorship. Poetry Project–affiliated writers deflated seriousness in an effort to enact an especially diffuse and amenable mood.[17]

Smith, on the other hand, worked aggressively to reinstate uniqueness to the figure of the poet. We see this through her identifying Rimbaud and Gregory Corso as the men she will "do" her reading for. Poets read consistently as agitating if not outright repudiating affiliation with a collective, Rimbaud and Corso are famous as much for their outlaw auras as they are for their poetry, if not more so. Rimbaud's dramatic departure from the poetic sphere for a life of trading and gun running in the Horn of Africa has become the stuff of legend. Corso's reputation as the bad boy of the Beat Generation, replete with endless retellings of his heckling poets at the Poetry Project, his womanizing, thieving, and drug use, is similarly well known and often overshadows the merits of much of his poetry.[18] All this is by way of saying that Smith—even within the context of nostalgic retrospection as we find it in *Just Kids*—emphasizes her affiliation not with the group but with solitary outlaws.

According to Anne Waldman, Patti Smith, despite being influenced to some extent by writers like O'Hara,

> was not coming out of the New American Poetry as so many of the other poets who were around the Project, and allied with the NY School or Black Mountain or Robert Duncan or the Beats in those days. Or inspired through the Modernists particularly—Pound, Stein, Williams, Stevens. . . . But her poems were iconic and she took on icons as subject matter. Every poet has their particular Rimbaud, and hers was the renegade *maudit*. Her themes often had to do with trials and redemption which I found interesting. She wore a cross around her neck. The poems were tough, working class, romantic, aspirational. Very different from the experimental work of Bernadette Mayer, Alice Notley who were more complicated on the page.[19]

The kind of position taking that Waldman describes would ultimately serve Smith well in the mid-1970s as Smith retooled her work for an audience accustomed to and hungry for the epic stance typical of the late-1960s rock star. Smith, aligning herself with predominantly male figures for whom poetry was always a grander "Poetry," drew a line between a poetics of sociability typical of the St. Mark's scene and her own favored world populated by outlaw deities.

Claiming that her performance at the Poetry Project marked the first time an electric guitar was used in St. Mark's Church[20] and describing the event as an upstart challenge to the poetry usually performed in the church's "hallowed ground," Smith admits she "was so filled with adrenaline that I behaved like a young cock. I failed to thank Robert [Mapplethorpe] and Gerard [Malanga]. Nor did I socialize with their people."[21] Smith's gendering herself male via the phrase "young cock" points back to the ways Smith yoked an essentialized masculinity onto her own androgynous body to set herself apart from the poetry pack.[22] Rejecting community in favor of reaching toward stardom, Smith figured early on that conventional femininity might not be the best way to be her generation's Mick Jagger. Smith thus acted like a cock in an effort to keep from being "shepherded" into St. Mark's Church by Waldman and friends.

A bootleg recording of the reading confirms that Smith approached the evening with real nervous aggression. Following her version of Brecht's "Mack the Knife," Smith announced she was dedicating the reading "to *crime*," moving on to align herself with an almost entirely male pantheon including Johnny Ace, Jackson Pollock, James Dean, Vladimir Mayakovski, Gene Krupa, Jesus Christ, Houdini, Blaise Cendrars, and Sam Shepard.[23] Smith's comparatively brusque entry into St. Mark's suggests she was already beginning to carve out a performance aesthetic for herself as rocking iconoclast aligned generally with male nonconformists. Crucially, Smith's success at this event was seen by some as marking a downgrading of poets and poetry itself in New York's counterculture. As Victor Bockris, in attendance that night, put it:

> Patti "took" St. Mark's that night. Malanga, whose reading was a superb and passionate rendition of some of his best work, was still the center of attention at Max's later on, but Lenny Kaye recognized that the changing of the guard started on that very evening. And within a year the rockers would have taken over Max's and other cultural outposts from the artists and poets.[24]

Such moves on Smith's part were, in the end, constructive. Smith recognized that small artistic collectives could be limiting to an artist eager to assert herself within a privileged lineage of literary and musical heroes, and she soon grew out of the social milieu that played such a large role in establishing her public persona. Recalling her participation in the 1974 New Year's Day marathon reading at the Poetry Project, Smith acknowledges, "I sat through much of it sizing up the poets. I wanted to be a poet but I knew I would never fit into their incestuous community. The last thing I wanted was to negotiate the social politics of another scene."[25] By 1975, the year *Horses* was released, Smith had very much managed to be both part of that "scene" while maintaining her distance from it. Even Malanga, whom Smith had opened for that fateful night in 1971, was consigned to irrelevance. "Someone like Gerard Malanga has 15 books of poetry published," Smith scoffed to Lisa Robinson, "and it doesn't mean shit in the face of history."[26]

By 1976, after *Horses* met with widespread acclaim, Smith seemed sick and tired of *all* art. "I love rock 'n' roll," she said in an interview with Robert Hilburn. "I love performing. I love communicating. To me, the most exciting and accessible form of communicating now is rock. I used to want to be an artist, but rock is freer and it reaches more people. You paint a picture and it ends up in a museum."[27] Where did Smith's aggressive iconoclasm come from? Why did she continue to participate in poetry events at the Church (as she does to this day) in spite of her dismissive posture? What, in the end, can Smith's relationship to the Poetry Project teach us about how Smith negotiated the journey from a collaboratively minded poetry scene to deific, male-inscribed rock 'n' roll stardom?

"I Pretty Well Hate Most of the Stuff You Guys Do"

Even during the early period of her tenure in New York in the late 1960s, Smith was grappling with the fact that the aesthetic at St. Mark's conflicted with her own sense of what was important in poetry. An undated letter from Smith to Waldman written when Smith had recently arrived in New York shows Smith consciously setting herself apart from the surface cool she associates with Frank O'Hara and the St. Mark's poets who followed in his wake. Smith emphasized how she loved Dylan Thomas and Vachel Lindsay despite the fact that Frank O'Hara famously stated in his essay "Personism" how he had always "hated" Lindsay. To love Lindsay and Thomas, as Smith well knew, was to run counter to New York School orthodoxy.

Smith continued in the letter by complaining that Waldman and her friends seemed tone-deaf to the possibilities of poetry as music. Nevertheless, Smith took care to point out how, despite that she "pretty well hate[d] most of the stuff you guys do," she still read the St. Mark's poets avidly: "I also love you guys," Smith confirmed, "cause you keep poetry alive. I think it's real neat what you're doing, I just got different theories."[28] This letter was in essence a performance where Smith juggled a variety of literary and social modes. She positioned herself as amenable to Waldman and the Poetry Project scene while simultaneously distinguishing herself from that world through self-consciously unfashionable references to writers frozen out of respectable avant-garde circles.

The notion of poetry as song was at the core of Smith's aesthetics, and Lindsay again serves as a useful sign that helps us see Smith as simultaneously linking up to and breaking away from Waldman and friends. While out of fashion at the time Smith was writing this letter, Lindsay was perhaps best known for what he called his "singing poetry." Lindsay was, at the turn of the twentieth century, invested in the history of the medieval troubadour (and was in fact referred to during his lifetime as the "Prairie Troubadour"). He essentially wanted to reinvigorate that intimate link between a populist audience and performer, traveling by foot throughout the United States delivering his verse.

One might argue that Smith's isolating Lindsay as distinct from what "you guys" (meaning Waldman and, one might assume, related figures including Lewis Warsh and Bernadette Mayer) were doing in the 1960s was unfair given that the Poetry Project was itself a site for the public performance of poetry. The Project, featuring at least three public readings per week, certainly maintained a space for poetry as a primarily performative act. Yet we need to make a distinction in terms of the *audience* associated with a troubadour like Lindsay versus the Poetry Project community. In fact, I want to step back a bit from the very word "community" as it is associated with the Project and suggest, following Lytle Shaw's work on O'Hara, that "coterie" might be a more appropriate framework through which to read the difference between the oral-poetics culture championed by Lindsay in the 1910s and the preponderance of poetry readings taking place at St. Mark's during the 1960s. Like Shaw, who traces "coterie" back to its medieval roots in peasant collectives agitating against their landlords, I also don't necessarily see any elitist, pejorative associations attached to the word.[29] Rather, I see "coterie" as having much more in common with the possibilities of a dissident microcommunity. Particularly given the collaborative nature of readings and publications at the Project, "coterie" resonates with the preponderance of actual communes in the late 1960s and early 1970s, social formations that are established in opposition to a wider consensus culture and defined as much by who is excluded as by who is included.

In light of Shaw's recuperation of the collective, even latently transgressive elements of the word "coterie," I would like to propose that the Poetry Project in the early 1970s be understood not as a privileged group of *littératures* but rather as an association of likeminded dissenters carving out temporary—and cheerful—autonomous zones of collective production and dissemination. This kind of work flew in the face of a dominant poetics and attendant politics that insisted on a construction of the poet as privileged, Muse-inspired genius. The Project's approach to the oral transmission of a poem compared to the one that Smith takes on through her privileging of Lindsay and Dylan Thomas was, in the end, fundamentally different. John Brinnin's recollections of a typical Thomas reading—in this case, one of Thomas's performances in New York's YM-YWHA—illustrates how Thomas's performance style was very much in the service of extending Thomas's practically shamanistic persona:

> At the appointed time he walked on to the stage, shoulders straight, chest out in his staunch and pouter-pigeon advance, and proceeded to give the first of those performances which were to bring to America a whole new conception of poetry reading. . . . When he concluded the evening with a selection of his own works—encompassing both tenderly lyrical and oratorical passages with absolute authority, it was difficult to know which gave the greater pleasure, the music or the meaning. Some of his listeners were moved by the almost sacred sense of his approach to language; some by the bravado of a modern poet whose themes dealt directly and unapologetically with birth and death and the presence of God; some were entertained merely by the plangent virtuosity of an actor with a great voice. In every case the response was one of delight.[30]

This is a familiar vision of the poet as isolated seer, a figure summoning an ecstatic social response and union while maintaining a shamanistic separation from community. These kinds of qualities associated with Thomas and Lindsay were, if not entirely discredited at the Poetry Project, nevertheless not part of the Project's overall culture and its celebration of mass readings, political poetry-reading benefits, and call-and-response ethos. It was this radical rejection of the mechanisms of stardom in favor of a poetics of sociability within the poetry community in New York that Smith was to find so dispiriting. Even as she recognized the Poetry Project was "the place to do it," she determined she should transcend it.

In a candid interview with Victor Bockris published in 1972,[31] Smith laid out her goals as they related in part to her negotiation with the Poetry Project at St. Mark's. Bockris seemed particularly interested in highlighting how Smith was "totally ignoring" the downtown literary scene despite her all-access pass to that desirable coterie. Bockris continued pressing Smith on this question by asking her point blank about whether she could actually learn anything from the downtown poets. The answer was an emphatic "no," in large part because of what Smith argued was the St. Mark's poets' inability to perform charismatically and because of what she perceived to be the poets' boring lifestyles. Name-checking rock 'n' roll gods including Jim Morrison, Bob Dylan, and the Rolling Stones and identifying Humphrey Bogart as someone she got "excited about," Smith acknowledged, "I'm not interested in meeting poets or a bunch of writers who I don't think are bigger than life. I'm a hero worshipper."[32]

Smith's candor here was refreshing. Not for her the collating parties, the group readings, the self-published small-circulation anonymous and pseudonymous publications. Rather, rock 'n' roll as a model for performance poetry helped Smith reestablish and celebrate the divide between privileged stage and underwhelming page. Rock 'n' roll, particularly by the late 1960s and early 1970s, had become a vehicle for deification, as the small-scale clubs, halls, and streets made way for the imperial grandeur of the amphitheater and festival. While much could be said for Smith's starting her music career in tiny clubs like CBGB, we should not forget that the end goal was to play—as the Patti Smith Group eventually did—in large arenas in the United States and Europe. That Smith wanted to imbue poetry with the bigger-than-life theatrics of the rock 'n' roll stage show suggests a creative intervention into and critique of the avant-garde poetics and attendant principles of the period.

Employing the kind of terminology we associate with rock 'n' roll, Bockris continued his interview by asking Smith which poets she would like to "tour" with. Naming Jim Carroll, Bernadette Mayer, and Muhammad Ali as her chosen three, Smith explained that it was their ability to perform captivatingly that was especially attractive to her. Carroll was particularly celebrated because his life as a heroin addict, hustler, and bisexual marked him out as a true Rimbaudian *poete maudit* in distinction to the other St. Mark's poets, whom Smith dismissed as "so namby pamby they're frauds." Smith took especial delight in mocking the St. Mark's poets' propensity for writing O'Hara-style "I do this, I do that" poems "about today at 9:15 I shot speed with brigid sitting in the such and such."[33]

It seems here that Smith looked to poetry not so much for what the art had to offer her as a model for her songwriting but for what the discourse of poetry could provide her with in terms of thinking about how to make actual lifestyle and performance choices. In a related interview with Bockris, for example, Smith acknowledged why she was initially drawn to French poetry and fiction. In response to Bockris's question—"Why are your influences mostly European: Rimbaud, Cendrars, Celine, Michaux?"—Smith replied that it was the French writers' biographies that proved so seductive for her: Their wild lives couldn't be matched by the contemporary crop of American poets. Again, show business was at the center of her critique, as she went on to celebrate how Bob Dylan and Allen Ginsberg revitalized a performance culture that had died out following the death of Oscar Wilde.[34] Smith's revisionary history is, of course, arguable. That said, what is revealing and useful in her account is how Smith marked the purported rebirth of muscular performance poetry. Ginsberg, perhaps *the* most recognizable American poet of the 1960s, was synthesized with Bob Dylan, the pop star most aligned, if problematically, to poetry. The two men had been friends for years, forming a kind of mutual-appreciation society that found Ginsberg handing the mantle of Beat spokesperson over to Dylan.[35] Dylan, for example, famously featured Ginsberg in the opening credits to D. A. Pennebaker's film *Don't Look Back* (1967), which situated Ginsberg all the more firmly in the pop firmament. In 1975 Ginsberg took Dylan to Jack Kerouac's grave in Lowell, Massachusetts, where the two men read from Kerouac's 1959 poem *Mexico City Blues* and sang together, a scene that was included in Dylan's film *Renaldo and Clara* (1978). These kinds of exchanges blurred the lines between poet and pop star all the more, as each figure profited from the cultural and popular capital attendant to their increasingly fluid roles. Who was the pop star? Who was the poet? Could we—should we— even bother separating the two roles anymore? "I don't want to get away from poetry," Smith insisted to Lisa Robinson in early 1975, "but there's no reason why the two have to be separated. I think I've proven it with what I do with 'Land of a 1000 Dances' . . . it's totally impossible to distinguish what is poetry from the poetry in that and the rock and roll. They're so integrated."[36]

Smith had a point. By 1970 Ginsberg was already issuing records of his weirdly Yiddische versions of Blake's *Songs of Innocence and Experience*, while Dylan in 1971 finally got around to publishing *Tarantula*, his widely boot-legged book of prose poems, with the venerable publishing house Macmil-lan. Smith wanted in on the "integrated" model personified by Ginsberg's and Dylan's works and friendship, and she went far in expanding their hy-brid poet/performer prototype. As early as 1973, a full two years before Smith released her first album, *Horses*, Ginsberg saw the potential power in Smith's efforts to collapse poetry into pop, pop into poetry. "What Patti Smith seems to be doing," Ginsberg proffered,

> may be a composite memorized, and the American development of Oral Poetry that was from coffee houses now raised to pop-spotlight circumstances and so declaimed from memory again with all the artform—or artsong—glamour that goes along with Liddy Lane . . . maybe. Then there's an element that goes along with borrowing from the pop stars and that spotlight too and that glitter. But it would be interesting if that did develop into a national style. If the national style could organically integrate that sort of arty personality—the arty Rim-baud—in its spotlight with make-up and T-Shirt.[37]

The "arty Rimbaud," bathed in the glow of the stage lights, was the way forward for poetry as far as Smith was concerned. The namby-pamby "I do this, I do that" New York School poets didn't stand a chance in Smith's ever-starrier poetic firmament. By the early to mid-1970s, as the music journalist Nick Tosches remembers, Smith's poetry-cum–rock 'n' roll per-formance had marked her out as something special—something that repre-sented a serious break with the poetry crowd.

> She was feared, revered, and her public readings elicited the sort of gut response that had been alien to poetry for more than a few decades. Word spread, and people who avoided poetry as the stuff of four-eyed pedants found themselves oohing and howling at what came out of Patti's mouth. Established poets feared

for their credence. Many well-known poets refused to go on after Patti at a reading, she was that awesome.[38]

And certainly by 1975, the year that brought the world *Horses*, Smith was actively cutting ties with the poetry community from whose stage she emerged. At a 1975 concert Smith gave at New York's Other End club (known formerly as the Bitter End), none other than Bob Dylan "stuck his head in the dressing room afterwards, a madhouse of journalists and photographers. 'Any poets around here?' [Dylan asked]? 'I don't like poetry anymore,' Smith blurted. 'Poetry sucks!'"[39]

"FUCK YOU JESUS!"

As Smith's comments to Bockris suggest, Smith was as interested (if not *more* interested) in poets' lifestyles as she was in their writing. Smith was as likely to stress her favorite writers' outrageous antics as she was to refer to their verse. In her foreword to Corso's *An Accidental Autobiography*, for example, Smith opens with an anecdote that illustrates and celebrates Corso's antiestablishment gestures:

> I first encountered Gregory long ago in front of the Chelsea Hotel. He lifted his overcoat and dropped his trousers, spewing Latin expletives. Seeing my astonished face, he laughed and said, "I'm not mooning you sweetheart, I'm mooning the world." I remember thinking, how fortunate for the world to be privy to the exposed rump of a true poet.[40]

Interestingly, Smith continues in her foreword to align herself materially with Corso: "My living space was akin to his—piles of papers, books, old shoes, piss in cups—mortal disarray."[41] This raggedy bohemia, in evidence most ideally in the rebellious figure of a poet-outlaw like Corso, would be absorbed and redirected by Smith into what would soon be called punk rock.

Despite Smith's ambivalent and occasionally openly hostile attitude toward the St. Mark's scene, Smith nevertheless chose to work within the loose institutional structures related to the Poetry Project. Crucially, Smith's first book of poetry, *Seventh Heaven* (1972), was published through Telegraph

Books, an imprint edited by Bockris and Andrew Wylie and for the most part committed to publishing figures affiliated with the second-generation New York School and the related Warhol scene.[42] "We had offered to print 1000 copies of her book in our uniform format and do our best to sell them at one dollar each, cheap even in 1971," recalled Bockris. "What Patti seemed to like about Andrew and me was our drive and energy. We came on like the City Lights of the seventies, calling ourselves the Electric Generation and talking big. Like Patti we believed in poetry passionately and were dead serious about what we were doing. Patti responded to our intensity."[43] By 1972 Telegraph Books had published books such as Berrigan, Padgett, and Tom Clark's *Back in Boston Again*, Bockris's *Face*, Gerard Malanga's *Poetry on Film*, Brigid Polk's *Scars*,[44] Tom Raworth's *Heavy Light*, Aram Saroyan's *The Rest*, Tom Weatherly's *Thumbprint*, and Andrew Wylie's *Tenderloin*.

Most of these little books emanated affection for a loosely defined experimentalism characterized by sociability. Even something as odd as Polk's *Scars* resonated with the collaborative turn in poetry. *Scars* was composed "from a selection of Warhol superstar Polk's collection of ink prints she made of celebrities and her friends' scars with accompanying explanations of the wounds by those who'd been scarred."[45] Thus, like the Berrigan/Padgett/Clark work, the idea of this book as something related to a stable subject named "Brigid Polk" was compromised as the reader scanned through a number of personages' scars, including Peter Fonda's foreskin scar, Jonas Mekas's thumb scar, Genevieve Waite's burn scar, Gerard Malanga's testicular scar, and so on. Smith was also included in this all-star roster.

Her contribution really stuck out—not because of the nature of her scar but because of the tone and diction of her submission: "On april 26 1967 / I bore my first baby / and ripped up the / left side of my belly / FUCK YOU JESUS."[46] The heretical petulance of FUCK YOU JESUS alongside the oddly archaic phrase "bore my baby" agitated very strongly against the otherwise faux-naïve, gentle, and generally whimsical contributions of the other featured figures. Even here, Smith was visible as both in and outside of the incrowd. Smith's inclusion in a book studded with "superstars" (to use Warhol's semi-ironic term) was a testament to her place among the glitterati of New York's cultural undergrounds. Yet her decision to use a somewhat dated diction alongside a punk posture that anticipated her cover version of Van Morrison's "Gloria" (beginning with Smith's line "Jesus died for somebody's sins but not mine")[47] marked Smith's refusal to become fully absorbed into the group ethos of the book. Smith didn't want to "fit in" too well; such acceptance ran the risk of erasing the heroic, individualist persona she was so committed to developing. That said, rubbing metaphorical shoulders with figures like Polk, Malanga, Warhol, and Mekas certainly added counterculture sheen to Smith's name. This approach to rejecting and participating in a wider artistic community characterized Smith's negotiations of the literary and musical spheres for a number of years.

The primary way Smith defined herself outside the potentially limiting circles of the downtown avant-garde was to embrace heroic representations of rock 'n' roll stars and project them via the purportedly "high-art" form of the poem. In a letter to the poet Michael Brownstein and his then-partner Waldman written in the early 1970s, Smith claimed that she was going to fight for a "musical" aesthetic and that her own work deserved the cultural status accorded to poetry: "I'LL rebel god dammit I'll call them poems even if they get on the top ten AM radio." Highlighting the musical sensuousness in Yeats and Dylan Thomas's work, Icelandic medieval poetry, Jesse James, and the Tex-Mex singing group Sunny and the Sunglows, Smith threatened Brownstein and Waldman with the promise "I'll fix you guys."[48] "I'll fix you guys," addressed as it is to Waldman and Brownstein, set Smith up as the voice of authenticity and poetic rebellion looking to enlighten the implicitly staid world at St. Mark's. This is not to say that downtown poets affiliated with St. Mark's weren't themselves interrogating the boundaries and associated cultural capital of poetry and rock-inflected performance. The emphasis on orality and performance underscoring the scene at the Poetry Project effected a serious if temporary challenge to the hierarchies that would situate poetry as a primarily high art form with connections to rock and popular culture. Innovative poets of the preceding generation, particularly Ginsberg, had also been vocal about their appreciation for rock 'n' roll.[49] However, for all the demotic chatter around avant-garde poetry in the late 1960s and early 1970s, no poet affiliated with the scene approached the synthesis of rock 'n' roll with poetry with Smith's single-mindedness.

Smith's efforts to imbue a vatic romanticism back into poetry, as has been suggested already, encountered the question of femininity. Smith needed to challenge what she perceived to be an inherently feminized aesthetics of (to borrow from Cixous)[50] diffusion and effervescence, an aesthetics that urges women to write outside self, outside center—in other words, an aesthetics that Smith understood to be at the core of the poetics affiliated with and promoted by the St. Mark's scene. Indeed, *Seventh Heaven* shows Smith employing straightforward narrative, a monologic speaker, and a general tendency to associate creative power with an idealized masculinity.

"Work your ass off to change the language," Mayer famously advised her students, adding, "and don't ever get famous."[51] Smith flouted Mayer's rules. Far from working her ass off to change the language, Smith, as we see in poems from *Seventh Heaven* including "female," "mustang sally," "fantasy (for allen lanier)," and "death by water" (Smith's paean to Jim Morrison), adhered to some fairly conventional literary practices in the service of both venerating a pantheon of star-touched men and (for the most part) relegating the female to the status of abject embarrassment, muse, or doomed beauty. And as so many of her idealized figures were men, part of Smith's process was working out how to align her own femininity with a value system that privileged the "male race."[52]

Her poem "female" anticipates Smith's later transformation into the gorgeous, boyish figure gracing Mapplethorpe's stunning cover for Smith's 1975 album *Horses*. The way she wore her shirt, suspenders, and jacket made Smith appear flat chested.[53] One could detect the outline of a slight mustache visible on her upper lip. She sported a vaguely confrontational expression on her face. Her narrow-hipped figure accentuated by her tight pants, Smith's self as it is enacted visually on the cover of *Horses* embodies the pose practiced initially within the pages of Smith's poetry. Smith insisted in numerous interviews during the 1970s that she had no interest in feminism and in fact relished a subordinate role. The exception was when she ventriloquized a male role herself, allowing her privileged access to women, which she could then exploit in kind: "I use women," as she put it bluntly to Bockris.[54] Again, contemporary reviews of Smith's poetry performances in the early 1970s attest to and revel over Smith's masculinist public style. As Tom McCarthy put it in 1974, "Looking like a female version of Keith Richards . . . Patti Smith is the poet as macho woman—hip, tough, sexy, raging."[55] The work that "poet as macho woman" produced was realized most ideally as song. "Still, Patti Smith is better heard than read. So see her if you get the chance. And hope that someday soon an adventuresome record company will sign her up and really give her a chance to wail."[56] Once Smith got that "chance to wail," the Richards effect was cultivated all the more as Smith began touring and recording in 1975. Beginning her life as a performer in the context of a sprawling, community-oriented poetry scene "shepherded" by a woman, Anne Waldman, Smith worked hard to define herself apart from it even as she used its stages to promote her developing punk/poetry style.

"Patti Signing Big Contract"

By 1975, Smith was well established as the downtown doyenne of performance poetry now making a name for herself as a bandleader at CBGB. New York's underground luminaries flocked to the Bowery to check her out—when Smith played CBGB for a seven-week residency, writers and artists including Burroughs, Ginsberg, and Warhol stopped by.[57] The legend grew across the Atlantic Ocean. Flicking through the April 5, 1975, issue of the British music journal *New Musical Express*, for example, a reader was likely to alight on the announcement "Patti Signing Big Contract" followed by the brief notice: "CULT New York poetess and songwriter Patti Smith is to sign an exclusive long-term contract with Arista Records, reportedly for a six figure advance." That "cult poetess" tag was something Smith was going to work hard to shake, particularly given the way "poetess" conjures up visions of a privileged monied dilettante with time to spare and cloying lyrics to write.[58] Smith was not going to put up with *that* characterization. In the months leading up to the release of *Horses*, Smith gave a series of interviews with music journalists where she worked hard to disassociate herself from her poetry apprenticeship. Lisa Robinson reported that "Patti has said that poets never had anything to do with her 'getting anywhere'; it was all people like Danny Goldberg (now the Vice-President of Swan Song, then the editor of *Circus*) who published her poems in his magazine, and Bobby [Neuwirth], and people in the music business."[59]

Smith was making a concerted effort to divorce herself further from the avant-garde ethos at St. Mark's, insisting on rock 'n' roll as *the* primary influence. Despite her refusals and repudiations, however, traces of St. Mark's can still be heard in Smith's *Horses*—and a decidedly feminist appropriation and parody of male authority emerged in spite of Smith's continued claims about wanting to join the "male race." Perhaps most curiously, parts of *Horses* were decidedly *funny*. Even in Smith's rousing reworking of the Belfast R&B band Them's 1964 hit "Gloria," for example, Smith undercut lead singer Van Morrison's narrative of scoring a hot chick with squeals, nasal intonations, and bizarrely extended vowel sounds. Philip Middleton rightly reveals how

Smith's performance was a way of contesting the ideology of Them's brand of leering cock rock, "in which a strutting male voice, dripping with demand, imposes his phallic authority on a female object of desire."[60] Smith's non-verbal ejaculations undermined Van Morrison's scopophilic and monologic authority. Smith's "use of a hard, nasal sound on the words 'me, me' at bars 15–16," Mark Daley points out,

> recalls the vocal idiosyncrasies of Mick Jagger, as Smith parodies Jagger's individu-alistic vocal swagger, itself so indebted to black American singing style. Her use of a confident low register seems oddly appropriate in a song where a female singer co-opts the role of a purportedly male-gendered sexual conqueror.[61]

Smith's potpourri of deranged sounds simultaneously paid homage to and critiqued male power through an inherently playful series of incantatory, "hard nasal," and yelping noises.

There is, as Daley recognizes, a spirit of play behind Smith's performance, one that "suggests a certain bodily pleasure in the sound and sensation of singing. Play becomes significant here not just for its own sake; it also func-tions as a critique and a grab for power . . . and she does it with a smile on her face."[62] Smith's smile stretched over a number of other songs in *Horses*, as if to provide a counternarrative to the arena rock–style songs on *Horses* like "Free Money" that would prove the rule rather than the exception on Smith's subsequent albums in her 1970s tetralogy (*Radio Ethiopia* [1976], *Eas-ter* [1978], and *Wave* [1979]). Take the song "Kimberly," for example. Opening portentously with images of the speaker holding her recently born sister Kimberly in front of a barn, Smith became Prospero-like as she prophesied a practically apocalyptic vision of the sky splitting, the universe cracking, life ending. At the first iteration of the chorus beginning with "Little sis-ter," the guitar and bass are modulated down to B-flat, then ascend in unison half a step to get back to the original key of the verses. Matching the instru-ments' ascension up the fretboard, Smith purred out an "Ahhhh" in a low reg-ister that slid into an ever-higher pitch over the course of about two sec-onds. Suggesting a kind of blasé attitude at odds with the mystic position adopted initially, Smith's "Ahhhh" contrasted with the insistent sincerity that characterized the song up to that point.[63]

These self-ironizing gestures were at play even in "Land," arguably her most ambitious and moving of songs. A boy assaults the character Johnny, introduced at the start of the song by Smith in a practically breathless whisper. Smith increased her pitch and tempo in sympathy with the cumulative violence, layering her narrative with overdubbed lines from the song to create an eerie echo chamber. The section climaxes with the vision of Johnny surrounded by horses. The apocalypse announced, the world afire, Smith practically panting the repeated word "horses" in a tone of rapturous surrender, it was hard for a first-time listener to figure out where Smith was headed next. What, then, do we make of where she went?

"Do you know how to *pony*"? Did Smith really just ask *that*? Not just that, but "Do you know how to *pony* like *bony maroney*."[64] Sung as gleefully and rhapsodically as the *Equus*-type narrative that opens the song, it is tempting to interpret Smith's use of lines from the R&B hit "Land of a Thousand Dances" as a kind of affectionate spoof on her own lament-like vision. Phrases like "do the alligator" and "do the mashed potato," particularly when Smith articulated them with the same urgency as the mystically inflected sections of the song, served to undermine the stentorian persona thundering about horses and Johnny. Smith was not forsaking her part as shaman necessarily, but she was certainly destabilizing the seriousness one usually ascribes to that role.

One wonders if the ludic moves Smith made on some of the songs in *Horses* had anything to do with the fact that Smith essentially rehearsed the album at the Poetry Project. Extant recordings of Smith in early 1975 find Smith simultaneously reifying and poking fun at her increasing fame, as she weaved lines and phrases from songs in *Horses* into her poetry performance. Reading at a benefit for St. Mark's Church on January 1, 1975, for example,[65] Smith—tongue firmly in cheek—dedicated her show to the Mummers Parade, a folk festival in Philadelphia. As if to undercut her own growing reputation outside poetry coteries, she continued by asking sarcastically, "Am I gifted, or merely mad? I'm feeling so carnivorous, I could eat live crows, *chomp chomp chomp!*" the "o" sound in "crows" pronounced precisely as she pronounced her "o's" in her song "Gloria."[66] Playing insistently to the crowd by assuring them she was as open to jokiness and self-effacement as the New York School poets it was enamored with, Smith then began quoting indirectly from the songs that would feature on *Horses* at the end of that year, including lines from Them's "Gloria."[67]

The energy of this performance, propelled in part by deep humor, self-deprecation, and boastful bravado, was intoxicating. Listening to performances like this illustrates why so many of Smith's contemporaries believe the period when Smith synthesized the roles of visionary bard and lackadaisical urbane poet on the Poetry Project stage was the most creative and interesting phase of her career. For many in the St. Mark's crew, Smith's shift from poetry readings like these to rock 'n' roll performances was troubling.[68] However, to remain in the Poetry Project coterie meant Smith would not have a shot at the fame she ended up so rightly securing after the release of *Horses*.

But what was lost in the wake of Smith's ensuing fame? Smith's subsequent albums found the playful Patti making way for the relatively straightforward and very serious rock 'n' roll Patti, major chords and Jim Morrison–style yowls interrupted only occasionally by performed poems such as "Radio Ethiopia"—but where were the redeeming giggles of earlier works? "Radio Ethiopia," featured on the eponymous album, began with drum rolls, cymbal washes, and a guitar riff that called to mind the prog rock of King Crimson more than it did the elated three-chord rock 'n' roll celebrated at CBGBs. Smith's poetry-infatuated critics called her on it. John Rockwell of the *New York Times* wrote, "The level of songs [on *Radio Ethiopia*] seems lower than on *Horses*. . . . And the shift away from declamation and minimal instrumental support to basic rock and roll robs Miss Smith's art of some of its individuality."[69] Charles Shaar Murray mourned that Smith "has not so much brought the qualities of imagination, perception, and emotion displayed on [*Horses*] into the hard-rock mainstream, but simply allowed the limitations of the genre to dictate restrictions to her."[70]

Smith in her later works seemed to have forgotten the golden rule of the New York School—never take yourself too seriously. Indeed, she seems to have self-consciously flouted the Gospel according to Frank O'Hara. Where O'Hara damned Robert Lowell precisely because Lowell assumed personal pain was a priori interesting, Smith in her post-*Horses* recordings performed angst all the more straightforwardly. Indeed, Smith's song "Revenge" (from her 1979 album *Wave*) opened nostalgically with a riff taken straight from the Beatles' opening to their song "I Want You (She's So Heavy)". Placing herself sonically in the company of the Fab Four, Smith then did a Lowell: The first line of "Revenge" found Smith declaiming the phrase "I feel upset" throatily. Smith assumed listeners would be interested in her song simply because she was supposed to be so upset.

Smith insisted that anyone who dared call himself a poet should be, ideally, an outlaw, a seer, and a visionary. Her promise in "Piss Factory" (featured on side B of her debut single "Hey Joe") that she was going to move to New York City and become a star was realized—by 1975, Smith had fully embraced music as her calling. "It's such a monstrous responsibility, because it's such an honour to me" she told Lisa Robinson, adding, "even now I still think that music is the highest art, and whereas I always thought of myself as a writer—and poet, I am now honestly starting to think of myself as a singer."[71] Smith was invested in the mechanics of stardom and the reification of hierarchies that always and forever raised the performer—materially and ideologically—above the audience.[72] The narrative of Smith's rise to prominence was predicated on an initial engagement with and ultimate rejection of a poetics of sociability that determined one didn't have to be an inspired mystic to engage with poetry. One didn't even have to be a "self," as it were, as poetry could be made in groups, could be part of the fabric of a local, ever-shifting, autonomous community/coterie. Smith pushed back on all that. She pushed back hard.

SIX

Giorno Poetry Systems

MUCH HAS BEEN said already about how New York poets influenced New York punks. How, then, did music—both in terms of its sound, its lyrics, and its associated recording technologies—encourage St. Mark's–affiliated poets to get their tracks on vinyl and ensure that their poetry and poetics became ever more oriented toward a punk-inflected performance aesthetic? To answer this question we must turn to John Giorno. Giorno, a perfor-mance poet active in the St. Mark's scene since the mid-1960s, was in many ways downtown's court jester. The star of Andy Warhol's durational film *Sleep*, lover to Robert Rauschenberg and Jasper Johns, founder of a pirate radio station broadcast from the bell tower of St. Mark's Church, organizer of LSD-fueled poetry-performance parties at the Poetry Project, Giorno was perhaps the preeminent figure in the downtown scene determined to refigure poetry as populist outlaw happening. "[One] of my first concepts in 1965," Giorno claims,

> when I began it all, was the idea that there was a poet and an audience, and the point of connection was many places, and many things and many possibilities. Previously the connection between the poet and the audience was through publication in some book or magazine. What I've been doing—Giorno Poetry Systems—is realizing a myriad of possibilities. *Dial-a-Poem* is one way that a poet can connect to millions of people. Or video. Or CDs. The albums are played in the living room, but are heard also on the radio.[1]

Giorno was moved to his various absurdist activities in large part because he felt the downtown poetry scene had become bloated, rigid, self-important, and, crucially, *boring*. Giorno recalled:

> I remember that around 1963, Andy Warhol and I went to some gallery to see John Ashbery, Frank O'Hara, and Kenneth Koch give a reading. It was really crowded, and it was the energy of this young New York School crowd, you know? We were standing in the back because it was really crowded, and there was no PA system. There was no thought given to presentation—it didn't exist. There we were, standing around with hundreds of people, and we couldn't hear a thing. Andy started whispering to me, "Oh John, it's so boring, why is it so boring?" Those words of Andy's, "Why is it so boring, *why* is it so boring," became one of those treasures that propelled me. I didn't know it at the time, but poetry readings didn't have to be boring—people were just making it boring.[2]

Part of contesting the monotony of the New York School poetry scene, as Giorno saw it, was to promote a more immediately accessible performance-poetry style characterized by insistent repetitions that owed more to the pop lyric than to poetry proper. Giorno's poetry from the mid-1960s through to this day employs an incantatory style built on the repetition and variation of a series of key phrases. Giorno's poem "I'm Tired of Being Scared" is one such example:

An unemployed
machinist
An unemployed machinist
who travelled
here
who travelled here
from Georgia
from Georgia 10 days ago
10 days ago
and could not find
a job
and could not find a job
walked
into a police station

walked into a police station
yesterday and said
yesterday
and said:

"I'm tired
of being scared
I'm tired of being scared"³

Akin to blues and pop-style call and response, repetitions like the ones we find in "I'm Tired of Being Scared" were ultimately there to entertain either as a complexly produced audio recording taking full advantage of studio technologies or, ideally, performed as a public spectacle. Giorno enthused, "When I talk of performance, I really mean *entertainment*! You know, you realize that it's the entertainment business! And I find that fascinating! Because one discovered, actually, that when you make people feel good, they *surrender* themselves to you! And then you're in this shameless position, which is wonderful!"⁴ Giorno, inspired in part by Brion Gysin and William Burroughs's experiments with recorded sound, matched pop musicians in their use of the recording studio as an instrument. "The idea of using the tape recorder and the possibility of layers of sounds," Giorno explained, was gleaned from Gysin's own use of sound recording. In 1965, after meeting Robert Moog, who invented the Moog synthesizer, Giorno would

> go up to where his factory was in New York, and we used to work on synthesizing the sound through the various oscillators and whatnot. We fed the words through the synthesizer and changed their modulation in terms of oscillations, and then put down various layers of the straight voice and then under that, the layers of modified voice. I used sound, experiments in sound, to create a *sound piece*, to create a musical score.⁵

Giorno made the move to vinyl and live performance not just because of earlier examples drawn from the broader history of performance poetry but because he was determined to mark a break from the urbane literariness associated with the first-generation New York School poets—especially Frank O'Hara. Making allowances for the shaggier, more working-class and pop-oriented second-generation New York School poets like Ted

Berrigan, Giorno was becoming increasingly contemptuous toward and paranoid about Berrigan's beloved precursors.[6] Over and over again in letters written to Brion Gysin from late 1965 through 1967, Giorno heaped scorn and oozed resentment over what he felt was the unnecessarily rarefied hot-house atmosphere swirling around O'Hara:

> Went last night to Fischbach [Gallery] party for Edwin Denby. O'Hara oiled sweet hostility, John Ashbery (back in NY as editor of Art News)'s frozen politeness is a change from his always trying to get me in bed, the rest look at me shifty eyed. But then all the young kids, Ted Berrigan, Mother, etc think my poems're great. . . . If it's the last thing I do I'm going to kill those bastards THE NEW YORK SCHOOL of Poets. Hope I can get them before they get me.[7]

Giorno's efforts to "kill" the New York School were driven in part by his deep suspicion over what he perceived to be the poets' efforts to humiliate him and mock his performative, incantatory style:

> NY's getting unbearable. Whenever I go out, I have to prepare myself for a whipping. My birthday was last Saturday. Donald Droll gave me an elegant birthday dinner party. Nine people, Frank O'Hara and crew. The whole thing was staged to put me on, rigged to humiliate me. Spent 6 hours in hell.[8]

So what to do? Given what Giorno perceived to be the preciousness of the staid poetry reading and its place in the "narrow New York Manhattan Museum of Modern Art artworld cocktail ballet scene"[9] identified by Ginsberg, Giorno worked hard to transform the poetry reading into a rule-breaking bacchanal, aligning it more to multimedia events like Andy Warhol's Exploding Plastic Inevitable than to beatnik coffee-shop readings typical of the Lower East Side scene through the 1960s. Foregrounding sex and drugs in a visual environment evocative of the psychedelic light show, Giorno staged his events in part to undermine the very status of the New York School as downtown poets par excellence. Challenges were overt, as Giorno proposed collaborative performance and noise as antithetical to the queer if comparatively staid erudition of the New York School:

> Had a poetry reading at the Folklore Center. Played the tape of 15 people reading the Pornographic Poem (Henry Geldzahler, Bob Rauschenberg, Patti Oldenburg,

Nina Thurman (Tim Leary's ex-wife) etc). The room was dark and I had an electronic strobe with a blue jell popping slowly in front. Peter Schjeldahl read before
me, his New York School of Poetry garbage. The comparison was fantastic. It
was a successful reading.[10]

The success of Giorno's reading as he sees it in comparison to Schjeldahl's is
telling, as it reveals a poet determined to liberate poetry not just from the
page but from the very genre it is defined as and contained within. In Giorno's view, the poetry scene was still enthralled with the discrete poem and
had failed to take advantage of technical advances exploited by the other
arts: "There was almost never any sound system. . . . Poets actually just
performed . . . with no microphone and nobody could hear anything but
the echo . . . poetry was 75 years behind painting and sculpture, dance and
music."[11] Simply standing there and reading a poem out loud from a book
did not, in Giorno's terms, count as performance. Rather, it was a statement
of defeat, an admission that the poet was physically bound to the page.

Giorno's "Pornographic Poem," appearing in print in 1964 when gay sex
was still widely believed to be a mental disease and a full five years before the
Stonewall riots revealed to the wider American public that angry queers
existed, is interesting enough on the page. Beginning with a description of
a sexual supplicant surrounded by seven Cuban army officers, the poem
quickly becomes a narrative of a gay gangbang. The speaker, on his knees,

shivered
looking up
at those erect pricks
all different
lengths
and widths
and knowing
that each one
was going up
my ass hole.[12]

Things got all the more exciting "Once they put me / on the bed / kneeling, //
one fucked me / in the behind / another / in the mouth, / while I jacked off /
one // with each hand / and two / of the others / rubbed / their peckers / on

my bare feet // waiting / their turns / to get / into my can."[13] The poem is significant for its very directness. Depictions of homosexual sex within the New York School were, after all, never *this* overt, never *this* abject and funny. All was camp and secret passwords—think O'Hara's "At the Old Place," for example.

O'Hara's poem begins by describing how a group of bored friends decide to go to the "Old Place," a gay dance club in Greenwich Village. "The Old Place," identified in O'Hara's poem initially as an acronym, is framed as a kind of key signifying entrée into a fairy-world underground: "Button's buddy lips frame 'L B T TH O P?' / across the bar. 'Yes!' I cry, for dancing's / my soul delight. (Feet! Feet!) 'Come on!'" The gang then goes to the club and dances the lindy, the rumba. The final lines of the poem feature its characters gossiping: "Jack, Earl and Someone drift / guiltily in. 'I knew they were gay / the minute I laid eyes on them!' screams John. / How ashamed they are of us! we hope."[14] As O'Hara's friend Joe LeSueur recalls it, "the Old Place was sweet and innocent, more limp-wristed than S&M or pseudo-macho, and it was about as wild as a high school prom of years past."[15] Giorno's "Pornographic Poem"—an "I do this, I do that" work in its own way—stands as a direct contestation of the "limp-wristed" New York queer culture O'Hara was so fond of depicting elliptically in his poetry. Where O'Hara wrote with his tongue firmly in cheek, Giorno was more tongue in ass.

Giorno was not without poetic models for explicit homoerotic imagery. Allen Ginsberg's "Howl," first published in 1956, was a radical alternative to O'Hara's "limp-wristed" mannerisms. Yet Giorno's "Pornographic Poem" repudiated the high-flown style attendant to Ginsberg's work. Ginsberg, after all, insisted on raising queer sex to the status of sacrament. One wasn't merely "fucked in the ass" by motorcyclists but rather "fucked in the ass by *saintly* motorcyclists."[16] Sailors featured in "Howl" weren't just sailors but "human seraphim."[17] Cruising gays didn't go to the Turkish Baths to get buggered but to meet "the blond & naked angel came to pierce them with a sword."[18] While Ginsberg aimed to redeem pornographic images from the proverbial gutter, Giorno was intent on doing just the opposite. Poetry, Giorno argued, could actively benefit and learn from pornography, a more immediately satisfying and entertaining genre.

Sucking out any traces of rhetoric approaching the "poetic," Giorno worked actively to tone diction *down* as he described double-anals and multiple fellatios. The Cuban army officers, after all, did not sport Romanesque phalluses or vision-inducing throbbing totems but rather "erect pricks / all different / lengths / and widths."[19] The supplicant's anus was not a portal to heaven but simply his "ass hole." Giorno attests tamely, "The positions / we were in / were crazy."[20] True, there is *one* instance where Giorno leaves the matter-of-fact routines behind and uses a word that evokes Beat theatrics of yore, arriving in the final lines. With "two / big fat / Cuban cocks / up my ass / at one time," the speaker attests, "I was / in paradise."[21] Yet following as it does the almost aggressively mundane affect of the poem overall, the word "paradise" seems designed in part as a parody of texts that tame representations of gay sex by transforming it into either camp (O'Hara) or mystical revelation (Ginsberg). Given that the poem is free almost entirely of basic poetic devices (analogy, metaphor, rhyme) and is marked overall by a matter-of-fact diction, Giorno's "paradise" manifests all the more strongly the very inappropriateness of adorning pornographic sex with pretty words and forms.

Giorno was not merely writing a pornographic poem but engaging with and critiquing his elders' poetry and politics actively and provocatively. All that said, a work like "Pornographic Poem" was not fully realized until it became sounded, distorted, and mediated through multiple voices. Giorno was very clear that his works were more akin to scores than they were poems traditionally understood, and he used the multisensory possibilities offered him by the new rock 'n' roll performance spaces and, crucially, the recording studio to propose his works as technologically innovative group efforts. The way "Pornographic Poem" is recorded on the Giorno Poetry Systems' album *Raspberry and Pornographic Poem* (1967), for example, reveals the profound challenges Giorno was making to conventional understandings of how a written text should be staged. One after the other on Giorno's recording, various speakers—including Robert Rauschenberg, Yvonne Rainer, Brice Marden, Patti Oldenburg, and, ironically enough, Peter Schjeldahl—approach the mike and read the poem in its entirety. Their voices are recorded through a reverb and stereo delay with varying delay times and feedback to create the illusion of multiple voices.

"Pornographic Poem" becomes less a poem than a challenge to lyric poetry—if by "lyric poetry" we mean texts affiliated imaginatively or literally to a single poet's body. The welter of voices attendant to the enunciation of a poem shocking in its very directness dissolves the poem into a babelogue. The straightforward (if "pornographic") narrative is similarly reduced at times to nothing more or less than noise as the disorienting re-cording effects that Giorno imposes on the production overwhelm sense. The recording process here becomes a way for Giorno to offer an alterna-tive to what he believed was an inherently alienated model of the poetry reading bequeathed to him by O'Hara et al.

What is of particular interest here is the way in which Giorno used the genre "poetry" against itself, actively undermining the cultural capital the lyric had accrued by contaminating it with sonic special effects tradition-ally accorded to the recording studio. This jarred with the literary turns rock 'n' roll music was making in the mid-to-late 1960s, following Bob Dylan, Leonard Cohen, Jim Morrison, and their ilk. As Simon Frith appreci-ates, lyricists like Dylan are recognized as "poetic" "by a particular sort of self-consciousness; their status rests not on their approach to words but on the types of word they use; rock poetry is a matter of planting poetic clues. . . . Dylan is the poet because his images are personal and obscure rather than direct or commonplace—his words are not plain."[22] Giorno's efforts to frame his text as a collaboratively produced, plain-spoken, and sexually ex-plicit record served as an antithesis to the bard-idolatry of 1960s musicians like Dylan. Paradoxically and complexly, "Pornographic Poem" can be read as an argument with Dylan's, Morrison's, and related musicians' use of ornate, obscure and "poetic" language and their insistent invocations of Rimbaud, Paul Verlaine, Dylan Thomas, and related others as high-priest deities.

"Pornographic Poem," especially in terms of its employment of rock-ori-ented sound, challenged Giorno's poetic contemporaries to consider how nonliterary (and perhaps even antiliterary) rock 'n' roll music could inform poetic practice in such a way as to make it more entertaining. The pur-ported complexity and intelligence of poetry—particularly when that po-etry was performed dryly as a "reading" and distributed as text within relatively small artistic and intellectual communities—was, in the end, *boring*. This did not mean that poets should be eliminated. As extreme as Giorno's performances could get, they were still widely understood to be connected intimately to poetry. "Despite the technologically enhanced na-ture" of Giorno's recordings and performances, "Giorno still conceived of them primarily as readings, as evidenced by his handing out copies of the texts at many of the events. Contrary to Sontag's conception of happenings, their 'emphasis on spectacle and sound' [did] not carry the cost of 'disre-gard for the word.'"[23]

Considering the ways Giorno was challenging normative definitions of what constituted poetry, one might fairly ask—as the *New York Times* reporter McCandlish Phillips did—"What is a poem? Is it words? Is it sounds? Is it moods? Is it images?" Phillips, having attended a Giorno "Poetry Event" held in Central Park, continued: "Questions about the nature of poetry could not be avoided last night."[24] In a letter to William Burroughs chronicling one of his readings at the School of Visual Arts in New York, Giorno wrote:

> New tapes of new poems, tapes made on this electronics machine the Rolling Stones use to make their music. Played tapes on big stereo speakers and as the audience was banked at a 45 degree angle and curved like an amphitheatre, I rented two huge follow-spotlights with changing color gels and had two guys move the beams over the people focusing on whoever they wanted to for as long as they wanted to. It worked very well.[25]

This brief description of a "poetry reading" illustrates how Giorno sought to find novel and innovative ways

> to connect with an audience using all the entertainments of ordinary life. His first attempt to achieve this goal was a series of Electronic Sensory Poetry Environments, or ESPEs, taking place between 1967 and 1969 in New York City and elsewhere, which infused the poetry reading with the energy of both Fluxus-style happenings and the psychedelic rock experience.[26]

The disorienting rock 'n' roll show went further than the LP in terms of expanding the range of lyric practice. The pulse of the poem became synaesthetic, appearing as sound, light, and even smell. The psychedelic lights Giorno used were "augmented by different combinations of striplights, light panels, and electroluminescent tape, while the various scents—from strawberry and peeled oranges to Frankincense and Chanel No. 5—were delivered to the audience through aerosol, fog machines, bubble machines, and incense."[27] The poem was no longer sacred, even as it was produced during a period when rock musicians like Dylan, Morrison, Cohen, Lennon, and McCartney were beginning to identify poets as heroes.

And, as was the case with Giorno throughout the 1960s and 1970s, these performances were as much repudiations of the New York School as they were redefinitions of what a poem could do. Following O'Hara's death after being run over by a dune buggy on Fire Island in July 1966, Giorno seemed positively *relieved*. In a December 1967 letter to Burroughs, Giorno celebrated the fact that "With Frank O'Hara dying the New York School of Poetry has all but disappeared haggling amongst themselves and writing their dumb poetry which everyone now admits is dumb."[28] Seeing O'Hara's death as just what was needed to encourage second-generation New York School poets to think more creatively about the possibilities of the public poetry reading, Giorno went further. "The next reading [of 'Pornographic Poem'] is at the Architectural League," he told Burroughs, adding: "We got them to start a poetry series (John Perreault, Ted Berrigan, Anne Waldman) in which they give us money to rent equipment. Maybe if the poets have to spent [sic] money they'll do something other than read their dumb poems to a lot of dumb people."[29] Released from the sophisticated and urbane chains held by first-generation New York School writers into the stink and noise of the rock scene, Giorno positioned himself as a punk pied piper leading the formerly obedient second-generation poets toward a wildly electric, outrageous future.

Unlike Ed Sanders, who formed the poetry-inflected rock 'n' roll band the Fugs but fancied himself a budding rocker and peer to Lennon, Grace Slick, Jerry Garcia, and others, Giorno maintained an identity as poet but fed off of—and adapted his writing to—the environment and energy of places like the Fillmore East and, later, CBGB and the Peppermint Lounge. By the early 1980s, late-night poetry events including special "Beat Nights" were being held fairly regularly at punk- and new wave–oriented clubs including the Mudd Club. Musicians like Tav Falco of the southern-gothic punk band the Panther Burns performed on the same bill as the Beat heroes Allen Ginsberg, Tuli Kupferberg, and Ed Sanders,[30] while poets like Giorno delighted in the rock 'n' roll reception accorded to them by association with the musicians. "[What's] turned out to be the best audience" for poetry, Giorno told an interviewer,

is the audience of, like rock 'n' roll clubs or new wave clubs or punk clubs or whatever you want to call them. An audience that's drunk and stoned and goes to a rock 'n' roll club or whatever, is very receptive to you, if you perform well. And in the passing years one's performances sort of got more skillful and developed.[31]

Poets and the people that went to listen to poetry readings were simply not as exciting as their musician counterparts. "Rather than poets," Giorno declared simply, "one is interested in music people."[32]

The Dial-a-Poem Poets and *The Destruction of America*

As the sixties made way for the 1970s, Giorno continued producing poetry LPs that foregrounded the performed poem as a troublemaking break with and challenge to tradition and authority. Of course, Giorno was not the first poet to put the LP and the poem together. Vachel Lindsay's recording of "The Congo," exulting in sensuous, nonreferential sounds, anticipated 1950s rock 'n' rollers like Little Richard, the Big Bopper, and Screamin' Jay Hawkins. It prophesied the Beat poets' experiments with African- and jazz-inflected neologisms—Kerouac's poems in *Mexico City Blues*, for example, or Gregory Corso's poem "Bomb."

Yet the way Lindsay transcribed "The Congo" and recorded it on LP was practically opposite to Giorno's group dynamics. Lindsay condemned the telephone, radio, "talking movie, or other mechanical intruder" as "all a part of the mechanical weight against which poetry and the spoken word has to struggle."[33] As Tyler Hoffman reads it, "for Lindsay, these items tamper with the auratic purity and humane quality of the authentic unenhanced voice, and he sees himself as leading a battle against the amplified forces of consumer capitalism."[34] True, Lindsay ended up recording some of his performances anyway, but this was more for practicality's sake to ensure his place in the canon.[35]

In distinction to Giorno's wholehearted embrace of recording technologies, Lindsay—like many of the poets who went on to have their poems recorded on vinyl, including Dylan Thomas and William Carlos Williams—did not use the recording studio as an instrument in and of itself. In Lindsay's case, the recording apparatus was there simply to *reify* the sanctity of the text and its association to the privileged body of the poet by inscribing the unadorned author's voice within the grooves of the tape or LP, theoretically in perpetuity. Authenticity—Lindsay reading Lindsay's poetry—was everything in terms of selling the product.

Over and over again in the history of recorded poetry we find the LP used to establish further the authority of the solitary bard. Ezra Pound's lively recordings of works like "Cantico del Sole," for example, were celebrated by the poet Donald Hall because "the voice is there, the *man* is there."[36] Edna St. Vincent Millay's recordings were adored by listeners, who wrote gushing letters to Millay pleading, "Don't, don't ever change, and become stiff or formal or eloquent. . . . You sound so real, so natural, so—so very much alive."[37] Following Hall, Derek Furr celebrated Millay's records because they revealed how "her voice was 'there,' the woman was there."[38] Even the more interdisciplinary jazz-poetry recordings of writers such as Kenneth Rexroth, Lawrence Ferlinghetti, Kenneth Patchen, and Jack Kerouac were often disappointing efforts that tended more toward celebrating the poet and the poem than toward transforming the ways we conventionally distinguish between the genres of poetry, music, and performance. While the poet David Meltzer identified Kerouac as successfully combining music with poetry, most of the Beat-affiliated recordings in his opinion "failed either to swing or sing. They recited or declaimed verse while a jazz combo vamped behind them."[39]

Giorno's use of the recording studio and the LP format, on the other hand—particularly in terms of his efforts to challenge the way cultural capital was accorded to poetry—was of an entirely different order. Multiple voices, feedback, and delay refused listeners' identification of the given poem as a static text brought to life by the poet's own voice. Instead, the poem was materially diffused. Any number of people, the Giorno recordings imply, could give voice to the text simultaneously. Giorno's recordings often foreground sonic effects so that the actual poem and whatever narrative or lyric qualities the poem embodied receded from the listener's attention. Sound was not employed as "background only" but rather used to destroy the primacy of the word.

Giorno's challenge to the conventions of the recorded poem had a visual aspect as well. Take, for instance, the 1972 *Dial-a-Poem Poets* LP.[40] At first glance, one might conclude that Giorno was invested in the revolutionary-chic aura of bands like the MC5 or the Last Poets, given that the cover featured a bearded grinning Giorno and included text at the bottom linking the record to "Movement" politics and the Vietnam War. However, what to make of the young black woman in sunglasses standing in front of Giorno and, given the perspective of the photograph, looming large over him? The woman, seen from the torso up, sported a bouffant shock of orange hair

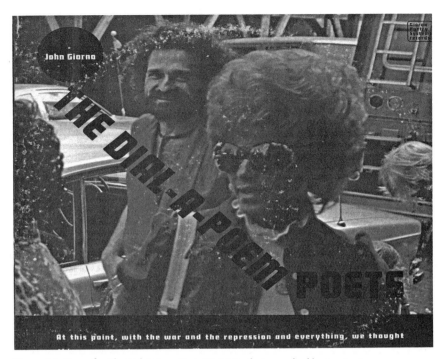

Figure 6.1 Cover for *The Dial-A-Poem Poets* LP, 1972, photographed by Les Levine.
Source: © John Giorno.

and wore a white shirt with a frilled Victorian collar. Giorno was practically overwhelmed here by a character whose mix-and-match appearance contested anything even purporting to be natural. Giorno—whether he intended to or not—seemed literally to be stepping back to make way for a proto-punk look that marked a break from the hippie pastoral style so common to the era.

This is not to say that the record cover was somehow without a politics or a sense of its own history. Inscribed on the bottom of the album were the words: "At this point, with the war and the repression and everything, we thought this was a good way for the Movement to reach people." Yet even here one has to wonder about the sincerity of Giorno's gesture. There is a marked casualness to the phrase "the war and the repression and everything." It is a kind of noncommittal shrug masquerading as earnest statement, the very vagueness of "the repression and everything" undermining its purported activist intent. Was Giorno being ironic? Was he making *fun* of poets whose self-regard was so at odds with reality that they actually thought their words could have a progressive political effect?

After all, "this was a good way"—that is, this *record* was a good way—implied contempt for the book as a vehicle for communicating progressive goals. If poets really wanted to have an effect, Giorno's message suggested, they should act more like rock 'n' rollers and get their tracks onto a record. From the way Giorno marketed the poets in the context of an LP and in the emphasis Giorno placed on the "sound" of the writers,[41] *Dial-a-Poem Poets* implicitly challenged poets' adherence to the written word and the discrete poetry reading. True, Giorno made much out of the fact that the featured writers were "from the New York School, Bolinas and West Coast Schools, Concrete Poetry, Beat Poetry, Black Poetry and Movement Poetry." However, what was *really* fun here? What was catchy? What carried within it intimations of menace, evocations of anarchy? Ultimately, the poetry featured on this record was curated in such a way that even New York School, Bolinas, and other coterie-affiliated poetry seemed more in thrall to anti-establishment, anti-ideological proto-punk aesthetics than it did to New American writing.

Take, for example, John Sinclair's performance of "The Destruction of America," recorded at the July 1965 Berkeley Poetry Conference and included in the *Dial-a-Poem Poets* LP. Now, while John Sinclair was just about a year away from becoming the outspoken manager of the MC5, his punk charisma had already marked him out to at least some second-generation New York School poets as a figure to respect and emulate. Talking about his own performance at the conference, Ted Berrigan admitted, "I had this totally competitive eye on Ed Sanders and John Sinclair, he used to come read at the [Lower East Side coffee-shop] Le Metro sometimes, and I knew him."[42] Berrigan was jealous, if sweetly so. Both Sanders and Sinclair had made their mark as bards by this time. Sanders had formed his proto-punk band the Fugs in 1963, and by the end of 1965 the band had established itself by performing in multiple venues across the country. Sinclair was a major force in Detroit's counterculture scene, particularly after he became involved in the mimeograph revolution. Sinclair recollects how he and his wife Leni

were thrilled because we were part of an arts community centered on a place called the Detroit Artists' Workshop, and we were proponents of the mimeograph revolution advanced by Edward Sanders here in New York City at the Fuck You Press. So we learned from him that you could publish off a mimeograph without it costing you very much money, especially if you could steal the paper and ink. We published books of our own poetry and other writings. We published a poetry magazine, an avant-garde jazz magazine—we did all this with mimeograph.[43]

Sinclair and Sanders were, by 1965, aiming for and achieving a level of populist acclaim rarely accorded to poets. That Berrigan's "competitive eye" roved around the Berkeley Poetry Conference, then, was no accident—particularly since the conference was more like a festival than an academic gathering.

The Berkeley Poetry Conference was the Woodstock of avant-garde poetry. Most of the (middle-aged) New American elders were there—Robert Duncan, Gary Snyder, Creeley, and Ginsberg, just returned from a triumphant trip to Czechoslovakia, where he was crowned "Kraj Majales" ("King of May") by thousands of Czech students. Connections were made by younger writers hoping to rub shoulders with the Beats and Black Mountaineers—Lewis Warsh and Anne Waldman, for example, met and fell in love at the conference, and Waldman was to cite Charles Olson's reading as a transformative event. "I date my empowerment or confirmation of a life in poetry, not simply my own, to Charles Olson's reading in 1965 at the famous Berkeley Poetry conference."[44] Sinclair attended mostly because he venerated Amiri Baraka and Charles Olson and wanted to be close to his heroes. For two weeks, the Berkeley Poetry Conference staged writers who, as Libbie Rifkin puts it, "were positioned as the wild Other of the academic poetry establishment."[45]

By 1965, the older writers looked and sounded like the kids who loved them. Bearded, stoned, bedecked and bejeweled in head-turning fashions, the New American poets at least superficially seemed more aligned with dissolute rock 'n' rollers than they did with erudite scribes. Charles Olson, whose 1950 essay "Projective Verse" had become a kind of manifesto for avant-garde New American poets moving away from the formalist poetry that had become the norm throughout that decade, was one of the main features at the conference. Given top billing—his reading closed out the two-week long conference—he did not disappoint those audience members looking for shambolic, performative intensity. "No, I wanna talk," Olson insisted drunkenly during his hours-long improvised tour de force. "I mean, you wanna listen to . . . a poet? I mean, you know, like, a poet, when he's alive, whether he talks or reads you his poems is the same thing." Olson then slapped the table hard for emphasis, which encouraged an audience member to shout out excitedly, "RIGHT!" "Dig that!" Olson responded delightedly, adding:

And when he—and when he—and when he is made of three parts, his life, his mouth, and his poem, then, by god, the earth belongs to us. And like—and what I think has happened is that that's—wow, gee, hmm, one doesn't like to claim things, but god, isn't it exciting? I mean, at least I'm—I mean, I can, I feel like a kid. I'm in the presence of an event, which I don't believe, myself.[46]

From insisting that poetry is as much a demotic speech activity as it is a material literary text to evoking a vague, transcendental, and community-oriented ecstatic *beyond* ("I feel like a kid. I'm in the presence of an event, which I don't believe, myself"), Olson's rhetoric here seems almost self-consciously in tune not just with countercultural lingo but with the very values of spontaneity and community so intrinsic to that evocative phrase "the sixties."

This is the context in which Berrigan cast a competitive eye on Sinclair. Sinclair had proved his poetry chops and was already making his mark as an authority on free jazz and as a countercultural icon. Indeed, Sinclair's Berkeley performance demonstrated the possible and actual links between radical politics, jazz, popular music, and poetry. Opening his reading by explaining to the audience that the title of his poem, "The Destruction of America," was taken from LeRoi Jones's novel *The System of Dante's Hell*, Sinclair then dedicated his reading "to Malcolm X Little . . . Malcolm X is one of the few political figures that I ever had any respect for."[47] Marking a break from the integrationist politics and ethos of white mainstream liberalism, Sinclair's dedication, made some years before militant revolutionary rhetoric became common among white counterculture activists, seemed as much designed to shock the Berkeley attendees as it was to mourn militant Malcolm X's passing.

Reading his poem to a hushed audience, Sinclair presaged punk's critique of the hippie era as much as he was rejecting the nonviolent ideology of the Freedom Summer. As if issuing a retort to Martin Luther King Jr.'s phrase "Darkness cannot drive out darkness; only light can do that. Hate cannot drive out hate; only love can do that,"[48] Sinclair in section 2 of "The Destruction of America" had this in part to say (the following selection is composed of the first five and a half and final four stanzas of the nineteen-stanza section that Sinclair read out in its entirety at the festival):

make the music hard, make
it burn. to sear the ear. to

make me scream. murder silence
don't stand for it, killers of

insane stupid dreams. move
my hands, & feet, make them work

to keep up. focus on the act of
violent music, the act

of making it. the kick
in the balls, where the feet

shd go. slitting fat throats.
. . . .

too late, for tears. For anything,
but simple action. war. the

filthy noise of "compassion,"
when the song runs out. to the ends

of silence. cracked lips, bloody
fingers, broken drums, blow,

Musicians, blow, till the racket
drowns us out. then KILL[49]

Performed at Berkeley in 1965, the same year Amiri Baraka wrote his notorious and threatening poem "Black Art" ("We want poems that kill / Assassin poems. Poems that shoot guns / Poems that wrestle cops into alleys / and take their weapons leaving them dead / with tongues pulled out and sent to Ireland"),[50] Sinclair's style was very much on the fringes of the various poetic registers competing for attention at the festival. Neither rhapsodic visionary à la Olson, Robert Duncan, or Allen Ginsberg; nor West Coast Beat-hippie like Gary Snyder; nor light-hearted New York School aesthete like Ted Berrigan, Sinclair pretty much in a class of his own. Sure, Sinclair was borrowing quite a bit from the New American poets. Robert Creeley's halting, heavily enjambed style is in clear evidence, as is Jones's jazz-inflected poetics. However, for a white poet to be doing what Sinclair was doing here was virtually unprecedented in 1965.

This is especially the case when we see how Sinclair is thematizing *music*. Now, it's not rock 'n' roll he's talking about here—it's free jazz, an "act of violent music" played by musicians with "cracked lips bloody fingers broken drums." Free jazz was in some sense the punk rock of the early to mid-1960s, a noisy squall to most audiences and practitioners across the critical and popular register—including dyed-in-the-wool jazz fans, many jazz artists beloved by the Beats such as Dizzy Gillespie and Miles Davis,[51] and beyond. Musicians such as Milford Graves, John Tchichai, and especially Ornette Coleman were regularly singled out for mockery. This is particularly significant given that Sinclair's "The Destruction of America" was published initially in a chapbook entitled *This Is Our Music*, the title of the free-jazz pioneer Coleman's breakthrough 1960 album.[52] As the trumpeter Roy Eldridge said of Coleman, "I listened to him high and I listened to him cold sober. I even played with him. I think he's jiving baby. He's putting everybody on."[53]

The language used to put down free jazz was remarkably similar to the criticisms lobbed at punk some ten years later. Coleman's music and free jazz more generally speaking, for example, "was described as anarchistic and nihilistic. Critics spoke of [Coleman's] technical inadequacies and the 'incoherence' of his saxophone playing. The revered jazz writer Leonard Feather said that 'his rejection of many of the basic rules, not merely of jazz but of all music, did not entail the foundation of specific new rules.'"[54] To celebrate free jazz and link those sounds to an idealized political violence was Sinclair's "fuck you" to the pacifist Berkeley scene considered generally and to the assembled poets who had yet to dig the new sounds of free jazz or commit themselves to Revolution.

This moment in 1965 was one early manifestation of how free jazz, in part as it was mediated through John Sinclair in his role as the manager and promoter of the proto-punk band the MC5, looked ahead to punk style. Part of the attraction free jazz held for nascent punk rockers was the fact that free-jazz musicians to some extent proposed that virtuosity was no longer a requirement to create soulful, angry music. Generating an untrained and primitive effect even if those musicians were otherwise skilled was part of the radical charm of free jazz. As Rob Wallace notes, the drummer Milford Graves consistently gave breaks to and celebrated untrained musicians. "How do you explain it when a musician that's only been playing five or six months comes out and plays something on his horn and someone can dig it?" Graves posed, adding: "Or someone who don't know *nothing* about music, getting up there and banging on the drums and five million people start moving and yelling? . . . You can't put that [criticizing lack of technique] on a musician who moves the people."[55] With Graves and other musicians as a model, one could dig deeper into the past to identify and celebrate punk-rock moments in jazz from the 1940s and 1950s. Waxing lyrical about the "raw, fartlike, obscenely loud and unquestionably tasteless and vulgar 'HONKs!' and 'SQUEEEs!' immortalized by Flip Phillips and Illinois Jacquet in the old Jazz at the Philharmonic concerts," Lester Bangs declaimed:

> That's right, I love punk rock, and I'm not apologizing to anyone. As far as I can see, what Philips and Jacquet were doing on those Jazz at the Philharmonic sides was kind of the punk rock of its day. What's more, I don't give a good goddamn if somebody can barely play their instruments or even not at all, as long as they've got something to express and do it in a compelling way.[56]

Bangs was identifying brief free moments in otherwise rule-bound jazz as premonitions of the free jazz to come. Moving on to celebrate the "garbage noise" of bands like the Sex Pistols and free-jazz improvisers including Archie Shepp, Bangs married the two genres with characteristic negative praise: "beyond a certain point both punk rock and free jazz give up all sense of structure. Result: atonal anarchic spew."[57] Clearly, free jazz's "atonal anarchic spew" resonated with proto-punk, punk, and post-punk musicians including Lou Reed, the Stooges, the MC5, and Thurston Moore. Performative amateurism and discordant, noisy sound had social and political implications, too. As Rob Wallace understands it, "the revolutions of free jazz and punk represent part of a historical continuum . . . where loud music, anarchic passion, and disciplined abandon can potentially always be regenerative in the face of aesthetic, economic, or political stagnation."[58] Not only were free-jazz musicians offering new ways of thinking about improvisation; they were also setting up independent distribution and marketing networks.

> As would the later DIY punk ethos, free jazz encouraged artists to take control of the means of production. [Independent recording and publishing free-jazz collectives] were part of a wider network of artists and community activists. The [Association for the Advancement of Creative Musicians in Chicago], an important model for many of these organizations . . . is merely one of many organizations that preceded punk rock's valorization of the DIY attitude.[59]

Sun Ra, Ornette Coleman, and other "free" musicians offered a sonic evocation of a revolutionary politics that was at odds with the far gentler anarcholiberalism typical of the New Left and the New American Poetry. Sinclair's reading "The Destruction of America" at the Berkeley Poetry Conference was not simply an anticipation of the later 1960s militant counterculture in response to the expansion of the Vietnam War. It was also an early instance of and premonition of the role that sonic "anarchic spew" could play in articulating and enacting a radical critique of polite, civic-minded society.

Fuck Fuck Fuck

Giorno curated the *Dial-a-Poem* LP to highlight populist radical outlaws like Sinclair and to invite critical assessments and redefinitions of the very genres "poetry" and "pop." In that spirit, Michael Brownstein's performance of his poem "Geography," also featured on Giorno's album, seemed designed to be placed in conversation with Sinclair's "The Destruction of America." "Geography" as it is heard on Giorno's album seems to mark a break with the enthused patter and love for quotidian detail marking so much second-generation New York School poetry and sounds indebted to a louche rock vibe. Brownstein pronounced lines including "Ripped out of my mind again /

'Ripped out of my mind again'— / how many people have said that?"[60] in a codeine-thick drawl. He interrupted otherwise complex lines with snotty phrases like "Did you say something? Did you say something?"[61] Following his Whitmanesque line "I can hear the disembodied populace in the trees / Blowing their golden horns and pieces / Bounce their music across the grass / into my EAR,"[62] Brownstein immediately undermined his own vatic gesture with "Not Van Gogh ear / just me // What is that supposed to mean? / What is that supposed to mean?,"[63] accenting the "that" in a languidly exasperated style. Over and over again, Brownstein's gestures toward transcendence and immanence were undermined by skeptical blather—at one point, for example, an amphetamine rush comedown was limned tragicomically as Brownstein mourned

Now I don't feel it so much
Now I don't feel that way anymore
Now I don't feel that way anymore
Now I don't care
Now I just don't care anymore
Who gives a fuck now
Who gives a fuck anyway?
Now I don't give a fuck
Now I don't know
Now it sounds pretty heavy
Now it's getting very heavy
Now it's horrible
Really horrible.[64]

Given that the poem is a *drug poem*, one wonders whether Brownstein was pointing back to lines like that great statement of ennui "I really don't care anymore" from the Velvet Underground's "Heroin."

The bouquet of "fucks" in Brownstein's "Geography" also revealed—ironically enough given the poem's place as a "spoken-word" LP recording marketed as a counterculture rock 'n' roll album—that poetry could go further than pop in terms of its ability to use "obscenities" freely. Even the Velvets could not, for commercial and legal reasons, repeat the word "fuck" over and over again in their songs, despite their manager Andy Warhol's famous advice: "Just make sure you keep the dirty words in."[65] Similarly, bands with revolutionary commitments and postures had to make concessions to get their work out, even if those concessions meant vacuuming out the "dirty words." Take Sinclair's MC5, who proved hugely influential on subsequent punk bands in the United States and abroad. The title track of their 1969 LP *Kick Out the Jams*, recorded live at Detroit's Grande Ballroom, kicked off with lead singer Rob Tyner screaming out, "Kick out the jams, *motherfucker!*" Elektra Records could not distribute such filth as easily as Grove Press could by then distribute the most scabrous routines of William Burroughs to every boho living room in America. In fact, Elektra executives understood that if the song were to get airplay, they would have to remove the "*motherfucker*" from the lyrics. Rob Tyner dutifully went back to the studio and rerecorded the opening phrase as "Kick out the jams, brothers and sisters."

Brownstein's "Geography" illustrates how poetry—thanks to its status as literature and following the outcome of any number of famous obscenity trials that found authors as various as D. H. Lawrence, William Burroughs, and Allen Ginsberg "not guilty"—could push the boundaries of good taste and civility more than its populist cousin pop music. Going further than the Velvets, the MC5, and pretty much any other band of the era, Brownstein's "Geography," Sinclair's "The Destruction of America," and much of the other work on Giorno's *Dial-a-Poem Poets* LP set the stage for a punk-inflected poetics that informed downtown poet/musicians.

Big Ego

By 1978—the year Blondie scored a number-one hit with "Heart of Glass," the Talking Heads charted in several countries with their version of Al Green's "Take Me to the River," and the Ramones entered the charts with their single "I Wanna Be Sedated"—Giorno's poetry recordings revealed an ever-increasing fascination with blurring the boundaries between high and low art, poetry and punk, minimalist music and rock 'n' roll. The mainstreaming of punk meant that Giorno could draw on his contacts in the underground to foreground even more how easily poetry and punk were linked to and nourished each other, as it enabled Giorno to market poetry as a pop-culture commodity. Giorno's 1978 LP *Big Ego*, which included figures as purportedly distinct as Philip Glass, Patti Smith, the Fugs, Robert Lowell, and Frank O'Hara into one attractive package, demonstrated how poetry generated some of the more interesting sounds coming out of downtown. It revealed New York School–affiliated poets ever more attuned to the punk attitude—not really a surprise considering the majority of the recordings on *Big Ego* were produced in the mid- to late 1970s as punk blossomed out of CBGB and onto national and international stages.

Kicking off *Big Ego* was none other than Patti Smith. Drawn from a recorded performance at the 1975 New Year's Day benefit for the Poetry Project at St. Mark's Church, Smith's contribution began with a riff describing Egyptian women from antiquity being smeared from head to toe with a mixture of opium, salad oil, and henna. Smith bobbed and weaved from one topic to another hyperactively. After a lively five-minute introduction, Smith broke out into an early version of "Seven Ways of Going" (a song included on her 1979 album *Wave*). Accompanying herself by rhythmically banging on what sounds like a piece of wood,[66] Smith interrupted her performance throughout to regale the audience with tales of her dreams of being a sixteenth-century Japanese archer "ninja boy," descriptions of aiming darts at a king's heart, and so forth. Proffering advice to audience members as to how they too could act out their own hilarious improvised routines, Smith then moved on to insist that the St. Mark's poets should read the visionary prose and poetry of Alexander Trocchi and Violette Leduc while masturbating.[67] Clearly enamored with the Beats and their reading lists, Smith consistently evinced a refreshing lightheartedness and jokiness that fit in well with the overall tenor at St. Mark's. Visionary, drug-addled, and sexually explicit poetry and prose were proposed primarily as material for developing a performative style. Smith was teaching a lesson to the St. Mark's poets. The poetry this crowd loved, Smith implied, must not remain ghettoized within the context of the poetry reading or poetry coterie. Rather, it must be something that, ideally, becomes a sexy, pop-inflected spectacle. A *show*.

Giorno's own contribution to *Big Ego*, the poem "Grasping at Emptiness," was of a piece with Smith's. Recorded in 1978, Giorno's work can be read alongside the photographer Robert Mapplethorpe's famous 1977 image "Jim and Tom, Sausalito," particularly since Giorno was friends with Mapplethorpe and was a great fan of the photographer's work. Mapplethorpe had achieved some acclaim with his now-famous black-and-white cover photograph for Patti Smith's first album *Horses*, and his "Jim and Tom" was already making waves in the downtown scene.[68] Mapplethorpe's photograph "depicts two men, dressed in leather, engaged in sexual activity in a beautifully lit military bunker. Jim is standing with his pelvis pushed slightly forward; he holds his penis in a gloved hand and urinates into the open, bearded mouth of Tom, who kneels before him. A stream of urine, in sharp focus, connects the bodies."[69]

For "Jim and Tom," Mapplethorpe employed a sophisticated use of geometric forms and lighting to depict, gorgeously and ethereally, an unconventional sexual activity. Similarly, Giorno's poem also aestheticized urolagnia, evoking Mapplethorpe's practice of cruising gay bathhouses in part to find photographic subjects ("you're cruising the baths and you're cruising the baths," Giorno chants in his poem, "looking in the dimly lit rooms . . . these guys looking like / they're posing for pornographic pictures").[70] By using a series of delays, overdubs, reverb, and echo, Giorno created a formally complex sound environment that imbued the abject content of his text with religious gravitas. Opening with the declaration "My new poem is called 'Grasping at *emp*tiness!,'"[71] as if introducing a new song to an expectant audience, the work begins by immediately disorienting the listener with a series of looped repetitions and accented cries. The narrative promise of the opening line "And you're walking down Lafayette Street" quickly disintegrates as Giorno's enunciations are layered over with other shouted, whispered, and jagged repeated phrases including "and you start *crying*," "*tears* running down your cheeks," "there ain't nothing worse than a relationship," "stupidity stupidity stupidity stupidity," "I never want to *see* you again," "If I wasn't a fucking Buddhist I'd love to put a gun in my mouth," and so on. The poem then takes an erotic turn. "And I like *dirty* sex and I like *dirty* sex," Giorno proclaims midway through the poem, continuing, "I like it when you cum when I'm pissing in your mouth I like it when you cum when I'm pissing in your mouth."[72]

Yet in large part because of the plangent reverberations created through Giorno's special-effects recording techniques, the patterns that he creates take on a weirdly celestial feel. Giorno seems not exactly to be parodying but drawing on the authority of religious sung refrains and litanies to reposition piss-swigging as a kind of Eucharistic exchange. As Luc Sante saw it, Mapplethorpe's image "Jim and Tom" might be said "to refer to holy communion: the standing donor, half-extending his arm, stands over the supplicant, who kneels and presents his upturned face, eyes reverently closed."[73] Like Mapplethorpe's use of visual forms conventionally understood to be in the service of the holy and beautiful, Giorno's evocatively religious repetitive annunciations challenge listeners to reframe how they might ordinarily respond to abject sexual acts as it proposes "*dirty* sex" as an eminently religious experience.

Throughout *Big Ego*, Giorno selected the poets, musicians, and composers to emphasize abjection, nihilism, sonic and political dissonance, and iconoclasm. Even the "high-art" composers and writers included on the album were framed as conductors of chaos—viz. Robert Wilson's and Christopher Knowles's performance of "The Sundance Kid Is Beautiful," recorded at the same 1975 New Year's Day benefit at St. Marks Church where Smith goaded her audience to jerk off while reading Trocchi and Leduc. Trading off lines including "Yeah the Sundance Kid is beautiful," "because the Sundance Kid was beautiful," and "The Sundance Kid could dance around the room," Wilson and Knowles ended up drawing from the crowd derisive laughter, sloweddown clapping, arguments among audience members, jeers and whistles, and catcalls including "conceptual bullshit of the sixties!" and worse. Obdurate in the face of the audience's indignant responses, Wilson and Knowles soldiered on in what seemed increasingly a willfully provocative performance, again revealing the power of minimalist repetition to elicit productive disapproval.

Confrontational, not sociable, these poetic and musical works anticipated—and influenced—the punk-rock acts that were soon to follow. As John Holmstrom, the cofounder of the seminal magazine *Punk* explained it to Steven Heller: "One cultural influence [on punk] that's been forgotten is Seventies minimalism. There was a concerted effort by bands like Suicide, Ramones and Talking Heads to follow the aesthetic that 'less is more' and to strip music down to its core."[74] By 1978 influence had come full circle—punk bands were showing the way to some New York School poets looking to get out of the quotidian poetics of Frank O'Hara. "When I first was scared of death I just fucked someone in the ass," sneered the poet Michael Lally during his 1978 performance at St. Mark's Church of his poem "All of the Above," sounding for all the world like Lydia Lunch's boy-toy.[75] No longer simply the case that poetry influenced punk or that punk influenced poetry, by 1978 the relationship between the two genres had become a complicated conversation that would leave its mark on poetry and popular music in successive decades.

Giorno continued through the 1980s to engage actively with punk as music, aesthetic, and politics. Albums like the 1980 Dial-a-Poem LP *Sugar, Alcohol, &*

Figure 6.2 The John Giorno Band.
Source: Copyright © Stephanie Chernikowski.

Meat, for example, featured the poet Tom Carey singing a song about trans-vestitism that could have easily passed as one of Wayne/Jayne County's gen-der-bending ditties from the early 1970s.[76] Up-and-coming writers includ-ing Kathy Acker, a regular on the downtown art-gallery punk-rock club circuit, spat out the short story "I was walking down the street" at a CBGB benefit for the St. Mark's Poetry Project, her demimonde reportage pro-nounced through dramatic extended vowels that called to mind the man-ner in which Patti Smith elongated "o" and "e" sounds in her song "Gloria." To hear Acker scoff "'Look,' a young dark haired *maahhn* said to me, releas-ing his erect cock from his pants, 'see what you do to me'?" is as much to hear the ways punk attitude made its way into downtown literature as it is to hear how punk vocal articulation formed part of the new literary perfor-mance style.[77] In 1984 Giorno joined the party by forming the John Giorno Band, playing gigs in places including New York's Bottom Line and CBGB.

Giorno's albums applied rock 'n' roll marketing strategies throughout the decade. His 1984 *Better an Old Demon Than a New God*,[78] which included recordings by the punk stalwarts David Johansen, Richard Hell, and Lydia Lunch, echoed the narrative of countless LP covers that found band members standing behind their charismatic lead singer—Lunch, Johansen, Carroll, and Giorno appeared on the jacket looking for all the world like a cool if dutiful backup band, their lead singer William Burroughs seated front and center. All of them, naturally, were glowering, as punk musicians should.

Drawing on the sounds coming out of downtown, Giorno proffered examples of what could happen when one yoked poetry to punk, rock 'n' rollers to lyric nerds. Giorno's LPs, exemplars of a postmodernism that Andreas Huyssen has identified as operating "in a field of tension between tradition and innovation, conservation and renewal, mass culture and high art in which the second terms are no longer automatically privileged over the first," were, in the end, a radically demotic assault on the privilege accorded to poetry as a "high art" and the purported innocence, primitivism, and spontaneity of three-chord rock 'n' roll.[79]

SEVEN

Eileen Myles and the International Fuck Frank O'Hara Movement

ON JULY 27, 1978, near the end of a half-million-dollar restoration of St. Mark's Church to upgrade the building and church steeple, a worker using an acetylene torch accidentally ignited a wooden cornice on the second-floor gallery of the main sanctuary. What followed was a three-alarm fire that many in the neighborhood were sure spelled the end of St. Mark's: flames spread into the steeple and the roof, which collapsed.

The fire was disastrous not just for the church itself, which had served as a sanctuary and space for worship for the community for almost two centuries, but for the second-generation New York School poets who called St. Mark's home. While

> the [Poetry] Project's tape archive was neither heat nor water damaged . . . the Project's office was . . . destroyed. . . . The parish hall sustained water and smoke damage, and the new hardwood floor in the sanctuary was completely destroyed by water and falling debris. Ron Padgett was in Vermont when he heard the news, Anne Waldman in Boulder, in a swimming pool with Robert Duncan. The cost of repair: somewhere over $2 million.[1]

It would be some time before the thrice-weekly readings would start up again at St. Mark's.

However, the Poetry Project had been running a good twelve years by this point, and many of its founding figures had moved on. This change was not lost on a new wave of poets descending on the Lower East Side, a number of whom were simultaneously indebted to and eager to break with their New York School heritage. The poet Eileen Myles, who had moved to New York from Boston in 1974, put it succinctly: "St. Mark's burned down . . . it was like a dividing of the generations, because those of us who were younger were like 'Yeah, this is great!,' and the older people were like, 'This is the end.'"[2]

Myles's comments should be taken with the proverbial grain of salt, of course. Her poetry and prose is clearly indebted to the quotidian, talky, and vernacular-oriented side of New York School–affiliated writing. Any playful hostility toward the earlier generations did not stop Myles from working as James Schuyler's assistant in the late 1970s. And when the opportunity came up in 1984 to serve as director of the Poetry Project, Myles grabbed it. For the next two years, Myles welcomed New York School–enchanted poets from the West Coast to St. Mark's, including Dennis Cooper.

That said, Myles's comments should also be taken seriously, given how relatively quickly the oppositional stances of the New York School were, by the late 1970s, being commodified as nostalgia by New York City authorities eager to promote the city as a bastion of culture. Officiating at the 1980 ceremonial bell raising following the 1978 fire, for example, Cultural Affairs Commissioner (and former curator of the Metropolitan Museum and early mentor to Andy Warhol) Henry Geldzahler "invoked the names of Isadora Duncan, Edna St. Vincent Millay, Allen Ginsberg, Ted Berrigan and other creative artists who found audiences at St. Mark's, adding, 'I've had a lot of pleasure and a lot of thrills from this church as a cultural center.'"[3] The pill-popping, Vietnam War–protesting, dope-smoking, long-haired hippie freak poets were now folded safely into an official cultural narrative. A blank space was opening up for a new generation of writers to stand willfully outside the institutional mainstream. The scene and sounds coming out of CBGB—particularly as the club made way for the even more extreme and nihilistic sounds of "no-wave" bands like Ut, Teenage Jesus and the Jerks, the Gynecologists, and James Chance and the Contortions—helped Myles and her friends stage their discontinuity from the New York School visibly and volubly.

By 1978, the Patti Smith Group, Blondie, Talking Heads, the Ramones, and many of the other figures associated with CBGB had found fame. CBGB had become too small a space for them to stretch out as they tamed and/or developed their music in ways that broke with punk orthodoxy. Figures as disparate as Rhys Chatham (whose band the Gynecologists' first gig was at St. Mark's Church late in 1977) and teenage runaway Lydia Lunch, having learned much from the initial punk scene and the literary world that swirled around them, took to making music that made even Richard Hell's most cacophonous moments seem tame by comparison. While Lydia Lunch shared similar literary tastes with the local poets and punks who had called CBGB and St. Mark's home, she was nevertheless less interested in fitting into the scene than in challenging it. As Thurston Moore put it, Lunch "called Patti Smith a barefoot hippie chick and Television a bunch of old men playing wanky guitar solos. . . . I was amazed there was a new punk person trashing Patti Smith! I had moved to New York to fucking marry Patti Smith and now Lydia was saying Patti was most definitely uncool."[4] While CBGB had not burned down like St. Mark's Church had, Lunch and her fellow travelers were at the very least aiming their destructive sights at what was already by 1978 a punk institution. As they saw it, they were the new phoenix, rising up out of the ashes of an already moribund New York punk scene.

This both/and approach on the part of these upcoming poets and musicians—both acknowledging their literary and musical inheritance and arguing provocatively that it had become stale—manifested itself on October 26, 27, and 28, when CBGB hosted a weekend benefit for St. Mark's Church featuring poets and writers including Kathy Acker, John Ashbery, Ron Padgett, Allen Ginsberg, and Ted Berrigan alongside bands including Richard Hell and the Voidoids, Lou Reed, John Cale, and the Stimulators. The St. Mark's benefit was arguably the moment when practically all the New York–based poets and punks, who had lived alongside and referred to one another in song and in verse for years, finally got the opportunity to mingle under one roof. Eileen Myles remembers fondly: "The Fire Benefit at CBGBs for St. Mark's . . . as part of a fundraising mechanism, they had a giant benefit at CBGBs, and it was *fantastic* . . . it was Andrei Voznesensky, and Elvis Costello, it was such a mishmash . . . and Allen of course . . . I read in it . . . it was great."[5] In contrast, Ron Padgett, one of the primary figures affiliated with the Poetry Project during the 1960s, had a much less rhapsodic reaction to the three days of peace, love, and music at CBGB:

Figure 7.1 Rock & Roll Music and Poetry Benefit flyer.
Source: Samara Kupferberg Collection.

What I do remember is how dark, raucous, and smelly CBGB was, and how out of place I felt, not only in terms of the venue but also the other performers, who could be gritty and let's say aggressive on the podium. The music was tremendously loud, too. The audience seemed to be shouting for anything that was raw and loud. I changed my game plan, ditching the poems I had chosen at home and going instead with my adaptation of Mayakovsky's "Screaming My Head Off," which I tried to read with a manic intensity. When I came down from the stage, Voznesensky told me he thought the poem was great and Allen said that he himself was surprised by my performance, though it was hard to figure out if his surprise was good or bad. I left the club through a back entrance as quickly as possible, relieved to be out of there and walking back toward my apartment.[6]

That Padgett's and Myles's recollections of the benefit were so radically different speaks volumes about the shift taking place at the Poetry Project. The poetics of figures like Padgett or Berrigan, at once surface oriented and intensely allusive of a real-time social field and literary heritage, was receding in the face of a much more raw approach.

The International Fuck Frank O'Hara Movement

The shift to a narrative, punk-inflected style was recorded both on downtown stages and downtown pages, perhaps most memorably in the typeset journal *Koff*, edited by Elinor Nauen, Magie Dubris, and Rachel Walling. *Koff*, according to Eileen Myles,

> was *the* punk magazine, it was really funny and great. Their antecedent was Ed Sanders's *Fuck You: A Magazine of the Arts*, so what they had was a series of naked male poet pinups, like they got every man on the poetry scene to pose naked. I remember being angry because they didn't ask me, and they were like, "But you're not a man."[7]

With a print run of just three issues published in 1977 and 1978 (the fourth issue was a limited-edition T-shirt),[8] *Koff* actively took down first- and second-generation New York School heroes, using punk overtly to stage their assaults.

As Myles points out, Sanders's *Fuck You* influenced the overall look and layout of the journal.[9] The twist, however, was that Sanders's misogynist satires were now being co-opted by female poets who were both delighted and disgusted by the shenanigans of their literary predecessors. No more "Slum Goddess" centerfolds, as there had been in the *East Village Other*. This time around, naked men would feature in all their priapic glory. Paul Violi, standing naked in a sylvan lake setting with mountains in the background, graced the first issue. In the second issue, Lewis Warsh lay au naturel on a couch with a baby poised sweetly in front of his stomach. Included in the third issue, the "1979 KOFF Calendar" showcased no fewer than twelve naked poets, including Michael Lally ("Mr. January"), Bill Berkson ("Mr. March"), and John Godfrey ("Mr. June"), splayed out in a variety of poses and settings. Men were now the objectified bodies on display to satisfy women's desires. Yet one couldn't escape the feeling that as silly as these images were, there was also a powerful critique of male power as it was distributed through the avant-garde networks specific to the New York School. Lally, Warsh, Violi, Berkson, and the rest were now not the names on the editorial masthead or the ones making decisions about who got to read at St. Mark's, publish in *The World*, and so on. Rather, with readers' eyes now focused on their limp penises and their naked bodies framed overall in the context of a poetry journal run by women, the boys seemed somehow sweetly, strangely, vulnerable.

Female authority as performed in *Koff* pointed back to pre-punk precursors like *Fuck You* and Berrigan's mimeographed *C* magazine as it made clear that punk rock, particularly the new sounds coming out of England, marked a break with Berrigan and his band of troubadours. This had a lot to do with the fact that Nauen and Dubris were as active in the music scene as they were in the poetry world. "Most of the poets were in bands," Nauen points out. "That was what we all did. It was a Sign of the Times. The coolest people were Punks & Poets, & who didn't want to be cool?!?! I don't think I thought there was a connection except that we had complicated, poets' lyrics."[10] For Dubris,

> Music in general had a huge influence on my work. The early New York punk scene (Patti Smith, Television, Richard Hell, Talking Heads) opened up the music world, which had fallen into a pretty boring place by the early/mid 70s. I remember seeing Patti Smith at the New Years reading very early on doing Piss Factory and being blown away. I realized you could be a real poet and a rock performer. I was in bands from the mid-70s on, and the scenes were fairly

intertwined. There were many bands featuring poets and artists—both well-known ones like Television (Verlaine was a poet), Voidoids (Richard Hell a major writer), 3 teens kill 4 (artist David Wojnarowicz), the EgoTones, the Tom Carey band, etc. My last band in the 90s, Homer Erotic was specifically formed as a poets' band by the poet Barbara Barg and myself.[11]

Poetry made its way into punk as punk made its way into poetry. Take, for example, Ted Arwulf's poem "SEX LUST AND ORTHOPEDIC SHOES / SEX LUST AND ORTHOPEDIC SHOES / SEX LUST AND PORNOGRAPHIC BLUES," published in *Koff* 1. Arwulf is described in the contributors' notes as someone "who wrote this poem and hundreds of others at the age of 13" and who "is not necessarily dead." Could readers really be sure who Arwulf was?[12] Presenting him as an adolescent poet who "is not necessarily dead" might also suggest the editors were playing a joke, acting out the role of proud editors showing off their own little punk Rimbaud. (The historical Rimbaud, of course, died figuratively a number of times. His disappearing acts from family and poetry communities, along with his ostensible deaths, played a strong part in his enduring status as *poète maudit*.) In fact, the first two stanzas of "SEX LUST AND ORTHOPEDIC SHOES" read like a Rimbaudian pastiche, replete with nihilistic rejections of sociability emphasized in part by a quotation from the Sex Pistols' song "Problems":

Forget the
ideas of the multitudes
Let's let our
own become
the problem:2.

We'd never start to
pine the
rascal's jew
and what is
his latest
prob-e-lem?[13]

Where Walt Whitman in "Song of Myself" declaimed, "I am large, I contain multitudes,"[14] Arwulf urged readers to dwindle Whitman's "multitudes" down to an implicitly unpleasant coterie of "our own." Don't care, don't bother, don't "pine"—these were the negations that determined the tenor of these two stanzas and the poem as a whole. That these negations were impelled in part by a punk posture is evident in the final line of the second stanza—"prob-e-lem" was clearly an effort to transcribe the way Johnny Rotten enunciated the word "problem" as a three-syllable epithet at the end of the song "Problems" featured in the Sex Pistols' LP *Never Mind the Bollocks*—"*prob-e-lem, prob-e-lem, prob-e-lem, prob-e-lem*," Rotten croaked repeatedly, relentlessly. Arwulf's poem was an intertextual punk event, as the ideal reader familiar with the song "Problems" layered Rotten's own dismal lyrics over Arwulf's. "Too many problems why am I here?!" Rotten asked, going on to claim scornfully, "I can see / There's something wrong with you / But what do *you* expect *me* to do?" As Rotten answered his own rhetorical question by making it clear that he was not going to do anything to solve your/our contemptible *prob-e-lems* ("the problem is *you*! Watcha gonna do?" Rotten sneered), so Arwulf told his readers to "forget" about the idealized other. Arwulf's text drew on punk to refuse and mock the Whitmanic poem's attempts to formalize a universal identity.[15]

Koff's editors worked hard to undermine the heightened status of the poetic lyric by invoking Rotten and punk throughout the magazine's first issue. A subscription advertisement featuring a doctored image of Rotten wearing a T-shirt bearing the slogan "Consumptive Poets League Lower East Side Chapter" proved an opportunity to take a swipe at the "Rimbaldian script" that by this late date had become something of a cliché. The accompanying text explained how "Poor Johnny has never owned a book by Rimbaud in his life! He had to pawn his X-rays to buy his t-shirt! You can help poets like Johnny by subscribing to KOFF at only $3 for the next three issues. Consumptive Poets League t-shirts at $8, or both [a bargain!] for $10."[16] In the same issue a series of quotations from figures including Garcia Lorca, Mayakovsky, Byron, and Paul Verlaine organized under the title "Konsumptive Kwotes" ended with a Johnny Rotten bon mot: "How would you make me look like a bigger cunt than I already am? The joke's on you." Quoting directly from Johnny Rotten's song "Bodies," Maria Mancini—who was in fact a literary alter ego created by Nauen and Dubris to project their own playfully hostile attitudes and ideas about punk and the New York School—wrote in her poem "Men": "I'm not an animo / I'm not an animal / I'm not an animo / I'm not an animo / I'm not an animal."[17] These moves, interestingly

Poor Johnny has never owned a book by Rimbaud
in his life! He had to pawn his X-rays to buy his
t-shirt! You can help poets like Johnny by subscribing
to KOFF at only $3 for the next three issues. Con-
sumptive Poets League t-shirts ar $8, or both
(a bargain!) for $10.

Consumptive Poets League
312 E. 9th St #14
NY, NY 10003
Send manuscripts (SASE) and centerfold photos to
above address.

Figure 7.2 Consumptive Poets League subscription advertisement, *KOFF* magazine.
Source: Copyright © Elinor Nauen, Maggie Dubris, 1977.

enough, went hand in hand with the editors' assault on their New York School brethren. While Arwulf was alluding to Whitman, his characterization of company as, at the very least, problematic and vaguely dishonest can also be read as a critique of the very poetics of sociability informing so much of O'Hara's and related writers' works.

This critique became overt in *Koff* 2. While engaged with the New York School ethos (the editors made sure to acknowledge "benefit readers" of *Koff* including Ted Berrigan and Alice Notley, and Ron Padgett's translations of the New York School's favorite Frenchman, Pierre Reverdy,[18] were included in the issue), it was clear that *Koff* was not simply going to serve as yet another belated "I do this, I do that" poetry mimeo, as the following "Letters to the Editor" letter articulated rather explicitly:

> Dear KOFFers,
>
> Hello, I am president (national) of the International Fuck Frank O'hara Movement, & it has come to our attention that you have misappropriated & other-wise ripped off our slogan, demeaning attitudes, & so forth. However, in the interests of killing off vestigial interest in this (faggot) & paean of the "people" (unverified) we wd gladly join forces for a giant burn-in', or, a suck-THAT-cock-baybee day, or screw you too you little greeps & if you think yr gonna get away w/ that kinda crap well you gottanother fuckin THINK comin & I for one (2) hope it comes SOON & then you drop dead too you little bastards.
>
> Thank you for yr kind attention to this problem of mutual concern to all of us here at the Baptist Convention, & hoping for a speedy resolution of the matter.[19]

Signed "Ms. M. Mancini," it would be too easy to dismiss this letter as nothing more than a mean-spirited homophobic joke. As serious in its own way as O'Hara's jokey but profoundly influential pseudomanifesto "Personism" was, "Mancini's" letter assailed downtown poets' assumptions that all they had to do to attain poetry cred was write about whom they had sex with or what they ate and drank. "Mancini" was in this sense echoing Patti Smith's own complaints to Victor Bockris (see chapter 5) about the very ease with which O'Hara's style could be commodified and oversimplified.

"Mancini" (in *Koff* 3) continued her argument with O'Hara by publishing a parody of O'Hara's much-loved poem "Having a Coke with You." (Dubris and Nauen recall that the poet Simon Schuchat authored the parody and that Schuchat gladly went in on the "Mancini" hoax.) Where O'Hara wrote in a high cosmopolitan style that "Having a Coke with You" "is even more fun than going to San Sebastian, Irún, Hendaye, Biarritz, Bayonne / or being sick to my stomach on the Travesera de Gracia in Barcelona,"[20] "Mancini" countered that "Having a Coke with You"

> is better than being thrown off the Orient Express
> at top speed at midnight at the border and it's raining
> getting beaten on the ground and tossed into filthy Turkish prison cell
> where the guards piss on my sleeping hands and the others
> hold me down while they gang fuck me with a splintery broom handle
> and I accidentally bite off my tongue trying not to scream.[21]

Koff editors delighted in this misbehavior, reveling in the refutation of poetic lineage. "We almost automatically rejected everything that came from our elders," Nauen points out. "O'Hara was held in such reverence that we almost automatically had to make fun of him. He was before our time, personally, so we didn't have any compunctions." Dubris concurred:

> I admired our near-contemporaries (in whom I include Paul Violi, Bill Zavatsky, Ron Padgett) and of course the poets who began with us. But I didn't have a sense of history, and I felt like O'Hara, in addition to apparently having been beatified for getting run over by a dune buggy, was responsible for a lot of bad imitators. All of whom invoked him. It was also largely a joke—it seemed like he was the perfect person to make fun of, as he was dead, none of us ever met him, and he seemed a sacred cow. Remember we were quite young when we put out *Koff*.[22]

With texts like "Mancini's" "letter" and Arwulf's poem, *Koff* clearly set out to challenge what Dubris and Nauen perceived to be an increasingly lame, derivative style. O'Hara's approach had, in the hands of his young followers, arguably become more a compulsive tic than an interesting poetic deployment of quotidian and demotic modes. This did not mean the New York School had ceased to be important for the writers collected within *Koff*. Take the opening lines to "Bill Kushner," a collaborative poem written by Yuki Hartman, Kushner, Bill Duckworth, and Mike Slater. Clearly playing off of John Ashbery's, Kenneth Koch's, and related writers' collaborative poems, "Bill Kushner" was marked by easily recognizable tropes—the emphasis on lightheartedness, vaguely abject naughtiness, etc.:

> Bill Kushner goes to the bathroom.
> One more day to live, Bill Kushner thinks.
> In that wet angry mirror that holds up the future
> Before our naked eye, Bill Kushner sees
> Something terrifying in the landscape of
> His pubic crater. Bill Kushner breaks down
> Instantly and just falls apart into
> Thousands of weepy pieces that fall nervously
> To the floor, there they chatter among one another
> In voices loud and strident.[23]

Given that readers wouldn't necessarily know who wrote what line, the self-referential humor in lines like "Bill Kushner breaks down / Instantly and just falls apart into / Thousands of weepy pieces" was pretty self-evident. Kushner as a lyric speaking subject has been dispersed, has fallen apart in the textual stew of the collaborative poem. While the poem has its rapscallion charm, it is also, years after Ashbery and Koch's *Locus Solus*, Berrigan's *C*, and Warsh and Waldman's *Angel Hair*, an instantly recognizable New York School piece. The presence of poems like this in *Koff* suggests its editors weren't quite ready to forsake the poem as a vehicle for entry into and signpost for a specific poetic community.

Yet as much as a debonair undifferentiated friendship was celebrated in works like "Bill Kushner," there was always an Arwulf, a Rotten, or, in *Koff* 2, a Rachel Walling to present an ornery counternarrative. "In the city I drink and take drugs," Rachel Walling wrote in her poem "Washing Machine." Situating herself in O'Hara's pleasure-soaked polis, however, Walling almost immediately contested the assumed joviality of such activity: "a city light begins to show / a bare bulb behind a haze / I take baths every day / I love my friends from a distance / It's taken me a lifetime to get this way."[24] Where O'Hara framed the poem as an intimate event—"the poem is at last between two persons instead of two pages," O'Hara wrote in "Personism"[25]—Walling and her *Koff* friends, pushed and prodded by the sounds and words of punk, confronted too-easy jollity head on with sneers, curse words, and unabashed,

Figure 7.3 *Koff* T-shirt, issue 4.
Source: Copyright © Elinor Nauen and Maggie Dubris.

straightforward expressions of loneliness and alienation. "It sucks. / I have no reason to be anything,"[26] Maggie Dubris stated flatly in her poem "They Said That He Was Bad." Or perhaps the final words on the final page of the penultimate issue of *Koff* said it best: "FUCK OFF TIL NEXT ISSUE."

And what of that next issue? No issue. Instead, a T-shirt. Dispensing with poetry entirely, *Koff* 4 began and ended as a blast of punk style. Featured on the front of the T-shirt were, as Nauen characterized them, "the dead poets who didn't get buried": "St Pound," "St Rimbaud," "St Williams," and a polyce-phalic monster composed of the heads of Allen Ginsberg and Frank O'Hara that Dubris and Nauen simply christened "St Marks."[27] All the poets were emblazoned with bullet marks to the head, neck, or face. The message was clear. Poets including Ginsberg and O'Hara had, according to Donald Allen in his seminal anthology *The New American Poetry*, "shown one common characteristic: a total rejection of all those qualities typical of academic verse. Following the practice and precepts of Ezra Pound and William Carlos Williams, it has built on their achievements and gone on to evolve new conceptions of the poem."[28] Those "new conceptions" found a very public face and stage at the Poetry Project at St. Mark's Church, where Beat and New York School aesthetics were embodied in over a decade's worth of poetry readings and parties. *Koff* marked a break from all that—avant-garde poetry saints from Rimbaud on were no longer that compelling to the younger writers making a new scene. It was time, *Koff* made clear, to kill your idols.

"It Was a Biker Bar!": Eileen Myles and CBGB

For Eileen Myles, an avid reader of *Koff*, the journal's strange pairing of literature and punk rock made sense. Recounting a poetry reading group in Boston that she attended in 1974 before she moved to New York, Myles describes a participant "dressed in all black with a medallion [who] said in this kind of ponderous way that her work was influenced by the New York rock poet Patti Smith. And I just—those words seen next to each other, I'd never heard of that but it sounded so perfect."[29] Smith's music found a home in Myles's poetry and prose. Myles's short story "Robin," for example, features a sex scene in which Robin, the narrator's lover, sits on the narrator's face. Describing what she thought was the taste and texture of come on her lips and in her mouth, the narrator moves on to register how the come was actually

> pee and now I had drank it for the first time. I swallowed some, but then no I don't really want to drink piss. I wiped the edges of my mouth and then kissed her. I think she said I'm sorry but grinned at me wiping my face. Do you have

any music she said. Take a look—the tapes are on the refrigerator. I lay on the bed, fascinated by the acrid taste of piss, yet horrified at the inadequacies of my tape collection. Da, *duh-duh*, Da, *duh-duh* came the opening notes of [Patti Smith's song] "Kimberly" and Robin walked naked across the length of my apartment like she was the real Patti Smith.[30]

The New York School as it developed at St. Mark's, with its innumerable odes to joy, casualness, and collaboration, was forced to make way for a markedly punk-inflected new style that went even further then the first wave of CBGB musicians did in foregrounding vulgarity, base intensity, raw passion—piss in the mouth without any attendant rhetorical fireworks, wacky jokes, or poetic justifications.

Little remarked upon in accounts of New York's downtown literary history is the fact that Hilly Kristal, CBGB's owner/proprietor, organized regular poetry readings in the bar during the same period that he opened the door to Richard Hell, Tom Verlaine, and other punk originators. "Today, fan-boys need only hearken to the Ramones' 1974 CBGBs debut and an oft-documented story unfurls," Brandon Stosuy rightly points out, adding crucially that "Eileen Myles's first New York reading at CBGBs also occurred in 1974."[31] Readings at CBGB, as Myles recalls, were based on a hierarchical model similar to St. Mark's. Open readings were open to all comers, but coveted solo readings were by invitation only. According to Myles, CBGB

> was a very funky place at the time . . . it was still kind of . . . it was a biker bar! There were big dogs walking around, and they had a reading scheduled before the band. . . . The bands would go on late, the readings would go on earlier. . . . There was an open mike, and if you were good they would invite you back to do a feature. . . . I had read at various open mikes but my first feature was at CBGB. . . . Hilly was always there at the poetry events, very supportive of my work.[32]

Myles enjoyed CBGB in part because of the way the place denoted a break, in her eyes, from second-generation New York School poets too comfortable and invested in relatively bourgeois artistic pursuits and lifestyles:

> As a poet in my twenties, when I would talk to older poets like Ted Berrigan, Alice Notley, Peter Schjeldahl, they were always like, "Get involved with the art

world." Don't be like a whore, junkie, alcoholic poet on the Lower East Side, you know, become something, get involved with the art world. That was like, a proper host to feed on. But the thing was, we were all involved with music! What we saw ourselves as was we were the people without bands. The whole move from, like, Patti Smith to her band, from Richard [Hell] to the band, it was like an extra step that plenty of people tried to take.[33]

This did not mean that Myles necessarily looked up to Smith and related punk scribes as poets per se. "There was also a silent or not-so-silent critique on my and my poet friends' part that we were the poets and Patti Smith wasn't. . . . Everyone loved who she was, but we all . . . nobody wanted to read the books of Patti Smith . . . that was for kids in the suburbs. . . . Everybody understood that her work was not on the page."[34] Dismissive of Smith's writing, Myles nevertheless highlights the significance of being part of the social text defining the musicians' world, a world of glamorous dissolution, romanticized ugliness, and populist possibility.

All the poets had favorite bands. . . . Everybody followed a band. . . . I loved the Talking Heads, and Blondie lived in my building. . . . Also, we all lived in the same vile, dangerous, junkie neighborhood, and there were plenty of poets who were doing heroin. . . . [Musicians and poets] were next to each other in the Kiev restaurant, that was open twenty-four hours, it was like beautiful Ukrainian waitresses, and bands, and every junkie and poet . . . that was what you did when you were up speeding all night, you'd go to the Kiev. . . . Everybody was eating at these restaurants that we all saw each other in.[35]

While very few poets could make the leap from performance poet to rock star—and while poets and musicians may not have actually talked that much to one another even if they were sitting side by side in the Kiev—Myles insists, "I think that . . . the *feeling* . . . we *felt* affiliated . . . they [the musicians] felt affiliated with us, we felt affiliated with them. . . . Robert Mapplethorpe was like, 'Do you have a band?' and I said, 'No,' and he said, 'Why?' *What else could you be doing?* was the implication."[36]

Myles's heralding poets, musicians, and a "dangerous junkie neighborhood" as a new and exciting scene points to the actual uses musicians and poets made of their environment. By 1979, the East Village was regularly described in apocalyptic terms. An article in the local *East Village Eye* described "a bright Thursday morning on Avenue B," the sun shining on "rubble-strewn lots," "empty shells of burnt out tenement buildings," and

> blackened interiors that are now filled with rotting garbage and piles of debris. Block after block, from 14th Street to Houston Street, from Avenue A to Avenue D, one can see, smell, and feel the devastation of the neighborhood. Many of the residents are gone now. Some remain, though, trying to hold on to the homes that have not yet burned. Others will burn their buildings down themselves so that they will be moved out of the area by the City.[37]

While we should be careful not to make *too* much out of Myles's first reading taking place at CBGB,[38] we should at least consider how she characterized the filth and noise typical of the Lower East Side as she developed her poetic persona. "The city was in despair, but we *loved* the city in the '70s because it was a mess . . . that's why we loved it," Myles exulted.[39] And as Myles loved the city because it was trashy, she and her fellow poets

> loved the Poetry Project before it burned down because it was *dirty* . . . you could smoke cigarettes, you could crush them out with your feet on the floor, you could bring your beer cans in, Alice Notley's workshop was awash in drugs! We would bring beer cans and amphetamine on Friday nights and pass around the pills, give Alice pills, we were all ripped sitting there . . . and the thing that was hard about the institutionality of the Poetry Project after the fire was that suddenly it was pristine . . . all these rules, all these things you couldn't do.[40]

Myles, aghast at the polite turn St. Mark's was taking after the fire, would begin to create a body of work in the late 1970s and 1980s that rhymed as much with New York's punk scene and the decrepit neighborhood she lived in as it did with the New York School "Manhattan Museum of Modern Art artworld cocktail ballet scene" she had been bequeathed.

Laughing at Poetry in the Laundromat

In the summer of 1977, the year Richard Hell and the Voidoid's *Blank Generation*, Television's *Marquee Moon*, the Clash's eponymous album, the Sex Pistols' *Never Mind the Bollocks*, and the Ramones' *Rocket to Russia* were all released, Myles got some of her friends together and arranged to have them filmed reading their poems in a basement Laundromat in SoHo.[41] As she recalls it:

> The Laundromat reading was my idea . . . it was my Laundromat in SoHo. . . . You would sit there and do your laundry and think, "It would be amazing to do a reading here," and I happened to know the lady who ran the Laundromat, and she said that we could do it an hour before it opened. . . . I of course expected something a lot more Robert Wilson and minimal, but as soon as you put the poets in the room everybody started goofing and throwing things and making jokes about. . . . I was the person passing around amphetamines so everybody came in one state and became more excessive. . . . I had the idea, and I was like, "We should do this we should do this," and people I knew were also, "We should do this we should do this." I hooked up with Bob Holman, who, the thing that Bob is really great about, he's like [claps hands] "SATURDAY." He had $20 to get the tape, and Rose Lesniak and Barbara Barg had the camera, so they shot it.[42]

Arguably a minor event in the history of literary New York, the Laundromat reading nevertheless revealed a young group of poets undermining their own genre by performing like iconoclastic punks. Myles certainly looked the part—sockless, wearing dirty sneakers, jeans, and a distressed T-shirt, she was filmed at one point during the reading pouring ketchup into a laundry machine. Some of the poets arrived initially on skateboards, kicking their boards up just before walking down the few stairs into the dark and dingy space. Some took up positions lying down on top of the machines; others started dutifully doing laundry. No one was introduced as, one by one, poets simply grabbed the mike being passed around and read from their work. At the end of Myles's performance of a poem ending "What is blue? What is yellow? What is your favorite kind of music?,"[43] Myles looked at the camera with unbridled hostility, threw her papers on the floor, and stomped off-camera—the next reading began with a poet slipping a banana into a washing machine.

The poets in the Laundromat treated their and their friends' readings as jokes, particularly when the content of the poems being performed pointed overtly to the de rigueur literary tradition inherited by the writers associated with St. Mark's. For example, a section of the video documented the poet Rose Lesniak reading one of her works excitedly. The assembled reaction, however, was antithetical to her performance style. Painfully blasé, the other writers in the Laundromat ignored Lesniak. They hammed it up for the roving camera by variously stuffing their laundry into the washing machines, picking up magazines that were lying around, and drinking cans of beer. After Lesniak proclaimed, "Poetry is in the lungs of *all of us*,"[44] the assembled poets finally responded—not with applause but with an overwhelming burst of hacking and coughing.

While their response pointed fairly literally to the content of the poem, the poets' expulsions also suggest a literary and social critique. Consider Charles Olson's seminal 1950 essay "Projective Verse," practically a liturgical script for New York's downtown, performance-oriented poets. In it, Olson thundered:

> And the line comes (I swear it) from the breath, from the breathing of the man who writes, at the moment that he writes, and thus is, it is here that, the daily work, the WORK, gets in, for only he, the man who writes, can declare, at every moment, the line its metric and its ending—where its breathing, shall come to, termination.[45]

Emphasizing how breath determines the shape and form of the poetic line—and by extension how poetry was in essence an embodied activity— "Projective Verse" provided a theoretical ground for the kind of live, utopian, and spontaneous poetry-performance aesthetics that characterized Beat and New York poetry reading scenes throughout the 1950s and 1960s.

The Laundromat poets' response to a reiteration of Olson's breath-based poetics ("Poetry is in the lungs of all of us!") was one of total mockery that, given the punky aura oozing out of this literally underground space and the playful aggression exhibited throughout the video, was analogous to the way punks (especially in England) spat at band members as both a show of appreciation and derogation. The Laundromat poets refused (albeit elliptically) not just the authority of Olson but the very authority embedded in a male-centered, purportedly natural breath-based poetics. The Laundromat reading, in other words, was a great big fuck you to intensity, to the purported immediacy of a performed poem, to *poetry itself*, even as it was a celebration of it. Or, as Myles put it, "you had to kind of laugh at poetry and debase it, in order to occupy it."[46]

This debasement took place both in terms of performance and on the page itself. Myles's poem "On the Death of Robert Lowell," from her 1981 book *A Fresh Young Voice from the Plains*, reiterated O'Hara's complaint that Lowell expected readers "to be interested [in his poetry] because he's supposed to be so upset" and suggested an alternative that aligned Lowell positively *against* O'Hara's suspicion of sincerity:

O, I don't give a shit.
He was an old white haired man
Insensate beyond belief and
Filled with much anxiety about his imagined
Pain. Not that I'd know
I hate fucking wasps.
The guy was a loon.
Signed up for Spring Semester at Macleans
A really lush retreat among pines and
Hippy attendants. Ray Charles also
once rested there.
So did James Taylor . . .
The famous, as we know, are nuts.
Take Robert Lowell.
The old white haired coot.
Fucking dead.[47]

While its title promised elegy, the poem's first line appeared obviously and vulgarly to flout readers' generic expectations. "O, I don't give a shit" might seem to resonate more with any number of nihilist punk claims—say, the Ramones' insistent barks of "I don't care," Richard Hell's "I can take it or leave it each time," the Dead Boys' "I'm so sick of romance / And I'm gettin' real sick of you"[48]—than it does with conventional elegies. Yet we should be careful *not* to read this poem as a straightforward repudiation of elegiac convention generally and Robert Lowell's confessional style specifically. Rather, Myles's opening the line with the exclamation "O" hinted at the possibility that Myles's punk O'Haraisms masked an actual *affection* for the "old white-haired coot."

Beginning a poem with "O" is typical of what Jeremy Prynne calls "emphatical expression" tied both to poetic apostrophe considered broadly (when the poet addresses the often inanimate or mythical other) and "in the impassioned utterance of much Romantic poetry." Similarly, if perhaps more subtly than the annunciatory "O," is when the "O" is designed as a "more inward-facing or solitary figure of exclamation, in which sorrow or wondering admiration are expressed in utterance pitched up in elevated contemplation but not addressed directly either towards surrogate recipients inside the poem or towards an acknowledged reader outside it."[49] Myles's "O" had no obvious addressee—it was a desperately lonely interjection that served to qualify the adolescent insolence of "I don't give a shit" and subsequent punk-inflected lines with real elegiac weight. Her "O," linked allusively to Wordsworth's, to Shelley's, to Keats's "O's," suggested a surprising alignment with and sympathy for Lowell despite Myles's echoing a New York School–connected coterie distaste for Lowell's uncool confessional exhibitionism. Myles relied on genre conventions even as she debased elegy with "shit," "nuts," and "fucking."

Punk should not be swept aside as we recover the pathos generated by Myles's "O." "On the Death of Robert Lowell" was as much a complication of elegiac literary tradition as it was a sophisticated reapplication of punk's strategy of insistent negation to poetry. Repeated over and over again (think once more to the Ramones' "I don't care / I don't care / I don't care / I don't care"), punk's purported negativity becomes its opposite, affirmation. That is, to repeat "I don't care" over and over again is to reveal you care very much. Similarly, opening a poem with the emphatical "O" and then defiling the expected mournfulness of elegy with lines like "I hate fucking wasps" is to witness a poet memorializing her elder brutally—the elegy as genre, informed by punk style, incorporated a new and startling set of expressions and possibilities in Myles's poem.

"On the Death of Robert Lowell," while funny, was born of rage and sympathy. Myles, like Lowell, knew very well what it was like to be "filled with anxiety," alcoholic, a "loon"—her often thinly disguised autobiographical writing, as Terry Castle rightly points out, was a testament to such awareness:

As anyone familiar with Myles's precocious, punked out, exquisitely risible oeuvre will know, her aggression is inevitably tempered by a paradoxical fellow feeling. The poet's own histrionic travails—with alcoholism, abusive homosexual relationships, mental institutions, and the ravages of a Boston Irish working-class childhood . . . link her with the coots and the loons.[50]

In a poem that on the surface seemed merely to reiterate the same kind of hostility toward Lowell that O'Hara, Gerard Malanga, Richard Hell, Lou Reed, and so many other downtown figures expressed, Myles's punk poetics were employed to refresh both the elegy as genre and to challenge Lowell's downtown fuddy-duddy reputation.

Myles and Schuyler

Turning back to the New York School, how, in the end, did punk musicians and associated writers read, love, argue with, and incorporate it into their work? Myles was openly "inspired by the poetry of John Ashbery and James Schuyler."[51] Schuyler's approach to writing, from his often straightforward, descriptive style of New York City streetscapes and rural idylls to his characteristically short, skinny lines, found a form in Myles's own verse. Yet Myles nevertheless contested Schuyler's work repeatedly. As with so many of the writers following in the wake of the second-generation New York School poets, punk in part provided Myles with ammunition to assault Schuyler's urban pastoral style,[52] or what Myles referred to as Schuyler's "values that seemed so 'Country Living.'"[53]

Myles, after all, knew what she was up against, having basically lived with Schuyler for about half a year. In an interview about her relationship to Schuyler, Myles recalls

I started working for him I think in May of '79 and then it was pretty constant for 5 or 6 months. By constant I mean like 7 days a week. . . . Basically my main function *really* was to give Jimmy his pills, because he had burned his previous room down by taking them all at once. So that was the deal, that was why I was there 7 days a week initially. I kind of invented this position of a person who was with Jimmy which continued long after I left. So I was there for 5 or 6 months pretty constantly, and then after that I handed the job on to Tom Carey and Helena Hughes, and then I'd just kinda fill in for them and just slowly became a friend of Jimmy's. It was just kind of a quick, intense marriage.[54]

Myles's presence in Schuyler's life entered Schuyler's own poetry. In his long poem "A Few Days," for example, Schuyler answers the question "Is that girl who comes and takes care of you your niece?" with "No, Eileen

Myles is / my assistant: she comes and makes my breakfast and lunch, runs errands / to the grocery store, the P.O., the bank, mails letters and always arrives with / that morning's *Times*."[55] Surprisingly, punk rock was also a tangible, if marginal, presence in Schuyler's poem as well—it was in the air: "Exhilaration: one night we took the toboggan and went to Emery Park, where / there was a long, long slide, on which we sped into the night. 'I'll / wash your face in the snow!' 'get away from me, you punk rock rabbit.'"[56] Schuyler also sang the praises of the Chelsea Hotel, his home from 1979, when the hotel was still favored lodging among the punk glitterati following Nancy Spungen's murder there in October 1978. (Her boyfriend at the time, the Sex Pistols' bassist Sid Vicious, was charged with her murder but died in prison before he took the stand.) "This old hotel is well built: if / you hold your breath and make a wish you'll meet Virgil Thomson in the elevator / or a member of a punk rock band."[57] Note how Schuyler did not so much as broach a distinction between his subjects in these gentle lines. Creating a sympathetic link between the modernist composer Thomson and the CBGB types now calling the Chelsea Hotel home, Schuyler's approach eliminated the division between popular and "serious" culture. While Schuyler by no means adopted a punk posture in his poetry, he at least made space for these various figures to jostle alongside one another comfortably in the urbane contours of the Chelsea.

That said, while Myles and Schuyler had an amicable friendship and valued each other's writing—"I got to show him my poems," Myles recalls, "and I got to see new poems of his, so that it was all those things. . . . I had massive respect for him. And it was reciprocated, he was very generous and admiring towards me and my poems and it was important to me"[58]—it was precisely Schuyler's gentleness, modesty, and decorum that Myles battered in her own work. Schuyler's elision of the city as loathsome and desperate territory, his fusing "urban and rural atmospheres, despite his recurring personal crises,"[59] is what Myles countered. Punk taught Myles trash was good. In the face of Schuyler's attempts to domesticate 1970s New York by sketching "pastoral solutions, plotting the coordinates of his 'inner geography' against a harsher reality with subtle shifts of rural and urban imagery,"[60] Myles refused the comfort of the pastoral sassily by foregrounding and privileging the urban over nature.

Contesting "Schuyler's urban idyll,"[61] Myles took direct aim at the pastoral mode. Actively and humorously polluting what Timothy Gray terms "the natural currents in the New York School" even as she employed an O'Haraesque disarming address, Myles went one step further by aligning her antipastoralism with a scathing critique of sociability and easygoing friendship, as we see in the opening stanzas of Myles's poem "Exploding the Spring Mystique":

Good Morning, World! Captain Eileen here
At her little morning desk
Dying to tell you at the crack of dawn
How dearly she hates it
How Spring truly sucks.

Here we have it outside my morning window
Birds twittering, buds newly greening on perky branches
    "Tweet," another fucking bird.

And I had to go through a whole night to get here.
That's the part that's really hard to swallow.
I had to lie awake for hours thinking of how I hate just about
Every man, woman and child who walks the face of this earth
Myself included, I find self-hate extremely motivating[62]

Myles creates a willfully inane landscape here in which the pastoral is practically regurgitated by the poet, who is determined to reclaim nihilism as a productive force. Debasing Eliot's opening line to *The Waste Land* ("April is the cruelest month") by following through on its implications without resort to heightened rhetoric of any kind, Myles insists instead on a poetics that aligns itself to the angry Day-Glo style characteristic of 1970s New York–based punk, in opposition to Schuyler's more genteel vision. Schuyler's tallying and praising nature's signs outside his window evoke what Emerson in his essay "Nature" described as an "occult relation between man and the vegetable." For Schuyler, following Emerson, nature enabled the poet to transcend his ego and connect intimately to the external world. "Among white lilac trusses, green-gold spaces of sunlit grass," Schuyler wrote in his poem "May 24th or So," continuing: "The shade side of a clothes pole, dark innards of a light-violet shell. / Everything trembles / everything shakes / in the great sifter."[63] The sun, the wind, the dear and darling April bud, shimmered over and redeemed the appreciated but ultimately provisional city: "April what an ice-cold promise / I saw a cherry almost in bloom today / one of its five magnolias opened all its buds / wide and pointing at the sun / going down in front of City Hall."[64]

Myles's rejection of the pastoral—"Spring truly sucks"—read in the context of her relationship to Schuyler and her contestation of the Gospel according to the New York School—seemed all the more like a vivid and overt break with the Poetry Project scene.[65] Even Myles's identifying spring as the most loathed season, followed by her refusal of sociability, appeared like a retort to Schuyler's invocations of his friends as they emanated out of his insistent odes to the seasons. In the face of Schuyler's pastoral tranquility, Myles was nothing if not direct: "Tweet—there goes another fucking bird." As Myles put it in talking about "Exploding the Spring Mystique,"

> the poem was definitely rejecting [Schuyler's] influence. Were you just going to take that on and try and be the blanket in the car, or are were you going to try and blow up the car? It did seem that was the way to do it. And a line like ["Tweet—there goes another fucking bird"] was part of it; that was how it felt like we were part of this community of musicians and filmmakers. Everybody in the neighborhood, if they weren't in a band, they were making Super 8 film, Scott B, Beth B., and Barbara Ess, all those people who were half music, half you know . . . Jim Jarmusch, who worked at St. Mark's movie theater, everyone remembers him as that guy who sold popcorn.[66]

Punk music, punk films, punk popcorn—this was the new scene. Poetry changed with it. Myles's "Exploding the Spring Mystique" echoed punk figures' rejection of 1960s hippie culture—a culture that, as any number of images showing second-generation poets in beads, bangles, flowing skirts, and long hair attest—held sway even at St. Mark's. As Richard Hell put it in his recollections of attending the first Central Park Human Be-In in March 1967:

> People were standing around eyeing each other and some of them were wearing little bells on their clothes. There was face paint and flowers and pot smoking. Some kids were waving their arms and singing. . . . Drugs were a theme, and people chanted about love. . . . Like George Bush's flag waving after the World Trade Center attacks, the Be-In was more repellent for its assumption of an axiomatic underlying basis of unity than for the dubious underlying idea itself.[67]

This distrust of "unity," similar to Lydia Lunch's "barefoot hippie chick" putdown of Patti Smith, was powerful and funny in large part because it was yoked to an over-the-top misanthropy and skepticism that characterized punk's response to 1960s pastoral counterculture. Consider Myles's lines alongside Allen Ginsberg's term "flower power," which the poet coined sometime around 1965. Imagine Myles's poem as it might have played alongside the street-oriented Bread & Puppet Theater, handing out flowers and balloons to its audiences, or the now-famous 1967 "Another Mother for Peace" organization's logo—a sunflower with the words "War is not healthy for children and other living things," which ended up on bumper stickers, key rings, and posters across the United States. The hope that simply invoking pastoral signs might generate feelings of peace and love were part of what Myles and her punk neighbors were resolute in condemning as hopelessly self-deluding and insincere.

No more easy friendship. Or rather, always and forever question sociability, the belief in the laid-back, name-dropping poem as vehicle for community. "Sure, I hate my friends and they hate me and there's no one around to / Fuck except the ones who won't fuck me and they like to torture me," Myles spat in the third-to-last stanza of "Exploding the Spring Mystique." Crucially, however, Myles's take on this potentially dismal friendless, sexless scenario was positive: "And I like it—my poems keep getting better and better."[68] The fantasy of always being at the party had made way for the reality of the artist's relative solitude as it played out in a collapsing city. However, this solitude thankfully was leavened by caustic humor and a continuing commitment to art—just not the art of the longhairs writing before Myles. The church had burned down.

EIGHT

"Sit on My Face!"

Dennis Cooper, the First Punk Poet

DENNIS COOPER CAME late to the party. "I only lived in New York for four years total, from '83 to '85, and then again from '87 to '90,"[1] he told his pal Eileen Myles, adding later, "I guess [it was] while I was living [in the East Village] that the whole New York School dream began to collapse or run out of gas."[2] It wasn't just that the heyday of Ashbery and O'Hara, Berrigan and Mayer was over. First-wave punk was finished, no wave was dead. Yet the lure of the New York School of poets and the 1970s punk scene was enough to bring Cooper east.

Readers scanning through the March 19, 1985, issue of the gay magazine *The Advocate* may have lingered over Cooper's provocatively titled article "The East Village and Its Gay Ways." In part addressing Myles's tenure as director of the Poetry Project at St. Mark's Church, Cooper took the opportunity to connect homosexuality and downtown poetry to a "punk aesthetic":

> Poetry has been a major force in the area for decades, centered largely around the Poetry Project, a literary/arts organization housed in St. Mark's Church. The Project's current director is Eileen Myles, a poet and lesbian in her early 30s, who originally developed her art by giving readings and attending workshops at the church.... In Myles' view, there are a number of distinctions that set the lesbians of her generation apart from those of previous ones. Lower East Side lesbians have been influenced in a very positive way by the emergence of the punk aesthetic, she feels.[3]

Figure 8.1 Dennis Cooper and Alice Notley poetry reading flyer.
Source: Fales Library and Special Collections, Dennis Cooper Papers, Box 11, Folder 802.

Cooper, a gay man whose poetry and prose ranges from mild representations of pin-up crushes to detailed depictions of extreme forms of sadomasochistic intergenerational sex, had a lot in common with those "Lower East Side lesbians" who loved punk as much as they did poetry. As he remembered, "Growing up in LA, and being heavily influenced by poets and musicians and performance artists associated with Downtown New York, the scene there seemed like a dream situation to me . . . my ideas and feelings about it are kind of inextricable from my early longing to be there."[4] Cooper had firsthand knowledge of those downtown musicians he referred to. As Diarmuid Hester notes:

> Cooper was in touch with the New York punk scene as early as 1974, having corresponded with Patti Smith over a shared interest in Rimbaud's poetry. In 1976 he traveled to England where he would experience punk first-hand. In London on July 4 he caught The Ramones supporting The Flamin' Groovies at London's Roundhouse, a gig that is widely recognized as a pivotal moment in the development of the United Kingdom's punk scene.[5]

A college student in Pasadena who discovered Ted Berrigan, Ron Padgett, Bernadette Mayer, Joe Brainard, and related writers in 1972 and who, a few years later, pogoed gleefully to the Ramones, Cooper was quick to see resonances between those writers' works and the world he occupied, which, as he described it to Myles, "revolved around rock music and drugs and rebellion and poetry."[6] Cooper told Myles:

> The more I found out about [the New York School poets] and their scene of mimeo poetry magazines and St. Mark's Church and all that, the more New York became an ideal to me . . . so there were the poets, and then the New York Dolls and Patti Smith came along, and I discovered Robert Wilson and Richard Foreman and the Wooster Group, and this picture of an ideal, incredibly fertile scene entered my head, and that was it. I was totally in love. . . . I was already into Warhol's films and the Velvet Underground by the time I found the poets, and it all seemed connected to me, which I guess it was.[7]

Cooper today is now better known as a novelist, though his punk stance, developed initially when he identified as a poet, remains a defining feature of his popular and critical reception. In fact, academics throughout the

1990s and beyond organized his and his fellow writers' works under the banners "Blank Generation Fiction" and "blank fiction," rubrics indebted directly to Richard Hell's song "Blank Generation."[8] What is lost in such a taxonomy, obviously, is the fact that Cooper's punk style had its origins in Cooper's *poetry*. How, then, was New York School writing and punk connected in Cooper's early lyrics? Did Cooper, like Myles, use punk to challenge the cultural capital commonly accorded to poetry? Was the latent literariness in punk recuperated in Cooper's verse? Similar to Myles's writing, can we understand Cooper's work as, in part, an argument with the New York School as it was an extension and complication of the pop culture–saturated second-generation scene? By 1978, after all, Blondie, Johnny Rotten, and other punk heroes that Cooper addressed within his lines of verse had become internationally known and were no longer underground. Cooper's evocations of these artists, combined with his markedly queer and even pedophilic paeans, made his poems irrevocably, unavoidably political and challenged conventional understandings of how a poem should act and sound.

Before the word "punk" was understood as music, and despite growing up in a California suburb, Cooper was already fusing poetry with the anger, glitter, and power of underground pop. Reading through his first book, *The Terror of Earrings* (1973), it seems clear that Cooper had already gotten his hands on Patti Smith's 1972 book *Seventh Heaven*. As Smith's poems invoked rock 'n' roll and pop figures like Mustang Sally, Edie Sedgwick, and Jim Morrison, Cooper included poems titled after and addressed to David Bowie, Todd Rundgren, and (following Smith) Jim Morrison.

Yet this was not mimicry on Cooper's part. Even Cooper's preface to the book suggested a shift away from the field of influences typical of Smith and the St. Mark's poets. Composed of a series of credits "& for influence and inspiration to james tate, jim morrison, william burroughs, jean genet, todd rundgren, clark coolidge, robin williamson, tom rapp, luchino [*sic*] visconti, tom clark, leonard cohen, kristoffer tabori,"[9] admittedly, Cooper's list was relatively familiar: denizens of the Beat Generation (Burroughs), their French counterparts (Genet), experimental New York School–affiliated poets (Clark, Coolidge, and Tate, to some extent), and pop counterparts (Rundgren). But Cooper's allusive field was more eclectic than the ones Smith and Hell put together. What, for example, was Kristoffer Tabori—a contemporary of Cooper's who made a name for himself as a character actor for film and TV shows—doing here? Why was Visconti the sole filmmaker on the list, particularly as his brand of cinema did not register much, if at all, in the work of Cooper's favorite poets? How did Tom Rapp end up here, given his role as psychedelic troubadour for the band Pearls Before Swine? Cooper's preface proposes the New York School gone SoCal, the amphetamine intensity of downtown jumbled strangely by the sunny psychedelic expansive fields of folk-rock.

As much as Cooper was indebted to the New York scene, he was also clearly determined not to ape his heroes. Cooper's yoking of '60s hippie music with the arch cool of Cohen, Clark, et al. was part of his contribution to an ongoing experiment in the debasement of poetry initiated by second-generation New York School writers and sustained by Myles and the third wave of St. Mark's poets. Cooper's "David Bowie" is accompanied on the facing page by a poorly reproduced image of Ziggy Stardust–era, makeup-caked Bowie. Cooper's combination of word and image positioned the poem as akin to an article accompanying a rock star's picture, typical of music magazines of the era such as *Creem*. Yet making matters all the more complicated is that one would be hard pressed to say unequivocally that Cooper's "David Bowie" was somehow "about" the singer. While the first stanza pointed to Bowie's glam monstrousness ("in quiet / the glittered eyes / seem evil"), the second stanza practically drew the reader's attention away from Bowie ("a boy, bearded, with a / Grateful Dead teeshirt manicures / the long piano fingers, / calmly praises with the words / genius and sway").[10] These lines were more like an assemblage of signs than they were a sustained meditation on a single artist. The bearded crusty with the Dead T-shirt was queered via an affiliation with Bowie's effeminacy, as Bowie himself was aligned with a hippie shabbiness anathema to his developing style. ("The hippies don't know what's happening," Bowie insisted in a 1973 interview with Patrick Salvo.)[11]

These moves determined the overall direction of Cooper's short poem, as Cooper darted toward and away from his subject in a disorienting fashion. The third-to-last stanza, for example, straightforwardly announced "a silver spacesuit, / skin tight & unreal" and then in the second-to-last stanza moved on to draw parallels between Bowie and Katherine Hepburn ("Katherine Hepburn and rock n roll / approach each other NOW, / proud legs gaped into the future / of teenage America"). OK, fair enough—Hepburn, at least in the 1935 film *Sylvia Scarlett*, did in fact look remarkably like Bowie did in the early to mid-1970s. These stanzas made a good ending to the poem, one that could be understood to use Bowie metonymically to herald a markedly androgynous queer nation emerging on the wings of pop and the movies. However, the poem didn't end there. Rather, Cooper finished on an entirely ambiguous note: "then stopping abruptly / to stare / at the bearded stranger / cutting his wrists / with a hubcap." It was as if Cooper was actively denying the reader's expectation for the poem somehow to generate or contain a clear, liberatory message. Anticipating Cooper's hostility to ideations of gay community in his later fiction works, "David Bowie" was more a gesture of obstinate resistance to readers' comprehension than it was a statement of gay pride or lyrical insight into a pop luminary.[12] Looking forward to the "no more heroes" slogans typical of punk, Cooper addressed his stars only to drag them off the page toward incomprehensibility.

Cooper developed this punk style further in his 1978 volume *Tiger Beat*, entitled cheekily after the popular 1970s teenybopper magazine.[13] Adapting techniques clearly indebted to the New American and New York School poets to texts centered on the vapidity of pop stardom and suburban teen ennui, Cooper managed to degrade and complicate mass culture and the heightened status of the avant-garde lyric. What, after all, were the implications of naming a volume of poetry after the magazine *Tiger Beat*? Ilana Nash's recollections of *Tiger Beat* and *16* magazines suggest what Cooper was up to in his yoking pop trash to the New York School poem:

> While *16* and *Tiger Beat* never discussed sex explicitly, the hints were sufficient to justify our assumption of sex as a central element of fandom. Color photographs, which the magazines always called "kissable color pin-ups," often showed idols shirtless or posed in bathing suits. One friend recently told me that, when his older sister read *Tiger Beat*, he and his friends used to flip through issues and laughingly call it "Tiger Beat-Off" because of its display of pretty boys' bodies. The magazine's lack of explicit sex clearly did not impede anyone from understanding what was implicitly being offered. In some regards, *16* and *Tiger Beat* served a similar function for us that *Playboy* did for boys, including the fact that the most privileged photographic space was the centerfold.[14]

Cooper, attracted to the images of topless teenage boys plastered across the centerfolds of *Tiger Beat*, applied his desire to a short series of poems focused on and/or addressed to teenage boys. Its cover sporting a disarming

picture of a smiling Shaun Cassidy, Cooper's *Tiger Beat* went far in presenting poetry as sexy, disturbing, and even crass. The poem "Boy Talk," for
example, opened memorably:

> At the BLONDIE concert
> I yell, "Sit on my face!"
> to the woman singer
> with chills on my skin
>
> and she doesn't even
> see me, or deem to
> answer my call 'cause
> she's above me, far above[15]

Using all capital letters to highlight the band's name and, probably, to
evoke the overwhelming gorgeousness of its lead singer, Debbie Harry, Cooper here might also be pointing in-the-know readers slyly back to Frank
O'Hara's "I do this, I do that" genre of poems, which also used all-caps to suggest the very materiality of the persons and places he listed in his poems.
Take O'Hara's best-known work, "The Day Lady Died." Going about his urbane
day at "12:20 in New York a Friday / three days after Bastille day, yes / it is
1959," O'Hara's dandy narrator treats himself to "a hamburger and a malted"
and buys "an ugly NEW WORLD WRITING to see what the poets in Ghana
are doing these days." He drops by the "GOLDEN GRIFFIN" bookstore to buy
some Verlaine, then stops at a tobacconist's to get "a carton of Gauloises
and a carton / of Picayunes, and a NEW YORK POST with [Billie Holiday's] face
on it."[16] This list—a litany, really—was clearly that of a sophisticate squeez-
ing as much joy out of New York City as he possibly could. However, this was
no paean to pop culture. Billie Holiday, while popular, was in no way analogous to the musicians ruling the *Billboard* charts in 1959 (songs such as Paul
Anka's "Lonely Boy," Elvis Presley's "A Big Hunk 'O Love," and the Coasters'
"Charlie Brown" were the order of the day). Rather, Holiday was the poets'
and artists' pop singer. Her gigs at the Five Spot were attended by regulars
including the "artists Willem de Kooning, Grace Hartigan, Alfred Leslie,
Larry Rivers, David Smith, and Harry Smith. . . . Writers at the bar included
Allen Ginsberg, LeRoi Jones, [Jack] Kerouac, Kenneth Koch . . . Frank O'Hara,
and Dan Propper."[17] O'Hara's invocation of Holiday's name, contained

within a framework of signs representative of the narrator's erudition (the French literature and cigarettes, the literary magazine, and so forth), was not so much in the service of a demotic poetics engaged and informed by mass culture as it was a containment of Holiday's voice within a grid of New York City streets and a circumscribed coterie of artistic and literary-minded aesthetes.

By incorporating O'Hara's use of all-caps and "I do this, I do that" style into a poem partly about BLONDIE, Cooper was democratizing not just O'Hara's elegy—the thinking person's Holiday replaced by the crowd-pleasing lead singer of Blondie, Debbie Harry—but, by extension, the very affect of urbanity O'Hara was such a genius at generating. Blondie, starting out as a punk new-wave band based at CBGB, had by 1978 released their multimillion-selling album *Parallel Lines*, which spawned such hits as "Call Me" and the glistening disco sensation "Heart of Glass." This was no longer music reserved for downtown cognoscenti. Rather, this was music open enough to draw audience members to yell out things like "Sit on my face!" The daily speech featured in Cooper's "Boy Talk" was a far cry from the implicit conversations taking place between O'Hara's narrator and characters like "Patsy" and "Mike" mentioned in "The Day Lady Died." Occupying and playing within the rhetorical spaces opened up by O'Hara's "I do this, I do that" poetics, Cooper offered readers a punk repudiation of O'Hara's sophistication. Cooper's "Boy Talk" paid attention to and was shaped by pop-punk, a *real* mass-culture form compared to jazz. Where Billie Holiday in the end of O'Hara's poem was conjured up in the sacred and practically silent space of a breathless "5 SPOT," Debbie Harry, in Cooper's text, was positively man-handled by a bunch of slobs. "Men have squeezed / her ass in bars," Cooper informs us in subsequent stanzas, "and smelled their palms / like evening skies // and she's kissed them; / she's slapped them; / they have been crude; / they've been right."[18]

Little Caesar

Cooper wrote poems like "Boy Talk" during a period in his life when he was immersing himself in the new sounds of post-punk and new wave. In diary entries written in a flat, affectless style, Cooper recorded his outings to record stores and commented briefly on his impressions of his various purchases. The following 1978 diary excerpts give a flavor of Cooper's doing this and that on the streets of Los Angeles:

> Then to Rhino where I got the new WIRE album which is excellent. Then home. Brian went to work and we talked, sat around I played him Pere Ubu's LP which he liked. . . . News yesterday that Syd [sic] Vicious (of Sex Pistols) was arrested in New York for stabbing his girlfriend to death is true. Very strange, disturbing. Will be interesting to see what comes of that. He'll have *real* trouble in court, being who he is. I feel really sorry for him.[19]

> Bought tickets for Talking Heads at Roxy, ran into Danny Wilde of The Quick . . . On the news: Sid Vicious tried suicide twice, once cutting his wrists and once trying to jump out of a hotel window. Poor Sid.[20]

> So we went out for dessert at the Cheesecake Factory and to Tower Records where I got the new Johnny Rotten single. Two listenings in it sounds real good.[21]

> Listened to old Stones—BETWEEN THE BUTTONS and Sex Pistols album, both of which sounded *tremendous* for different reasons. Great stuff![22]

> Went to Rhino, talked to Gary, bought some 45s and the new Buzzcocks album.[23]

Written in the same year *Tiger Beat* was published, Cooper's shopping clearly had an effect on the subjects addressed in the book itself. Critics found much to laud about Cooper's aesthetic and quickly homed in on the "punk" quality of his work. "Dennis Cooper is one of the bright lights—probably the *brightest* light—among American gay male poets in their twenties," enthused his fellow poet Rudy Kikel, going on to pinpoint punk as the quality that made Cooper so special:

> What accounts, I think, for the initial appeal of this Los Angeles–based writer is what I would call his work's "punk" *frisson*: there are, for instance, attacks on his "audience" ("The highlights of some of your lives" are considered inferior to a "French baby's dreams"), an acceptance of vulgar or circumscribed desire (the influence of rock 'n' roll, the press, television, and American cinema are felt in this poetry), and an unembarrassed association of sex and violence: Cooper

dares, in *Tiger Beat*, to find poetic subject matter in "Dean Corll, American Mass Murderer." In this respect, Cooper's work is closer to that of some older, legendary, or "oppressed" poets—Rimbaud, Genet, Wieners, and Kirby Congdon, particularly the Congdon of *Dream-Work*—than it is to that of the post Stonewall poets like Stan Persky, Ron Schreiber, or Aaron Shurin who have preceded him.[24]

Other writers and poets echoed Kikel. From an undated press-release flyer for *Tiger Beat*, readers were treated to a series of blurbs from Robert Peters, Gerard Malanga, Ian Young, Kirby Congdon, Tim Dlugos, Joe Brainard, and Allen Ginsberg. Highlighting the way the book *looked* and the punk ethos contained within, Malanga opined, "I really did get a rise out of it. I think the packaging of the book relates to the poems in a very specific way. [He] may very well be the first punk poet."[25] As punks marked themselves through ripped clothes, exotic haircuts, and piercings to signify their disaffiliation from mainstream culture, so Cooper, Malanga suggested, marked his allegiance by "packaging" his book in a way that served to point his audience to the punk scene. However, the flyer went beyond locating Cooper as sympathetic to punk. Ensuring readers would at least attempt to situate the book within a New York School lineage, the press release also included a wonderfully banal boost from Joe Brainard ("I like it a lot" was Brainard's entire contribution) as well as a plug from Ginsberg: "TIGER BEAT is imaginative, sexy, funny, TV pop high school masculine muscles and hair plus some high irony cadenzas out of the extravagances of 'N.Y. School' mind."

Unlike most small-press, self-published poetry chapbooks, *Tiger Beat* reached beyond the confines of the poetry world, attracting punk-music-industry types. Danny Fields, the renowned manager of the Stooges and the Ramones, began his letter to Cooper—typed on personalized stationary emblazoned with the word RAMONES at the top of the page—with the most fulsome of praise: "I must begin by telling you how much I loved 'Tiger Beat'—you are a great genius, and I can't wait to see your other works . . . if you can, please send me other things you've written, because your writing is the most thrilling and beautiful that there is."[26] Given this kind of attention and the excited focus on his fans' parts on the relationship between Cooper's poetry and the new sounds coming out of New York, London, and Manchester, it is little wonder that our "first punk poet" started *Little Caesar* in 1976. Hot off the presses the same year Cooper saw the Ramones in

London, *Little Caesar* (and later, Little Caesar Press) was a publication that, as we'll now see, was essentially a punk New York School poetry magazine.[27] And what better format for Cooper to explore the rhymes between the two genres? Unlike the single-author book or chapbook, the magazine as praxis necessarily embodies a group dynamic providing back-and-forth exchanges between poems and poets. Conceptualizing the little magazine as pop group was something that Cooper and Eileen Myles both shared. Recalling how Cooper sent her copies of *Little Caesar* through the mail when Cooper was still out in LA and she sent Cooper copies of *her* little magazine *dodgems* from her perch in New York, Myles offered: "It really seemed like, in lieu of having a band, you did a magazine that got your model out there of who and what you had in mind. You know? Then you put yourself in it." Cooper's response? "Yeah, totally. Totally."[28]

Following on the heels of the Poetry Project–based poets whose publications Cooper read so avidly,[29] *Little Caesar* broke new ground in its basic, untheorized assumption of affinity between poets and musicians. With Jim Glaeser, his coeditor for the first two issues, Cooper wrote a mini-manifesto calling for a mass-market poetry. "We want a magazine that's read by the Poetry fans, the Rock culture, the Hari Krishnas, the Dodgers."[30] It was not just any "Rock culture," mind you.

> I have this dream where writers are mobbed everywhere they go, like rock stars and actors. A predilection [*sic*]? You never know. People like Patti Smith are subtly forcing their audiences to become literate, introducing them to Rimbaud, Breton, Burroughs and others. Poetry sales are higher than they've been in fifteen years.[31]

Ensuring that *Little Caesar* would *not* be read as an extension of the idealized, romanticized San Francisco Beat scene initiated by Gary Snyder, Philip Whalen, Allen Ginsberg, and the like, Cooper and Glaeser took a potshot at Kenneth Rexroth himself, the Great Papa of the West Coast poetry reading: "We're not fifty year old patrons of the arts. We're young punks just like you, and just because Kenneth Rexroth's got a name in some crowds doesn't mean a wink's gonna get his rickety old crap in here."[32] Punk was invoked directly in an effort to rub out the creaking poetry behemoths still held in high regard by California literati. Paralleling punk musicians' own refusal of their bloated predecessors, Glaeser and Cooper invited readers to throw away their preconceptions of poetry as something in thrall to history and tradition. Poetry could transcend Poetry (with a capital "P") and become akin to punk.[33] Glaeser ended up leaving *Little Caesar* after the first two issues because he was "hit," as Cooper explained it in the introduction to *Little Caesar* 3, with "post Kerouacian wanderlust." It was Cooper's world now. The third issue revealed themes that were to obsess Cooper throughout his career—hot boys and punk rock. The cover alone, featuring a homoerotic image of sixteen-year-old John Kennedy Junior's face and torso, spoke volumes about the direction Cooper and *Little Caesar* were heading. Taking in Kennedy's full, juicy lips, his eyes looking just barely askance at the camera, his mop top of thick hair fluttering in the wind, his white Oxford shirt unbuttoned strategically at his neck and just above his jeans zipper, "John-John" as featured on Cooper's cover would undoubtedly appeal to ribald queer readership.

The cover was funny, too. Given that Kennedy's picture was centered just below the magazine title *Little Caesar*, readers were tacitly invited to think of John Jr.'s relationship to his father, former president John Kennedy (implicitly the Big Caesar of this latent tale). The cover of *Little Caesar* 3 announced its politics fairly outrageously by presenting the scion of a former president as available for visual consumption. That such a latently pedophilic posture was aligned to "Poetry, Fiction, & Interviews" served all the more to propose poetry and the literary arts more generally as aligned with an unruly perversity.

Queerness, poetry, and punk were linked inextricably throughout this and subsequent issues.[34] The editor's letter opening issue 3, for example, announced, "The Rimbaud Birthday Issue has been delayed," though "we still need poems for and about, translations, etc. Do you resemble the Great Boy? We'll be running a Rimbaud-Live-Alike Contest. If you wanna get in early just send photo, address and a 24 words or less testimonial. May the best boy or girl win."[35] On the facing page, Cooper placed an advertisement for the pop-punk band the Quick headlined "THE QUICK: Could you be their biggest fan?" Given the proximity of this ad to Cooper's letter, an implied dialogue was created that found the outlaw gay connotations inherent in the "Rimbaud-Live-Alike" contest echoed in the sullen, adolescent faces of the band members. "Thousands have seen 'the light' through what intellectual teenagers are calling the Coolest Rock Band in America," read the ad for the Quick, continuing by emphasizing aspects of the young men's bodies and miens—"Meet: DANNY WILDE, the smartest & skinniest lead singer ever"; "BILLY BIZEAUX, so bored you have to care." To read this ad alongside Cooper's letter inviting his readers to live like and *be* one's own Rimbaud was to go further than Patti Smith had gone in incorporating Rimbaud's persona into her music and style. Rimbaud, in Cooper's world, was no longer the idealized other about whom one dreamed, for whom one cheered GO RIMBAUD, and idolized. Rather, Rimbaud was now just another suburban "intellectual teenager" out in the streets, in the clubs, playing in a band.[36] The Quick—accessible, bored, singing, pretty punks—were proffered as examples of the new Rimbauds living among us. And importantly, one didn't have to be a Patti Smith–style demon-angel to be a Rimbaud. Adamantly lighthearted, Cooper's Rimbaud's could be a "girl" or "boy." All sexy, playful kids were welcome to enter the Rimbaud-Live-Alike contest.

Cooper's own contributions to the issue expanded on the range of characters able to assume the Rimbaud mantle. Set alongside images of cute teen male pop stars and actors such as Leif Garrett, Vince Van Patten, and Mark Hamill, as well as anonymous boys featured in gay-porn magazines, were a series of Cooper's short prose poems designed to be read as interior monologues. Take the prose poem accompanying Leif Garrett's photo, for example:

> I rake heaven's leaves and while I work the windows fill with people watching me. I see girls grow breathless at the sight of me among leaves. My friends tell me I'll be famous when the world learns my best angle. We're betting it's from the sky, over my heart breaking blond hair.[37]

Given the shadow Rimbaud casts over *Little Caesar* 3 as a whole, readers were invited to detect Rimbaud's influence on the form and content of this poem. The erotic ambiance of the text is unmistakable. Even the fact that Garrett looks no older than sixteen was meaningful, as this was about the same age Rimbaud was when he embarked on his tempestuous affair with Paul Verlaine. But Rimbaud is in Cooper's poem most clearly in the language itself. As the adolescent Rimbaud declaims lines in his *Illuminations* series, including "I am the saint, at prayer on the terrace,"[38] so Leif Garrett, as Cooper has him, shows off his own high-flown style in phrases such as "I rake heaven's leaves." Cooper's Leif Garrett poem encourages readers to identify heightened visionary poetic rhetoric as perfectly amenable to pop dreck. Moreover, Garrett's presence in the group context of the magazine sets up a funny dynamic between himself and the Quick. These two purportedly incongruent sets of musicians, situated in the "band" that is *Little Caesar* 3, are reconciled further by their mutual absorption into a sexy, funny Rimbaudian discourse.

Would Cooper so easily have employed Garrett's face as a kind of cartoon image to which he attached a speech bubble / prose poem had he not had Berrigan, Padgett, Brainard, and the rest of the gang as precursors, particularly in light of the fact that Brainard and related poets had already rejected the relatively recondite tastes of O'Hara et al. in favor of 1960s rock 'n' roll, junk food, pills, and poetry cartoons? While *Little Caesar* 3 did not feature many New York School poets (Malanga, Jim Carroll, Tom Clark, and Cooper himself were the only true representatives of that particular tradition), the New York School determined the tenor of the magazine more and more with each succeeding issue even as Cooper's commitment to punk and proto-punk grew.[39]

Cooper also worked to frame a wide range of poetry as being as interesting and as accessible as porn and rock 'n' roll were. The cover for *Little Caesar* 8, for example, featured a nude Iggy Pop. Inside the issue were scores of portraits of other punk stars (albeit clothed). Marcia Resnick's portfolio "Bad Boys" featured musicians and punk characters including Alan Suicide, Joey Ramone, Legs McNeil, and Pat Place. Malanga's portfolio "POPISM" historicized 1970s punk by including photos of 1960s antecedents including Mick Jagger, Lou Reed, Anita Pallenberg, and Andy Warhol. A reprint of Chris Brazier's *Melody Maker* interview with Johnny Rotten was incorporated into the issue for good measure and served to mark punk's shift from New York to an Anglo-American phenomenon. Yet even in the face of such a glut of images, New York School work was foregrounded throughout the issue to echo and make even stranger *Little Caesar*'s punk porno poetry theme.

Take Peter Schjeldahl's paean to fellatio "On Cocksucking." Admitting in the final lines of the poem, "Anyway I haven't done it in years," Schjeldahl continues by teasing, "but maybe—who knows?—I'll do it again, I reserve / the right and—who knows?—maybe, big boy, / I've got my eye on *you*."[40] Though buried on pages 62–63, do these lines perhaps encourage us to think of Schjeldahl's eye in relationship to Stooges songs such as "Cock in My

Pocket" and "T.V. Eye"? As Schjeldahl purred, "big boy, / I've got my eye on *you*," readers might be forgiven for imagining Iggy singing *back* that he has his TV eye on Schjeldahl.[41]

Similarly, the gay ribaldry characterizing some New York School–affiliated poems found a punk echo in Cooper's interview with the gay-porn director Toby Ross featured in *Little Caesar* 10. "My dream is to cast known stars in pornographic films," Ross enthused, adding: "To use a well known character in that situation would be very powerful. . . . I'd love to remake my *White Trash* with a few of those punk rock stars I see around."[42] Directly following Ross's comments was Brad Gooch's poem "Origami," which, read as connected materially and thematically to Ross's interview, becomes a kind of "I do this, I do that" New York School porn scenario: "Bill goes down on Greg. / Greg (statue) leans back against the wooden wall-board. White. / Greg. Then Bill let's Greg's cum fly all over his washboard stomach. / White stains on tan stomach."[43]

These kinds of editorial moves on Cooper's part challenged conventional assumptions underlying what Lawrence Grossberg argued was the overly simplistic if "most commonly observed division within rock and roll (and its fans)" as "between the punk—violent, sexual, and emotional—and the poet—critical, sensuous, and intellectual."[44] Crucially, Cooper employed both word and image to assault the divide Grossberg identified. While the cover of *Little Caesar* 6, for example, featured John Wieners, a fellow traveler of the New York School of poets,[45] the first thing readers saw when they opened the magazine was a full-page picture of the British punk singer Billy Idol, then lead singer for the band Generation X. With Idol's and Wieners's faces as guides, readers were encouraged to assume and think about affinities between a specific set of characters published throughout *Little Caesar* connected specifically to American and English punk and the New American and New York School poetry communities.[46] One could now envision how sexually suggestive and transgressive lines from, say, Wieners's poems "With You Gone" and "An Evocation" included in *Little Caesar* 6 might look ahead and speak to what Dick Hebdige recognized early on as a "great punk signifier—sexual 'kinkiness'" disseminated by punk musicians from Sanders through Reed through Hell through Idol.[47] This is not to say, of course, that Wieners himself would be open to such an affiliation. Rather, strictly within the locale of *Little Caesar*, Wieners's lines like "I saw blood smeared on her eyelids and mouth. Woman what have I done to you" or "I hymn the fates / that try to explain us. // in golden trousers, / doing Arabesques" could now be seen as anticipating and resonating with the edgy, violent, and transgressive glam style of 1970s punk.[48]

Cooper's juxtapositions of punks and poets forged new connections between artists and genres circulating traditionally within separate cultural economies. Speaking retrospectively about the new forms of negotiated reading that *Little Caesar* engendered, Cooper said proudly, "People have told me that connecting those made writing seem kind of cool, opening up the whole idea that poetry could be connected to these other things that are more popular."[49] By pulling underground poetry into a shared spotlight enjoyed by pop-punks, Cooper staged a populist takeover of postmodern poetry, liberating it from what by the late 1970s and early 1980s had already become its institutionalized academic and critically approved home and dragging it, metaphorically, to New York's CBGB and the Mudd Club, LA's Masque, London's Roxy and 100 Club.[50] Cooper did not so much grace music with the authority of the literary underground as much as he proposed that New American and New York School poetry could be as fun and up to the minute as the music made by Generation X, Blondie, and Iggy.

"Oh God It Got Really Terrible"

By the 1980s and 1990s Cooper had left poetry behind to focus on prose fiction, most notoriously the radically abject five-book George Miles cycle *Closer* (1989), *Frisk* (1991), *Try* (1994), *Guide* (1997), and *Period* (2000). This period of his life also found Cooper working actively as a music journalist for magazines including *Rolling Stone*, *Spin*, and *Interview*. While his novels received their fair share of critical notoriety and praise, Cooper's fellow music journalists were corresponding with him about his bold experiments in prose. Jon Savage, whose account of British punk rock *England's Dreaming* (1991) is still considered by many to be the definitive history of the era, exchanged a series of letters with Cooper that deliberated on the influence of punk and post-punk on literature. In one candid missive, Savage acknowledged some misgivings about Cooper's *Closer*:

> Part of my problem [with *Closer*] may be the exposure I had to the late 70s brutalist aesthetic very early on, going right into the Sex Pistols and all that

[Throbbing Gristle] stuff and living with it for years with all the imitators, much of which I've exorcised in "England's Dreaming." Oh god it got really terrible. Maybe now that I have exorcised much of the psychic baggage that I still carried from those years, I can begin to appreciate again those dark places in the human heart—although I must still say that it is an aesthetic that, unless very well done, I'm bored by.[51]

We know what Savage is talking about when he expresses skepticism over punk's third-rate imitators and their continuing attachment to "those dark places in the human heart." After all, the pedophilic, incestuous, barbaric acts detailed repeatedly in Cooper's *Closer* take on a practically numb, flat patina. A typical example from *Closer*: "For instance, over my dad's shoulder, I'm trying not to distinguish a boy about my age. His back is turned and where his ass used to be there's this thing that looks half like drawn curtains and half like what's left of a cow once it gets to the butcher's shop."[52] Even at this early stage in the book, the sordid moments preceding the description of the boy's violently distorted ass-flaps are so numerous that the reader can barely muster the energy to say "Yuck." This is a far cry from Cooper's pop-inflected poems of the 1970s.

Cooper's repudiation of poetry in favor of an unflinching commitment to revolting fiction paralleled his growing stature as a music journalist covering literary-minded, punk-influenced bands like Sonic Youth and Pavement. Cooper's increasingly prosaic, violent (if consistently compelling) repetitiveness throughout the George Miles cycle may have been informed partly by post-punk rock 'n' roll—the late 1980s and early 1990s, after all, found formerly marginal sounds entering the mainstream, with some hailing 1991 as "the year punk broke."[53] Playing live music at ear-shattering levels, reconciling feedback and distortion with a marked pop sensibility, and writing lyrics that were as much about death cults (Sonic Youth's "Death Valley '69") and rape (Nirvana's "Polly") as they were about haircuts (Pavement's "Cut Your Hair"), Madonna (Sonic Youth's Ciccone Youth side project), and school recess (Nirvana's "School"), the bands Cooper wrote about and interviewed seemed to have figured out a way to seduce a large audience into a marginal world.

To be literate, to be noisy, to be "underground," to be a pin-up—to be all these things at once. Cooper and his writer friends were horrified by the prospect of being seen as pretentious and "literary," yet they were in love with poetry. Aware of and frustrated by second-generation New York School's poets' relegation to limited social coteries and audiences—"don't ever get famous,"[54] as Bernadette Mayer put it—Cooper saw in punk and post-punk bands' negotiations of the underground and popular spheres a model for a new sincerely populist sensibility. Bands from Richard Hell and the Voidoids through Pavement had always made space for the abject, the nihilist, and the scornful even as they reveled in being erudite, goofy, and hot.[55] For Cooper and his fellow writers, punk and post-punk bands' ability to contain these multitudes proved both influential and irresistible as they targeted not just the "mainstream" but the increasingly ossified poetic avant-garde itself.

People Who Died

My friends whose deaths have slowed my heart stay with me now.

—Ted Berrigan

Those are people who died, died
They were all my friends, and they died.

—Jim Carroll Band

MAKING IT ONTO *Billboard*'s Top 100 list in 1980, the Jim Carroll Band's hit single "People Who Died" had—and continues to have—multiple lives. "'People Who Died' . . . had people in radio tip sheets, like the influential *FMQB Album Report*, saying radio things like 'People Who Died is phono-matic sales stirring rock' and 'best new candidate for hot phones.'"[1] The fifth track on the Jim Carroll Band's first album, *Catholic Boy*, "People Who Died" is heard in films as various as Steven Spielberg's *ET: The Extra Terrestrial*, Fritz Kierch's *Tuff Turf*, and Zack Snyder's 2004 remake of George Romero's *Dawn of the Dead*. It is referenced in autobiographical reportage including Vanessa Gezarri's *The Tender Soldier*. It is name-checked in novels including Michael Muhammad Knight's *The Taqwacores*. Yet despite the way Carroll's "People Who Died" has resonated across the decades, few critics bother to mention that Carroll's song is inspired directly by Ted Berrigan's poem "People Who Died," first published in 1969. The last great punk song on the last great punk album was actually modeled on a New York School poem.

What explains the dearth of commentary on the Berrigan-Carroll connection? Could this elision be attributable to the fact that some music critics interested in punk so often see a life in poetry as an apprenticeship for the real job of rock 'n' roll? A 1981 feature on Carroll in *New York* magazine suggests as much. Its author, Chet Flippo, pointed out that Carroll's November 19, 1980, performance on NBC's *Tomorrow* show "was only his second New York rock-'n'-roll performance—as opposed to his poetry readings at St. Mark's and such places—but there was no doubt he was the hottest ticket in town."[2] Flippo's "St. Mark's and such places—but" says it all. You can have your fun reading your little verses to your little friends, but what you *really* want is to be a rock 'n' roll star. "Jim Carroll, former teenage junkie, whizz-kid poet, basketball legend who went from Lower East Side asphalt courts to hardwood-floored gyms and prep-school uniforms at Trinity, seemed to be about two minutes away from full-fledged rock-'n'-roll stardom."[3] Flippo inadvertently set up a kind of Virgilian triadic career ladder here. For the rock bard in training, the pastoral was represented by a hip childhood spent shooting hoops and shooting up, the georgic was represented by writing lyrics and reading them to the St. Mark's crowd, and the epic was represented by the artist's successful transcendence of these place- and time-bound scenes into rock 'n' roll stardom. While Flippo did invoke Ted Berrigan's name, it was only in the service of further idealizing Carroll's successful graduation from poet to pop star: "A young poet whom Ted Berrigan called 'the first truly new American poet,' who was signed to Rolling Stones Records, and whose New York rock debut, last July at Trax, featured no less a guest guitarist than senior Rolling Stone Keith Richards."[4]

Yet throughout Flippo's article, Carroll seemed to be at pains to identify himself as a New York School poet. Falling into line with the other St. Mark's–based writers of the 1960s and 1970s, Carroll told Flippo,

> I *followed* Frank O'Hara one day when I was first into poetry, followed him home from the Museum of Modern Art, because I knew he worked there. This was like two months before he died. I followed him in a taxi and he got off at Astor Place and I followed him up to 10th Street and Broadway, right across from Grace Church . . . I followed him to his house.[5]

Carroll made no real efforts to align himself to the rock 'n' roll stars he was being compared to. Instead, he played the humble card. "When I'd do readings, people would say, 'Mick Jagger reading poetry—you should do rock 'n' roll.' I said, 'No way, man.' I respected people's singing voices then. Forget it."[6] Carroll acknowledged here that he believed in maintaining the distinction most people made between "singing voices" and reading voices.

Carroll also believed that poetry accrued a cultural capital that was simply unattainable by mere rockers—and he seemed to like it that way. Referring to Patti Smith's early poetry career, Carroll admitted: "Her lyrics were better than her poems, to me. But Patti wasn't as accepted and didn't have a reputation in the poetry scene like I did."[7] Carroll was speaking the truth here—writing poetry from an early age, he performed regularly at St. Mark's Church before he ever dreamed about fronting a rock band. His poetry books were steeped in the New York School scene. *4 Ups and 1 Down* (1970), for example, was published by Anne Waldman and Lewis Warsh's Angel Hair Press. His *Living at the Movies* (1973), featuring a cover by Larry Rivers, established his place as a downtown player across the poetry and art scenes. His autobiography *The Basketball Diaries* made the rounds in the Lower East Side initially in manuscript form passed around from poet to poet to prose writer to poet; it was excerpted in the St. Mark's house journal *The World* and praised by William Burroughs and Jack Kerouac.[8] Carroll was everywhere, as his account of a particularly playful night at St. Mark's showed:

> Gloria Excelsior [Bridget Berlin], one of Andy Warhol's superstars, has been hanging around the poetry readings at St. Mark's Church. St. Mark's is, of course, my home away from home. I guess it was Bill Berkson, my provider of room and board, who first brought her around. One night she stayed with Gerry Malanga after the reading and, in a moment of stoned blasphemy, got Gerry and me to pose naked on the altar, standing on each other's shoulders against the giant wooden cross.[9]

Rock 'n' roll? Who needed it?

Nevertheless, following his departure in 1974 from New York for the pastoral idyll of Bolinas, California, Carroll caught the punk bug. "My connection with New York in my recluse period," he told Flippo,

> was reading about CBGB and punk rock and Television and Blondie and Talking Heads, and one by one they all got signed up by record companies and came out

to San Francisco to play the Old Waldorf. I checked them all out.... So I started to think, "Rock 'n' roll!" . . . It's just a natural extension of my work, of the images.[10]

Like Hell, Smith, and Giorno before him, Carroll was beginning to find poetry readings increasingly boring. "Poetry readings just don't cut it for me the way they used to," Carroll wrote in one of his diary entries.

> There are only a handful of poets who truly know *how* to read their work, who can take the audience *out there*. I've been a regular at the readings at St. Mark's Church, down on 10th Street, since I was sixteen, and it's astonishing how boring some of the really great poets are when they ascend that podium. I've heard an anthology of my favorite poems, so alive when I read them on the page, butchered en route from the poets' mouth.[11]

Even in his conversation with Flippo, though, Carroll insisted on a kind of intellectual gravitas. "By making images just obscure enough to be made personal," Carroll explained earnestly, "I have the street imagery, but you have to have that kind of mythology built into it, because that's what kids understand. I don't like to deal with any subject matter straight out, you know."[12] Carroll's rock lyrics were beholden to poetry, if by "poetry" we mean a genre that is by its nature indirect, allusive, and elusive. In other words, Carroll's rock 'n' roll poetics seemed the very opposite of the earthy directness and simplicity that made so many rock 'n' roll songs—from Elvis's "Hound Dog" to the Beatles' "She Loves You" to the Stooges' "No Fun"— irresistible. Hoping to appeal to "kids," Carroll nevertheless insisted that his rock lyrics were formally elliptical and heavy with the weight of legend. He wanted to tell the truth, but he felt bound to tell it slant.[13]

In light of Carroll's comments, it is easy to see why Berrigan's "People Who Died" proved so attractive to an artist looking to combine the mythic with the personal, the universal with the quotidian. Berrigan's poem was quite simply composed of a list of names, followed by a brief description of those names' relationships to Berrigan, followed by chronologically arranged phrases identifying cause and year of death. Berrigan's use of the list as a poetic form pointed back to Homer's use of the list as an elegiac roll call of the dead, even as his entirely flat style (at least until the final lines) repudiated the epic's at-times hortatory manner. The first five lines of Berrigan's poem referred entirely to Berrigan's friends and relationships:

Pat Dugan . . . . my grandfather . . . . throat cancer . . . . 1947.

Ed Berrigan . . . . my dad . . . . heart attack . . . . 1958.

Dickie Budlong . . . . my best friend Brucie's big brother, when we were
five to eight . . . . killed in Korea, 1953.

Red O'Sullivan . . . . hockey star & cross-country runner
who sat at my lunch table
in High School . . . . . . car crash . . . . . . 1954.

Jimmy "Wah" Tiernan . . . . my friend, in High School,
Football & Hockey All-State . . . . . . car crash . . . . 1959[14]

Berrigan's poem, characterized by a plainness of style and arresting use of typography, was a counterintuitive if ultimately successful contribution to the elegy as a genre. The names, isolated visually from the rest of the lines by ellipses, serve to emphasize the absence of the material bodies those names once signified. The ellipses themselves dramatize empty space, adding a crucial touch of pathos—the sentimental cliché "words cannot describe our loss" is here embodied by the dot, dot, dot. Through Berrigan's brief descriptions of the subjects' roles in his life and various causes of death, he refuses further to adorn grief with language. Rather than undermining the elegy's force, however, this refusal encourages the reader to intuit the chasms of sorrow that are here only hinted at. These are *repressed* lines. Inviting the reader to do most of the associative work, the poem becomes a moving example of the interactive and inherently social possibilities of a poem—someone like "Jimmy 'Wah' Tiernan," described so elliptically here, can easily stand in for one of our own high-school friends who died too early. Berrigan gives us the names and a hint of background, and we provide the narrative.

With the sixth line, however, the poem swerves quite dramatically. Leaving his friends and family behind temporarily, Berrigan starts to summon musicians, dancers, and poets from the Elysian Fields, even as he folds in subjects whom he actually knew and loved:

Cisco Houston . . . . died of cancer . . . . 1961.

Freddy Herko, dancer . . . .jumped out of a Greenwich Village window
    in 1963.

Anne Kepler . . . . my girl . . . . killed by smoke-poisoning while playing
                    the flute at the Yonkers Children's Hospital
                    during a fire set by a 16 year old arsonist . . . . 1965.

Frank . . . . . . Frank O'Hara . . . . . . hit by a car on Fire Island, 1966

Woody Guthrie . . . . . . dead of Huntington's Chorea in 1968.

Neal . . . . . . Neal Cassady . . . . . . died of exposure, sleeping all night
                    in the rain by the RR tracks of Mexico . . . . 1969.

Franny Winston . . . . . . just a girl . . . . totalled her car on the Detroit-Ann Arbor
                    Freeway, returning from the dentist . . . . Sept. 1969.

Jack . . . . . . Jack Kerouac . . . . . . died of drink & angry sickness . . . . in 1969.

My friends whose deaths have slowed my heart stay with me now.[15]

Including folk legends like Woody Guthrie and Cisco Houston alongside
Franny Winston and Anne Kepler, and complicating these associations even
further by incorporating Beat and New York School figures into his thren-
ody, Berrigan—ever so gently—challenges readers' perceptions of what
constitutes intimate mourning. The sorrow attendant to the loss of people
Berrigan loved on a day-to-day basis is equivalent to the sorrow felt over
the loss of those artists whose works formed the soundtrack to his life. They
are all, even the ones he has never met, "friends."

Speaking in 1971 about "People Who Died" to a BBC radio talk-show host,
Berrigan explained:

It was written very cold-bloodedly, but out of an idea which came to me not
so cold-bloodedly at all. Someone died and I felt this constriction in my heart

as if a big hand had reached down and squeezed my heart for a second. And everything slowed down. And then tears came to my eyes, and then after a day or a few days I was over it, I wasn't feeling that way anymore. The person had simply passed from my outside life to my inside life.[16]

Berrigan's reminisces further established the ways in which the act of naming could be used to elide the question of officially recognized achievement and status entirely. Berrigan didn't even bother mentioning "the last name" in this conversation—though that "last name" was none other than Jack Kerouac. Anne Kepler's flute playing, Freddy Herko's dancing, Frank O'Hara's poetry, Ed Berrigan's Daddy-ness . . . all so lovely, all so sad to lose.

It was Berrigan's ability to talk "straight" even as he was mythologizing his friends by associating them with literary and musical legends that proved so intoxicating to Jim Carroll and that so clearly informed his poetics as he explained them to Flippo. We should also note that before his move to Bolinas and his long-distance infatuation with punk rock, Carroll was encouraged by his friend Patti Smith to think about his poetry in relationship to music. "I have been considering lately writing lyrics for some rock-and-roll bands," Carroll wrote in his New York diaries of the early 1970s.

> Certain friends have prompted me toward this idea for years. Some, like Jenny Ann [Patti Smith], have even made the ridiculous proposition that I *sing* these songs . . . that I actually form a band! They tell me they see the possibilities when I give readings of my poems and diaries. The way I move. The phrasing. . . . But I respect craft. I believe in technique . . . and my singing abilities are so serious a handicap that it would take a whole new scale to make the entire thing less than ludicrous. Music without melody, where my voice would simply be another rhythm instrument, like a drum.[17]

Hearing the possibilities in Berrigan's "People Who Died," Carroll would go on to do precisely what he shied away from in the early 1970s. Combining Berrigan's efforts to enact a democratic mythos via poetry with the DIY speech-singing typical of punks like Lou Reed, Carroll produced his own "People Who Died."

As in Berrigan's poem, the characters in Carroll's songs were based on people he knew growing up. A couple of them are identifiable from Carroll's earlier diaristic writing. In *The Basketball Diaries*, for example, we find the following prosaic sentence: "Bobby died of leukemia. He got it two years ago but had such a strong body (he was always the best at sports) that he kept fighting it off."[18] Carroll allowed himself in his song to cut loose from the strictures of deadpan prose by breaking down a sentence into rat-a-tat syllables: "Bobby got leukemia, fourteen years old / he looked like sixty-five when he died / he was a friend of mine." So, how do lines like these evince an indebtedness to and complication of the source text, Berrigan's "People Who Died"?

Berrigan's poem sought to use the act of naming to grace its subjects with the light of literary posterity. Berrigan used ellipses and an overall economy of scale in an effort to engage readers more actively in realizing the potential narratives in the names for themselves—the name as a kind of predigital hypertext link. Carroll did something quite similar in his own "People Who Died." Following Berrigan, each line in Carroll's song began with a person's name and was followed by a brief description of how that person died. "Teddy" died when he "fell from the roof on east two nine" after a glue-sniffing binge, "Cathy" committed suicide after ingesting "twenty six reds and a bottle of wine," "G-berg and Georgie" died of hepatitis after shooting up with dirty works, Bobby "hung himself" in jail, and so on. As in Berrigan's poem, these characters were framed bathetically as friends—"he was a friend of mine," "two more friends that *died*." Berrigan ended his poem by shifting dramatically from matter-of-fact reportage to an almost mawkish sentiment, "My friends whose deaths have slowed my heart stay with me now." Carroll makes comparable turns, moving from flatly realistic descriptions of what happened to "all my friends" to hyperbolic clichés including "And Eddie I miss you more than all the others / and I *salute you, brother*!"

There are, however, distinctions to be made here. Somewhat amusingly, Carroll's song, considered conservatively, was more like a poem than Berrigan's poem. Carroll did what poets are supposed to do—he rhymed, and he followed a rough metrics by including four accented syllables in almost every line featuring a named friend. Beyond the obvious fact that Carroll's "People Who Died" was a recorded song and Berrigan's a published poem, Carroll's narrative featured a chorus, the paradoxically gleeful collective shout of "Those are people who *died! died!* / They were all my friends, and they just *died*." Berrigan pointed to a group experience—in Carroll's song, this effort toward initiating a communal mourning was made all the more literal by having the Jim Carroll Band sing the rhyming rhythmic song of sorrow together. Crucially, Carroll joined the chorus—not for him the role of classic hero whose actions the chorus explained to the audience. Rather, his sorrow was their/our sorrow.

Carroll broke from Berrigan as well by sticking entirely to names specific to his lived experience. Carroll saw no need to grace Bobby, Joey, Eddie, and all the others with the proximate authority of fame attendant to figures like Kerouac. His friends—all doomed, all latently beautiful—were dignified instead by the propulsive energy of the bass, guitar, and drums. The perfectly ordinary urban burnout was raised to the status of legend via the production of a collective sound and accompanying chant. Carroll's stripped-down version of Berrigan's already stripped-down elegy was an attempt to free elegy from the burden of literariness—an effort that Berrigan himself was making through his antipoetic flat affect—by taking Berrigan's poem and translating it into punk rock. With Carroll's "People Who Died," the implications of Berrigan's populist poetics of sociability found a new, intoxicating form that literally played out on the radio, on TV, and on the streets. The New York School poem became the song the million punk kids sang together.

∗   ∗   ∗

As tempting as it might be to wrap this narrative up neatly by proposing "People Who Died" was a signal that a certain moment in New York City's cultural history was dead—that the influence of poetry on punk rock had reached its climax in Carroll's chant—this is not the case. Postwar American poetry continues to cast a spell on punk and post-punk well past the 1980s. Contemporary poets still look to the music to inform their verse.

In particular, the New York School of poetry endures. In a 1997 interview with Dennis Cooper, for example, Pavement frontman Stephen Malkmus claimed John Ashbery as a direct inspiration in the composition of Pavement's album *Brighten the Corners*. "Often, I'll be thinking of what I've read lately," Malkmus explained, adding, "Like I'd been reading John Ashbery before we made the album. He's brilliant, and I took his work as like, okay, I can do something like that. I don't have to do something that's really formal."[19] Far from proposing Ashbery as an obdurately difficult writer, he is instead implicitly transformed into a parodist of poetic rhetoric whose model of composition is open enough for nonspecialists to emulate.[20] Malkmus's friend David Berman, who fronted the band Silver Jews, regularly invokes poets such as Kenneth Koch as inspirations. Thurston Moore's "Frank O'Hara Hit," featured on his short-lived band Chelsea Light Moving's 2013 eponymous debut album, memorializes O'Hara's 1966 death in part by linking him to rock legends including Bob Dylan and Mick Jagger. Moore to this day regularly performs and records with writers including Anne Waldman and Clark Coolidge.

Influence doesn't end with the great stylists of alt-rock. As the New York School scholar Andrew Epstein notes, the indie-pop band Rilo Kiley's 2004 song "More Adventurous" quotes from O'Hara's prose poem "Meditations in an Emergency," and the singer Greta Kline, better known as Frankie Cosmos, claims O'Hara as both the source for her stage name and a formal influence on her 2014 album *Zentropy*.[21]

Correspondingly, contemporary American poets like Nada Gordon, K. Silem Mohammad, Drew Gardner, and other writers associated with Flarf (a movement committed to composing poetry almost entirely by collaging words and phrases drawn from Google searches) look in part to the New York School and to punk aesthetics to inform their rabidly antipoetic low-brow styles. Todd Colby, the former lead singer of the punk band Drunken Boat (named after Rimbaud's 1871 verse poem "Le bateau ivre") who became a renowned performance poet in the 1990s, cites John Ashbery as a primary influence. The conceptual poet Trisha Low goes so far as to claim in her promotional materials that she wears a shock collar (seemingly drawing on punk style to foreground her assault on lyric preciousness) and insists, if parodically, that poems in her 2013 book *The Compleat Purge* "chronicle the sexual fantasies of indie rock fangirls, who may or may not be exorcising the effects of abuse through their blithe avatars (the guy from The Strokes, etc.)."[22]

This is obviously a partial list, and other punk-motivated poets and musicians beyond those included in this book deserve attention. Barely touched upon here, one might fairly complain, are the ways in which Beat Generation writers like Allen Ginsberg became involved in the punk scene—in Ginsberg's case, writing poems including "Punk Rock Your My Big Crybaby" and recording and appearing on stage with the Clash. Work remains to be done on the role the Beat Generation writers played in the punk imaginary and, congruently, on how punk informed the writing and performance styles of Ginsberg, William Burroughs, and related figures in the 1970s and 1980s.

Moreover, the exchanges between the British performance poet John Cooper Clarke and the various bands he toured with, including the Sex

Pistols and the Fall, are also an important part of a much larger story. Following Clarke, a group of performance poets and spoken-word artists with stage names including Attila the Stockbroker and Joolz came together around the British post-punk scene of the early 1980s. They shared the bill with bands at numerous punk gigs in the United Kingdom, recorded their own albums, and appeared on punk musicians' records. The 2000s find contemporary British writers such as Sean Bonney, who has written extensively on Amiri Baraka and whose book *Happiness: After Rimbaud* proves the "Rimbaldian script" is still being scripted, drawing directly on the histories of punk to stage their provocations. Bonney's poems in the influential British online magazine *onedit*, for instance, are composed out of a series of willfully sloppy typewritten pages on which phrases including "ok here;s 3 chordS" rub messily against other fragmented refrains aimed aggressively at the police/late-capitalist state.[23]

It is clear that the conversation between punk and poetry goes well beyond downtown New York and well past the 1980s. Punk-affiliated musicians continue to draw on poetry to shape their sounds and styles. Likewise, contemporary poets still employ punk and its offspring in part to interrogate the high-art status of the poem; to unsettle received notions about authorship as a solitary, visionary activity; and to foreground performance in the composition and reception of poetry. Studying the era this book examines enables us, I hope, to think more ambitiously about what is possible when one breaches the divide between lyric verse and performed song, poetry venue and rock club, page and stage.

Notes

Introduction

1. There is no shortage of historical and critical accounts of the musical eras considered here. A very partial list of such works, all of which at the very least point to poetic influence on punk sound and style, should include Simon Warner, *Text and Drugs and Rock 'n' Roll: The Beats and Rock Culture* (London: Bloomsbury, 2013); Bernard Gendron, *Between Montmartre and the Mudd Club: Popular Music and the Avant-Garde* (Chicago: University of Chicago Press, 2002); Carrie Noland, *Poetry at Stake: Lyric Aesthetics and the Challenge of Technology* (Princeton, N.J.: Princeton University Press, 1999); Legs McNeil and Gillian McCain, *Please Kill Me: The Uncensored Oral History of Punk* (New York: Grove, 1996); Michael Azerrad, *Our Band Could Be Your Life: Scenes from the American Indie Underground, 1981-1991* (Boston: Little, Brown, 2002); Jon Savage, *England's Dreaming: Anarchy, Sex Pistols, Punk Rock, and Beyond* (New York: St. Martin's Griffin, 2002); Greil Marcus, *Lipstick Traces: A Secret History of the Twentieth Century* (Cambridge, Mass.: Harvard University Press, 1989); and Will Hermes, *Love Goes to Buildings on Fire: Five Years in New York That Changed Music Forever* (New York: Faber and Faber, 2011). What none of these works offers, however, is an in-depth account and analysis of how the New York School of poetry influenced and informed New York–based proto-punk and punk rock and, correspondingly, how punk inflected New York School poetry and poetics in the 1970s and '80s. My focus on New York music and poetry from the 1960s through the 1980s will, I hope, serve as an extension and complication of the valuable abovementioned and related scholars' works.

2. Savage, *England's Dreaming*, 530.

3. In *Lipstick Traces*, Marcus claims the critique developed by the Situationist International, who "looked back to the surrealists of the 1920s, the Dadaists who made their names during and just after the First World War, the young Karl Marx, Saint-Just, various medieval heretics and the Knights of the Round Table," reappeared

"a quarter of a century later, *to make the charts*" via the Sex Pistols single "Anarchy in the U.K." (18– 19).

4. The no-wave chanteuse Lydia Lunch followed a similar path: "Prior to my arrival [in New York] I'd only been scribbling in notebooks, like all other delinquents if they weren't writing on bathroom walls or subway trains or notebooks," Lunch recalled. Qtd. in Maria Beatty, dir., *Gang of Souls: A Generation of Beat Poets* (Oaks, Pa.: MVD Music Video Distributors, 2008). Her adolescent jottings led to her pilgrimage downtown, with mixed success. "I was coming [to New York] to do poetry," she explained. "But no one would read my poems except [Patti Smith's guitarist] Lenny Kaye. He always had an ear that was so kind." Qtd. in Byron Coley and Thurston Moore, eds., *No Wave: Post-Punk. Underground. New York. 1976–1980* (New York: Abrams Image, 2008), 12. Having trouble finding a place to read her poetry, Lunch took it to "the stage of CBGBs, that's where I took my atrocities, I felt everything that had been inflicted upon me to date I would inflict back, sort of a product of my environment." Qtd. in Beatty, *Gang of Souls.*

5. Qtd. in Beatty, *Gang of Souls.*

6. Ibid.

7. "My House," Reed's paean to Schwartz, was included on Reed's album *The Blue Mask* (1982). Drawing biographical parallels between Reed and Schwartz, Jeremy Reed describes Schwartz as "a Jewish, seriously alcoholic writer, who remained a lifelong avatar to Reed's aspirations to make pop lyricism into a serious literary expression. Reed credited Schwartz with showing him how 'with the simplest language possible, and very short, you can accomplish the most astonishing heights.'" Jeremy Reed, *Waiting for the Man: The Life and Music of Lou Reed* (New York: Omnibus, 2015), 34.

8 Lou Reed to Delmore Schwartz, 1965, Box 1, Folder 99, Delmore Schwartz Papers, Beinecke Rare Book and Manuscript Library, Yale University Library.

9. Bernadette Mayer to Richard Hell, February 20, 1983, Box 6, Folder 373, Richard Hell Papers, Fales Library and Special Collections Library, New York University.

10. Waldman served as assistant director of the Poetry Project from 1966 to 1968 and then served as director through 1976.

11. Victor Bockris, *Patti Smith* (London: HarperCollins UK, 2008), 1.

12. Ted Berrigan, "Sonnet II," in *The Collected Poems of Ted Berrigan* (Berkeley: University of California Press, 2005), 27.

13. Eileen Myles, "Exploding the Spring Mystique," in *Maxfield Parrish: Early and New Poems* (Santa Rosa, Calif.: Black Sparrow, 1995), 142.

14. Quoted in Paula Court, *New York Noise: Art and Music from the New York Underground, 1978-1986* (London: Soul Jazz Publishing, 2007), 92.

15. Daniel Kane, "An Interview with Thurston Moore," *Postmodern Culture* 25, no. 1 (2014): n.p. Richard Edson was a participant in Lewis Warsh's poetry workshops held at the Poetry Project.

16. Rhys Chatham, "either hustle to like or don't," *Ear Magazine* 1, no. 3 (Summer 1975): n.p.

17. Bockris, *Patti Smith*, 121.

18. Randy Kennedy, "Max's Kansas City Recalled in Two Exhibitions," *New York Times*, September 1, 2010, http://www.nytimes.com/2010/09/05/arts/design/05maxs. html.

19. Lou Reed, foreword to *High on Rebellion: Inside the Underground at Max's Kansas City*, by Yvonne Ruskin (New York: Thunder's Mouth, 1998), xi.

20. Bryan Waterman, *Marquee Moon* (New York: Continuum, 2011), 120–121.

21. Kaya Oakes, *Slanted and Enchanted: The Evolution of Indie Culture* (New York: Henry Holt, 2009), 53.

22. Recordings featuring avant-garde poetry and punk music were available by the mid-1970s, thanks in large part to John Giorno's *Dial-A-Poem* recordings (considered in detail in chapter 6). Harvey Kubernik's 1983 and 1984 recordings *English as a Second Language* and *Neighborhood Rhythms* are a fascinating blend of poetry and music representing the Los Angeles community and reveal a commitment to a poetics of place that echoed New York's. West Coast punks like Henry Rollins, Chuck Dukowski, D Boon, Mike Watt, and Exene Cervenka read and sometimes sang their work alongside writers like Charles Bukowski, Amy Gerstler, and Dennis Cooper. Even on these recordings, however, New York casts its shadow. Dennis Cooper's recitation of his "Seven Poets Chosen by John Ashbery (Dedicated to Tim Dlugos)" on *English* not only refers to the New York School poet Ashbery but also is recited in a comically haughty nasal twang that practically ventriloquizes the manner in which Ashbery and Frank O'Hara sounded.

23. New York critics were quick to identify West Coast Johnny-come-latelys to the punk party—in a fairly scathing review in *The East Village Eye* of a Dead Kennedys show, David Katz set up a binary opposition between "art" and "politics" that served simultaneously to compare San Francisco unfavorably to New York: "The Dead Kennedys hate [California] but unfortunately are from the thick of it, or they've been out there in the sun too long. At Max's they sounded loud and muddy and very energetic but their numbers reek of political concerns or just plain sentimental concern; political concern being among the lower human endeavours [sic] and sentiment, however nihilistically marinated, being the opposite of rock. Who cares who the latest stooge in office is anyway; the Dead Kennedys big song, 'California Uber Alles' is full of dark brown knitting concern over wheat germ dictator Governor Brown. To me it's the same thing as 'MacArthur Park,' or 'Eve of Destruction.'" David Katz, "Dead Kennedys Alive," *East Village Eye* 1 no. 4 (September 1979), 9. Recent work by contemporary literary historians also makes an issue out of the East Coast–West Coast divide during the 1970s. Brandon Stosuy helpfully sets up a distinction between the psychedelicisms of Pynchon and the "minimalism" he associates with New York "downtown" writing and insists that New York punk had its effect on a developing literary style. See Brandon Stosuy, *Up Is Up, But So Is Down: New York's Downtown Literary Scene, 1974-1992* (New York: NYU Press, 2006), 19.

24. We should also address the fact that New York punks were older than their British counterparts and were more situated in a 1960s counterculture that looked to its poets as high priests. Caroline Coon notes: "While New York cultivates avantgarde and intellectual punks like Patti Smith and Television, the British teenager, that much more alienated from rock than America ever was, has little time for such aesthetic refinements. . . . There's an age difference, too. New York punks are mostly in their mid-twenties. The members of the new British punk bands squirm if they have to tell you they are over 18." Caroline Coon, *1988, the New Wave, Punk Rock Explosion* (London: Orbach & Chambers, 1997), 19.

25. Rudy Kikel, "Dennis Cooper: New Moves for the Poet of Distances," *Advocate* (November 24, 1983): 57.

26. During his interview with Rudy Kikel, Cooper revealed that he had spent the previous night at "CBGBs—a very important club in the mid '70s that's now on sort of hard times." Ibid., 57.

27. Anne Waldman, foreword to *Angel Hair Sleeps with a Boy in My Head: The Angel Hair Anthology*, by Anne Waldman et al. (New York City: Granary, 2001), xxi.

28. See Daniel Kane, "*Angel Hair* Magazine, the Second-Generation New York School, and the Poetics of Sociability," *Contemporary Literature* 45, no. 2 (2004): 346–347.

29. Ted Berrigan, Stephen Ratcliffe, and Leslie Scalapino, *Talking in Tranquility: Interviews with Ted Berrigan* (Bolinas, Calif.: Avenue B; Oakland, Calif.: O Books, 1991), 90–91.

30. Colin Murray, "Patti, the Stones, & Rimbaud," *White Stuff* 5 (September/October 1977): 12.

31. Quoted in Roberta Bayley, *Blank Generation Revisited: The Early Days of Punk Rock* (New York: Prentice Hall International, 1997), n.p.

32. Roman Kozak, "Anarchy at the Labels: Does This Mean I'm Out?," *Billboard* 90, no. 2 (1978): 49.

33. Seymour Stein, "Assault on the Record Industry!," *Billboard* 90, no. 2 (1978): 49.

34. Fugazi is perhaps the prototype for punk bands' hostility to "selling out." A 1993 *Washington Post* article on the band captured Fugazi's ethos nicely:

There are three facts about Fugazi you must know:

It only plays shows where age IDs are not required.

It charges $5 admission to its shows, always.

It will never, ever sign with a major record label.

Its rigid adherence to these precepts gives the band that most valuable of intangibles: integrity. The flip side of integrity is selling out, which can be loosely defined in the music business as putting yourself before your fans. Fugazi doesn't.

Eric Brace, "Punk Lives! Washington's Fugazi Claims It's Just a Band. So Why Do So Many Kids Think It's God?," *Washington Post*, August 1, 1993, https://www.washingtonpost.com/archive/lifestyle/style/1993/08/01/punk-lives-washingtons-fugazi-claims-its-just-a-band-so-why-do-so-many-kids-think-its-god/6c56fef5-780a-4a6e-8411-8c6b407e1eed/.

35. "[Kenneth] Koch calls Ashbery avant-garde and writes a literary memoir based on Apollinaire's 'Zone.' [David] Lehman [in his book *The Last Avant-Garde*] observes 'substitute Frank O'Hara for Apollinaire and Abstract expressionism for Cubism, and you get an eerie fit,' and in fact O'Hara, who was known as the New York School's Apollinaire, made numerous references to avant-garde writers such as Mayakovsky and Mallarmé." William Watkin, *In the Process of Poetry: The New York School and the Avant-Garde* (Lewisburg, Penn.: Bucknell University Press, 2001), 12.

36. Noland, *Poetry at Stake*, 3.

37. Ibid.

38. Simon Frith, "Music and Identity," in *Taking Popular Music Seriously: Selected Essays* (Aldershot: Ashgate, 2007), 301.

39. Berrigan, *Collected Poems*, 19. Berrigan received his master's degree at the University of Tulsa in 1962 for his thesis on George Bernard Shaw, but he ended up mailing his diploma back to the university, explaining in a note that he was the "master of no art."

40. Andreas Huyssen, *After the Great Divide: Modernism, Mass Culture, Postmodernism* (Bloomington: Indiana University Press, 1986), 164.

41. See, for example, Savage, *England's Dreaming*; Marcus, *Lipstick Traces*; Noland, *Poetry at Stake*; Gendron, *Between Montmartre and the Mudd Club*. Greg Shaw, "The Beat," *Bomp!* (November 1977): 4–5, argues irreverently and interestingly that high culture contaminates low culture, not the other way around. Claiming rock 'n' roll as a kind of avant-garde, Shaw insists the music succeeds in erasing the boundaries between "art" and "life":

> Although I've been typecast as one of the prime eggheads in this field and will admit to some inspirational responsibility for the excesses that have been committed in its name, I've always tried to draw the line between real bullshit—trying to "justify" rock in terms of modern art, film critique, literary tradition, "auteur theory," etc—and the kind of questions that any rock & roll fan who cares about the music, has a brain, and doesn't mind using it, is gonna want answers to.

> I don't think there's any great Meaning in rock & roll . . . and I have little patience with those who seek it in Dylan lyrics or the lost chords of the Moody Blues. To me, rock theory has always started from the fact that this music, when it's done right, has an amazing power to make me (and a lot of other people too, presumably) feel great in a way that nothing else can.

42. Lou Reed to Delmore Schwartz, 1965, Box 1, Folder 99, Delmore Schwartz Papers, Beinecke Rare Book and Manuscript Library, Yale University.

43. Victor Bockris, "The Poetry of Performance," *Carry Out* (1972): 12–13. Smith would repeat variations on the "hero" theme in a number of her interviews. "I've always been hero-oriented," Smith insisted to Penny Green. "I started doing art not because I had creative instincts but because I fell in love with artists. I didn't come to this city to become an artist, but to become an artist's mistress. Art in the beginning for me was never a vehicle for self-expression, it was a way to ally myself with heroes, 'cause I couldn't make contact with God." Patti Smith, interview by Penny Green, *Interview* (October 1973): 25.

44. Dan Graham, *Rock/Music Writings* (New York: Primary Information, 2009), 6.

45. Lenny Kaye, "Interview," *Punk* 1, no. 2 (March 1976): 8. Quotation appears in all capital letters in the original.

46. Frank O'Hara, "Personism," in *The Collected Poems of Frank O'Hara*, ed. Donald Allen (Berkeley: University of California Press, 1995), 498.

47. O'Hara, *Collected Poems*, 262.

48. Ron Padgett, *Collected Poems* (Minneapolis, Minn.: Coffee House, 2013), 103.

49. Aram Saroyan, *Complete Minimal Poems* (New York: Ugly Duckling Presse, 2007), 42.

50. Helen Vendler, *The Art of Shakespeare's Sonnets* (Cambridge, Mass.: Harvard University Press, 1999), 2.

51. Qtd. in Terence Diggory, "Elinor Nauen," in *Encyclopedia of the New York School Poets* (New York: Facts on File, 2009), 334.

52. Qtd. in Daniel Kane, "'Nor Did I Socialize with Their People': Patti Smith, Rock Heroics, and the Poetics of Sociability," *Popular Music* 31, no. 1 (2012): 111.

53. Bill Ogersby, "'Chewing Out a Rhythm on My Bubble-Gum': The Teen Aesthetic and Genealogies of American Punk," in *Punk Rock: So What? The Cultural Legacy of Punk*, ed. Roger Sabin (London: Routledge, 1999), 166.

54. David Johansen, "Punks Have It Out," *Punk* 1 no. 3 (April 1976): 8.

55. Waterman, *Marquee Moon*, 83.

56. Dee Dee Ramone, Tommy Ramone, et al., "Ramones," *Punk* 1 no. 3 (April 1976): 18. Quotation appears in all capital letters in the original.

57. Rossignol ended up running Some Records in New York City's East Village in the mid-1980s. The store built up a reputation as a welcoming hangout for hardcore punks.

58. Duane Rossignol, "Punk Poll Results," *Bomp* (November 1977): 37.

59. Lester Bangs, *Psychotic Reactions and Carburetor Dung* (New York: Vintage, 1988), 74.

60. Qtd. in ibid., 218.

61. Waterman, *Marquee Moon*, 143.

62. Greg Shaw, "The Beat," *Bomp!* (November 1977): 185.

63. Brent DiCrescenzo, "Sonic Youth: *NYC Ghosts & Flowers*," *Pitchfork* (April 30, 2000), http://pitchfork.com/reviews/albums/7342-nyc-ghosts-flowers/.

1. The Fugs Are Coming

1. Jeffrey Lewis, *Complete History of Punk Rock*, https://www.youtube.com/watch?v=88QLxLHQW_M, uploaded April 17, 2007.

2. Ed Sanders, *Fug You: An Informal History of the Peace Eye Bookstore, the Fuck You Press, the Fugs, and Counterculture in the Lower East Side* (Cambridge, Mass.: Da Capo, 2011), 228.

3. "One of the least recognized lines of punk's myth narrative tells how Ed Sanders, a young poet and activist who graduated from New York University with a degree in classics, opened a used bookstore on the Lower East Side of Manhattan and in the winter of 1964–65 teamed up with fellow poet Tuli Kupferberg to form the Fugs, the prototypical New York, beatnik, art-rock group, the precursors of the Velvet Underground and, through them, the entire New York and international new wave rock culture of the mid-1970s onwards." Steven Taylor, *False Prophet: Fieldnotes from the Punk Underground* (Middletown, Conn.: Wesleyan University Press, 2003), 38–39.

4. Richard Hell, "Intros to poetry readings," 1987–1988, Series 3D, Box 11, Folder 769, Richard Hell Papers, Fales Library and Special Collections, New York University.

5. For more in-depth histories of Sanders's *Fuck You*, see Sanders's *Fug You* and my *All Poets Welcome: The Lower East Side Poetry Scene in the 1960s* (Berkeley: University of California Press, 2003), 64–79.

6. Jack Godard, "Fug Rock from the Lower East Side," *Cavalier* (June 1966): 83.

7. The slogan, accompanying a diagram that showed how to play the A, E, and G chords, appeared in the December 1976 issue of the British punk fanzine *Sideburns*.

8. Dave Markey, dir., *1991: The Year That Punk Broke* (Hollywood, Calif.: Universal, 1992), DVD.

9. As the future Fugs guitarist Steven Taylor put it, "The Fugs prefigured punk in a number of ways. They championed musical amateurism, a disregard for mainstream decorum, and a radical politics. Most significantly, like the key New York art rock performers Richard Hell and Patti Smith of the subsequent generation, they were poets before they were musicians" (*False Prophet*, 48).

10. I should note however that bands like the Beatles were inspirational to Sanders and Kupferberg. Sanders was particularly moved by the fact that the Beatles spelled their name "Beatles" instead of "Beetles" because "the group's name had been inspired by Ginsberg, Kerouac, and crew. And that started me thinking about a blend of music and poetry. I couldn't help but notice how The Beatles' words were crystal clear! Intimately hearable! That would be my goal with The Fugs—that the words could at last star in the musical mix." Sanders, *Fug You*, 68.

11. Kupferberg is widely credited as the subject in Allen Ginsberg's "Howl" who jumped off the Brooklyn Bridge and helped set the stage in the late 1950s for the Lower East Side as the site for experiments in publishing and alternative lifestyles. Kupferberg's Birth Press was a precursor for Sanders's Fuck You press and magazine. As early as 1959, Kupferberg was making the kinds of links between Beat Generation poetry, pop culture, and nineteenth-century French poetry that would become practically cliché among the rock 'n' roll cognoscenti of the late 1960s and early 1970s. "The Beats," Kupferberg opined,

> link themselves & are linked to the new rising energies of Africa & Asia, to the primitive current life-loving peoples of Mexico & the Caribbean, to the old wisdoms of Asia, to the crazy Bohemian poets of 19th century France breaking their heads against the coming calamities & yet raging after joy, digging life. . . . Since the Beat is outside of society (aiming to create his own by main force) he is sympathetic to, understanding with & seeks the friendship & support the comfort and the aid of & to aid and comfort those others also on the outside.

Tuli Kupferberg, *Beating* (New York: Birth Press, 1959), n.p.

12. Sanders, *Fug You*, 69.

13. Ibid., 112.

14. Godard, "Fug Rock from the Lower East Side," 82–83.

15. Allen Ginsberg, *Howl and Other Poems: Pocket Poets Number 4* (San Francisco: City Lights, 1956), 12.

16. Frederick Whiting, "Monstrosity on Trial: The Case of 'Naked Lunch,'" *Twentieth Century Literature* 52, no. 2 (2006): 145.

17. Don Cusic, *Encyclopedia of Contemporary Christian Music: Pop, Rock, and Worship* (Santa Barbara, Calif.: ABC-CLIO, 2009), 27–28.

18. See, for example, Lawrence Lipton, *Holy Barbarians* (New York: Messner, 1959); Aldon Lynn Nielsen, *Reading Race: White American Poets and the Racial Discourse in the Twentieth Century* (Athens: University of Georgia Press, 1988); Jon Panish, *The Color of Jazz: Race and Representation in Postwar American Culture* (Jackson: University Press of Mississippi, 1997).

19. Tuli Kupferberg and Ed Sanders, "Notes on the Fugs," in *The Fugs Songbook* (Detroit: Artists Workshop, 1966), n.p.

20. Charles Olson, *Selected Writings of Charles Olson*, ed. Robert Creeley (New York: New Directions, 1966), 19.

21. Ibid., 19, 22.

22. Tuli Kupferberg to Barry Miles, n.d., Box 1, Folder 3, The Fugs Archive, Fales Special Collections Library, New York University.

23. Sanders, *Fug You*, 196.

24. "During the Newark ghetto revolt of 1967, Baraka was injured, arrested by the police, and indicted for unlawfully carrying firearms. An all-white jury convicted him, and after the judge read Baraka's poem 'Black People!' to the court, the poet was sentenced to 2–2½ years in jail without parole." Werner Sollors, *Amiri Baraka/LeRoi Jones: The Quest for a "Populist Modernism"* (New York: Columbia University Press, 1978), 6.

25. Imamu Amiri Baraka, *Transbluesency: The Selected Poems of Amiri Baraka/LeRoi Jones (1961–1995)* (Venice: Marsilio, 1995), 224.

26. Sanders, *Fug You*, 323.

27. Tuli Kupferberg to Barry Miles, April 13, 1965, Box 1, Folder 3, The Fugs Archive.

28. The LP was initially titled *The Village Fugs Sing Ballads of Contemporary Protest, Point of Views, and General Dissatisfaction*; in its second incarnation with ESP Records, it became *The Fugs First Album* (New York: ESP-Disk, 1965). All references to the Fugs' first album will be to the ESP edition.

29. Sanders, *Fug You*, 175.

30. The Fugs were so identified with their place in the East Village that "Slum Goddess" inspired a regular column "Slum Goddess of the Lower East Side" in the counterculture newspaper *East Village Other*. Parodying *Playboy* centerfolds, the column featured photographs of local young women accompanied by mini-interviews and the like. The first "Slum Goddess" was none other than the civil rights activist Suze Rotolo, the woman featured on the cover of Bob Dylan's *Freewheelin' Bob Dylan*.

31. John Gruen, *The New Bohemia: The Combine Generation* (New York: Shorecrest, 1966), 8.

32. Thomas Clark, "Allen Ginsberg, The Art of Poetry No. 8," *Paris Review* (Spring 1966), http://www.theparisreview.org/interviews/4389/the-art-of-poetry-no-8 -allen-ginsberg.

33. Ginsberg, *Howl and Other Poems*, 27.

34. Ibid, 9.

35. Algernon Charles Swinburne, *Poems and Ballads and Atalanta in Calydon* (London: Penguin, 2000), 310.

36. Analyzing the meter of the original poem on the page, R. Bruce Elder scans the opening lines dismissively as follows: "ta-BOOM-ta-ta BOOM-ta-ta BOOM-ta / BOOM-ta-ta BOOM-ta-ta BOOM—the Swinburne stomp, I call it. The rhythm is firm, the stresses heavy. Ten out of twelve lines begin with a noun (Or 'and' along with a noun) followed by an adjectival phrase. This sameness reinforces the heavy bass-drum 'BOOM-ta-ta' metre, hardly alleviated by the mixing of dactyls and trochees, or by the fact that rhythm almost bears being scanned as all trochees." R. Bruce Elder, *The Films of Stan Brakhage in the American Tradition of Ezra Pound, Gertrude Stein, and Charles Olson* (Waterloo, Ont.: Wilfrid Laurier University Press, 1998), 191–92. Elder's distaste is in part based on his incredulity that Ezra Pound, a poet that both he and Sanders very much admired, had cited Swinburne as an important predecessor and influence. "How far Swinburne's rhythms are from Pound's! . . . [In Pound's 'Canto XLVII'] we hear no hoof-beat echo, no thumping foot. Even when his song was furious, he avoided stomping out the metre" (192–93). But why would Sanders—the editor who loved Pound so much that he pirated Ezra Pound's final drafts and cantos and published them in *Fuck You*, repercussions be damned—treat his hero's hero in such an overtly mocking way, complete with slide whistles, shrieks, and absurd exaggerations? Perhaps Sanders's "Swineburne Stomp" was a way for Sanders to interrogate the authority Pound (and, by implication, other respected poets and critics) assumed in anointing the blessed and identifying the blasted.

37. Richard Aquila, *That Old Time Rock and Roll: A Chronicle of an Era, 1954-1963* (New York: Schirmer, 1989), 20.

38. Carrie Noland, *Poetry at Stake: Lyric Aesthetics and the Challenge of Technology* (Princeton, N.J.: Princeton University Press, 1999), 164.

39. Ed Sanders, "Ed Sanders Newsletter," 1966, Box 1, Folder 6, The Fugs Archives.

40. *The Fugs* (New York, N.Y.: ESP-Disk, 1966).

41. Sanders, *Fug You*, 258.

42. Qtd. in Michael Davidson, *Guys Like Us: Citing Masculinity in Cold War Poetics*, (Chicago: University of Chicago Press, 2004), 77.

43. Jonah Raskin, *American Scream: Allen Ginsberg's Howl and the Making of the Beat Generation* (Berkeley: University of California Press, 2004), xii.

44. Ibid, xx.

45. Raskin, *American Scream*, xxii.

46. Ginsberg, *Howl and Other Poems*, 16.

47. Bob Perelman, "On the Jewish Question: Three Perspectives," in *Radical Poetics and Secular Jewish Culture*, ed. Stephen Paul Miller and Daniel Morris (Tuscaloosa: University of Alabama Press, 2010), 50–51.

48. Ginsberg, *Howl and Other Poems*, 21.

49. Perelman, "On the Jewish Question," 49–50.

50. Sanders, *Fug You*, 239.

51. Ibid., 404.

52. This phrase and variations of this phrase appear throughout *Fug You*.

2. Lou Reed: "In the Beginning Was the Word"

1. I don't mean to suggest here that we should ignore the well-documented links between the Velvet Underground and the New York arts and music scenes that the band was so obviously a part of (from La Monte Young's experiments with the drone to Andy Warhol's work in serial repetition). Rather, I want to *add* to the historical record by including poetry as a genre that was important to the Velvets' development.

2. See Clinton Heylin, *All Yesterday's Parties: The Velvet Underground in Print, 1966-1971* (Boston: Da Capo, 2009), for a compendium of articles on the EPI and the Velvets.

3. Brandon Joseph, "My Mind Split Open: Andy Warhol's Exploding Plastic Inevitable," in *Summer of Love: Psychedelic Art, Social Crisis, and Counterculture in the 1960s*, ed. Christoph Grunenberg and Jonathan Harris (Liverpool: Liverpool University Press, 2005), 239.

4. Ibid, 239–40.

5. Gerard Malanga to Kenneth Koch, April 3, 1961, Kenneth Koch Papers, Berg Collection, New York Public Library.

6. Bill Berkson, e-mail message to author, August 1, 2013.

7. Lewis Warsh, e-mail message to author, August 1, 2013.

8. Ron Padgett, e-mail message to author, August 1, 2013.

9. Quoted in Wayne McGuire, "The Boston Sound," in *All Yesterday's Parties*, 75–76.

10. Quoted in Robert Greenfield, "C/O The Velvet Underground, New York," in *All Yesterday's Parties*, 137.

11. Heylin, *All Yesterday's Parties*, 23.

12. Gerard Malanga, interview with the author, July 9, 2013.

13. Qtd. in Victor Bockris, *Uptight: The Velvet Underground Story* (London: Omnibus, 2009), 47.

14. Ibid., 47–48.

15. Victor Bockris, *Transformer: The Complete Lou Reed Story* (London: Harper, 2014), 46.

16. Jack Kerouac, *The Subterraneans* (New York: Grove/Atlantic, 2007).

17. Quoted in David Rosenthal, *Hard Bop: Jazz and Black Music, 1955-1965* (Oxford: Oxford University Press, 1993), 77–78.

18. Jack Kerouac, *Mexico City Blues* (New York: Grove, 1990), 3.

19. Consider season 1, episode 10, of *The Many Loves of Dobie Gillis* (the episode, aired in 1959, was entitled "It Takes Two"). The conservatively dressed and coiffed Gillis waits in a courtyard for his raggedy, hep-cat companion Maynard G. Krebs to update him on a plan to meet a girl. Sporting a beatnik uniform of ripped dirty sweatshirt, baggy white trousers, and compulsory goatee, Krebs walks into the courtyard scatting "Peeya poo pee poo peeya poo poh poh," à la Betty Carter or Ella Fitzgerald. "Did you give Poppy the message?" Gillis asks Krebs. "Yeah, man," replies Krebs nonchalantly. "And you told her it was an emergency?" Gillis presses. "Oh, like life and death man," Krebs responds none too convincingly, adding that

Gillis's love interest will make a showing in about five minutes. "Good man!" a relieved Gillis declares, adding, "Oh Maynard, you oughta get yourself a girl." "Oh not me, big Daddy" responds Krebs. "I've tried girls and it's like, nowhere . . . You try girls if you wanna, me, I'm stickin' to jazz." This comment elicited a hearty guffaw on the show's laughtrack. By 1960, in large part because of its association with suburban alternative types aping their poetry idols, jazz had become shorthand for wooly, lazy literary pretenders looking to acquire easy countercultural cache.

20. Rosenthal, *Hard Bop*, 152.

21. Swados, brother to playwright Elizabeth Swados, was Reed's close friend and roommate at Syracuse University. Reed's "Harry's Circumcision: Reverie Gone Astray" on the album *Magic and Loss* memorializes Swados, who died homeless on the streets of New York in 1989.

22. Allan Millstein, "Five Authors in Search of a Campus Publication," *Daily Orange* (May 11, 1963): 1.

23. Ibid.

24. The quotation marks around "Luis" are Millstein's, indicating he was fully aware that Reed regularly went by the name "Lou." Perhaps Reed was trying, in the vein of the hipsters described in Norman Mailer's essay "The White Negro," to evoke a racialized authority predicated on the "other," in this case by trying on a Latino name. The fifth editor was Reed's friend Karl Stoecker, an art student at Syracuse. Stoecker would later make a name for himself as a photographer, shooting album covers for Lou Reed and Roxy Music, among others.

25. Millstein, "Five Authors," 9.

26. Lou Reed, "Prologue," *Lonely Woman Quarterly* (May 7, 1962): n.p.

27. Ibid.

28. "We were all in our early twenties. John Ashbery, Barbara Guest, Kenneth Koch, and I, being poets, divided our time between the literary bar, the San Remo, and the artists' bar, the Cedar Tavern. In the San Remo we argued and gossiped; in the Cedar we often wrote poems while listening to the painters argue and gossip." Frank O'Hara, *The Collected Poems of Frank O'Hara*, ed. Donald Allen (Berkeley: University of California Press, 1995), 512.

29. Lou Reed, "Prologue."

30. Ibid.

31. Lou Reed, "Michael Kogan—Syracuse's Miss Blanding," *Lonely Woman Quarterly* (May 23, 1962): n.p.

32. Lou Reed, "And What, Little Boy, Will You Trade For Your Horse?," *Lonely Woman Quarterly* (April 1963): 25.

33. Ibid, 26.

34. Ibid.

35. Other contributors to *Lonely Woman Quarterly* were openly contemptuous of Beat pretenders. John Gaines's "EXCERPT from *Village '60*," included in *Lonely Woman 3*, sneered that "the movement of 'beatdom,' whatever that may be, seems to have spawned a whole slew of griping 'poets' and pseudo-intellects whom I prefer to call exhibitchionists (with the emphasis upon 'bitch'). These persons and their followers seem to never read anything more stimulating than Peanuts cartoons and the drivel which passes off as stream of consciousness 'poetry.' The beat movement

seems to have taken the existential idea of man's personal aloneness and misconstrued it to mean 'Why try?'" (5).

36. Reed, "And What, Little Boy," 29.

37. Bockris, *Transformer*, 57.

38. During Reed's senior year at Syracuse, Reed took the leap "from making the short story his primary form to song lyrics, taking his knowledge of the short story structure with him. Dylan not only showed him a way to write lyrics, he legitimised being a singer/songwriter with intellectual credentials. That was the vital point. Lou needed to be recognized intellectually." Bockris, *Lou Reed*, 69–70.

39. Bob Dylan, who was awarded the Nobel Prize for Literature in 2016, took weeks to acknowledge he was even aware of the honor. Despite finally conceding that he was in fact touched by the award, he failed to show up for the ceremony, claiming preexisting commitments. Dylan's studiously dismissive response to critics who wished to invest him with poetic authority stands in stark contrast to Reed's efforts throughout his career to align himself to a privileged literary domain.

40. Lou Reed, *Between Thought and Expression: Selected Lyrics* (New York: Penguin, 1993), iv.

41. Jeremy Reed, *Waiting for the Man: The Life and Career of Lou Reed* (Woodstock, N.Y.: Overlook, 2015), 38.

42. Andrew Epstein, "'I'll Be Your Mirror': Lou Reed and the New York School of Poetry," *Harriet: The Blog*, http://www.poetryfoundation.org/harriet/2013/10/ill-be-your-mirror-lou-reed-and-the-new-york-school-of-poetry/.

43. Ibid.

44. Gerard Malanga, interview with the author.

45. As James Atlas illustrates, Schwartz regularly mined the intimate details of his past for material. Schwartz's "The March Beginning," which Atlas describes as "an ecstatic, Iliad-like catalogue of his mother's friends, his father's business associates, and his neighbors in the Washington Heights area of New York where Delmore grew up," finds Schwartz reveling in the "euphonious" qualities of proper names: "The Siegels and Rose Grauer / And Mrs. Berkowitz"; "The Kottles, the Davises, / Helene, her mother, and Irving, / The sister, her husband, their dog"; "Mrs. Guichester who had lovers like Molly Bloom." James Atlas, *Delmore Schwartz: The Life of an American Poet* (New York: Farrar, Straus and Giroux, 1977), 4.

46. Lou Reed and John Cale, *Songs for Drella* (New York: Sire Records, 1990).

47. Andy Warhol, *The Philosophy of Andy Warhol: From A to B and Back Again* (New York: Harcourt Brace Jovanovich, 1975), 178–79.

48. A useful counternarrative to this perhaps overly simplistic alignment of O'Hara and Warhol with urban space can be found in Timothy Gray, *Urban Pastoral: Natural Currents in the New York School* (Iowa City: University of Iowa Press, 2010). Gray sets out to revise both the legacy of the postwar avant-garde and the dominant readings of New York School–affiliated poems as inextricably bound to the city. Repainting New York School poets as modern-day Colins and Cuddies, Gray offers an important reconsideration of the possibilities of the pastoral mode as it engages with New York City as a material place and as a poetics.

49. O'Hara, *Collected Poems*, 197.

50. Warhol, *The Philosophy of Andy Warhol*, 31.

51. The articles, flyers, and advertisements for Aspen were all contained in a hinged cardboard box designed by Warhol to look like a box of Fab detergent.

52. Lou Reed, "The View from the Bandstand," *Aspen* 1, no. 3 (1966): 1.

53. Amiri Baraka, *The Autobiography of LeRoi Jones* (Chicago: Chicago Review, 2012), 232.

54. Marjorie Perloff, *Frank O'Hara: Poet Among Painters* (Chicago: University of Chicago Press, 1977), 13.

55. Reed, "The View from the Bandstand," 1–2. Perhaps Reed was following Bob Dylan's lead here, who in 1965 had described Smokey Robinson as "America's best living poet." Qtd. in Bob Gulla, *Icons of R&B and Soul: Smokey Robinson and the Miracles, the Temptations, the Supremes, Stevie Wonder* (Westport, Conn.: Greenwood, 2008), 258.

56. Epstein, "I'll be Your Mirror."

57. Ted Berrigan to Delmore Schwartz, 1964, Box 1, Folder 10, Delmore Schwartz Papers, Beinecke Special Collections Library, Yale University.

58. Delmore Schwartz, "Seurat's Sunday Afternoon Along the Seine," in *Screeno: Stories & Poems* (New York: New Directions, 2004), 122.

59. "Tom Clark in Conversation with Beat Scene Editor Kevin Ring," *Jacket* 21 (Autumn 2002), http://jacketmagazine.com/21/clark-iv1.html.

60. Ibid.

61. Geoffrey Cannon, "The Insects of Someone Else's Thoughts," in Heylin, *All Yesterday's Parties*, 201.

62. Lou Reed, "Murder Mystery," *Paris Review* 53 (1972): 20.

63. The Beatles, *Sgt. Pepper's Lonely Hearts Club Band* (Hollywood, Calif.: Capitol, 1967).

64. Byron, *Don Juan* (London: Penguin, 2004), 37.

65. Ted Berrigan, "Three Sonnets for Tom Clark," *Paris Review* 53 (1972): 163.

66. Bill Brown, *Words and Guitar: A History of Lou Reed's Music* (Brooklyn, N.Y.: Colossal Books, 2013), 17.

67. Charley Patton, *Charley Patton, Founder of the Delta Blues* (New York: Yazoo, 1970).

68. Nick Johnstone, *Lou Reed Talking* (London: Omnibus, 2005), 33.

69. Daniel Morris, "Whose Life Is Saved by Rock and Roll? An Essay on the Lyrics of Lou Reed," *Popular Music and Society* 16, no. 3 (1992): 25.

70. Reed's "I'm Waiting for My Man" similarly echoes "Howl" in that the speaker in Reed's song is in Harlem (Ginsberg's "negro streets") looking for his own angry fix. In his interview included in the documentary *Rock and Roll Heart* Reed reminded viewers, "I was influenced by Burroughs and Ginsberg, Raymond Chandler . . . that's what I wanted to do, but with a guitar."

71. Allen Ginsberg, *Howl and Other Poems: Pocket Poets Number 4* (San Francisco: City Lights, 1956), 18.

72. Matthew Bannister, "'I'm Set Free . . . ': The Velvet Underground, 1960s Counterculture, and Michel Foucault," *Popular Music and Society* 33, no. 2 (2010): 169.

73. John Ashbery, *Reported Sightings: Art Chronicles, 1957–1987*, ed. David Bergman (Cambridge, Mass.: Harvard University Press, 1991), 393.

74. Mark Silverberg, *The New York School Poets and the Neo-Avant-Garde: Between Radical Art and Radical Chic* (Farnham: Ashgate, 2010), 7.

75. As Tirza Latimer claims in a fascinating article exploring the iconography of the sailor in gay and balletomane culture of the late-nineteenth and twentieth centuries, "The sailor—thanks to a maritime hornpipe tradition of long standing—provides a credible pretext for male balletic virtuosity. The sailor's uniform, meanwhile, calls attention to the male body; its tailoring emphasizes buttocks, biceps, deltoids, and pectorals. . . . The figure cut by the sailor—'fully conscious of the attraction of his uniform to both sexes,' as W. H. Auden notes—articulates desire and indiscriminate sexual availability." Tirza True Latimer, "Balletomania: A Sexual Disorder?," *GLQ: A Journal of Lesbian and Gay Studies* 5, no. 2 (January 1, 1999): 185.

76. The 1950s saw sailor suits featured "in musicals, vaudeville, drag shows, pantomime, Hollywood films, and children's dress-ups . . . They had by this time attracted a certain ambivalence due perhaps to the prevalence of queens, gays, and cross-dressers in the navy and the custom of nautical drag shows, which, in turn, influenced the naval themes of musicals such as *HMS Pinafore* and *South Pacific*. . . . Despite these ambivalent connotations and diverse uses, the sailor suit remained a form of 'best' wear for children." Jennifer Craik, "The Cultural Politics of the Uniform," *Fashion Theory* 7, no. 2 (June 1, 2003): 60.

77. Lou Reed himself wore the sailor suit and cap: "One summer [Reed] worked as an attendant at Jones Beach, which entailed wearing a sailor's suit and cap." Howard Sounes, *Notes from the Velvet Underground: The Life of Lou Reed* (London: Doubleday, 2015), 8.

78. Smith "found a copy of Arthur Rimbaud's 'Illuminations' in a bargain book bin in the bus terminal, along with old copies of the *Evergreen Review*, a journal that in the early and mid-sixties was publishing Jean Genet and William Burroughs, and that had advertisements for bookstores and art galleries in New York." Sharon Delano, "The Torch Singer," *The New Yorker* (March 11, 2002), http://www.newyorker. com/magazine/2002/03/11/the-torch-singer.

79. As Fred Jordan characterized it in his introduction to *The Evergreen Review Reader*, in the late 1950s and early 1960s "*Evergreen* published writing that was literally counter to the culture, and if it was sexy, so much the better. In the context of the time, sex was politics, and the powers-that-be made the suppression of sexuality a political issue. The court battles that [*Evergreen Review*'s publishing arm] Grove Press fought for the legal publication of *Lady Chatterley's Lover, Tropic of Cancer,* and *Naked Lunch*, and for the legal distribution of the film *I Am Curious: Yellow*, spilled onto the pages of *Evergreen Review*, and in 1964, an issue of *Evergreen* itself was confiscated in New York State by the Nassau County District Attorney on obscenity charges." Fred Jordan, Barney Rosset, et al., *Evergreen Review Reader* (New York: Grove, 1979), ix.

80. Loren Glass, *Counterculture Colophon: Grove Press, the* Evergreen Review, *and the Incorporation of the Avant-Garde* (Stanford, Calif.: Stanford University Press, 2013), 28–29.

81. For a lively analysis of this curious period in American literary history, see Jed Birmingham, "Burroughs and Beats in Men's Magazines: William Burroughs's Appearances in Adult Men's Magazines," *RealityStudio*, http://realitystudio.org/bib liographic-bunker/burroughs-and-beats-in-mens-magazines/william-burroughs -appearances-in-adult-mens-magazines/.

82. Generally speaking, the poem's meaning as it was defined by its place in *Swank* has received short shrift from critics. The exception is Peter Middleton's account, which goes far in thinking theoretically about what the appearance of "Ave Maris" in *Swank* might mean in terms of reader reception and response. While Middleton was not able to track down the copy of *Swank* that O'Hara's poem was featured in, he does note helpfully that his overall impressions of the poem "are based on looking at another issue from the same year, the issue for January 1961 which contains poems by Ginsberg and LeRoi Jones ('Hymn for Lanie Poo' where he brilliantly satirizes the idea that black people have the jungle in their make-up), as well as articles with titles such as 'Plush pad for mobile playboys,' 'Big business takes a sex break,' and an article on London night life, 'The pleasures of Percy.' In this type of company, 'Ave Maria' would read as a literal incitement to (hetero)sexual pleasure and a celebration of cinema sexuality. The poem would also gleam like the expensive commodities in those bachelor digs, where new writing would be part of the lifestyle." Peter Middleton, *Distant Reading: Performance, Readership, and Consumption in Contemporary Poetry* (Tuscaloosa: University of Alabama Press, 2005), 14.

Noting that the poem then found a second life in Ted Berrigan's *C* magazine, Middleton moves on to reveal how crucial context was in ensuring O'Hara's poem would retain a provocative charge. By the time Berrigan printed O'Hara's "Ave Maria" in *C*, Berrigan's "front page announced that both *C* and Ed Sanders' even more sexually provocative *Fuck You*, had been nominated for a magazine award, thereby linking the two magazines in the mind of the reader" (15). Middleton makes a convincing case in showing how the publication context of "Ave Maria," both in its overground manifestation in a "gentleman's magazine" and its underground appearance in *C*, enabled O'Hara's poem to accrete and ultimately to synthesize a series of traditionally competing economies and registers.

83. Middleton, *Distant Reading*, 14.

84. Reed, "And What, Little Boy," 25. All misspellings *sic*.

85. One of the more prominent cartoons in the issue, for example, featured a buxom psychiatrist's secretary standing by the office door while the natty patient, lying on the shrink's couch in the background, quipped, "Part of my guilt complex concerns your secretary, Doctor." Its centerfold nudie, Marya Bruno, was pictured standing in a classical pose with a long purple train of fabric wrapped over her left shoulder and breast, her right breast fully visible.

86. "The Ostrich" was released in 1964 and featured Tony Conrad and John Cale. The name of their band was "The Primitives," essentially an ad-hoc group formed to release quickly penned and recorded singles modeled after the novelty hits of the day.

87. Lou Reed to Delmore Schwartz, 1965, Box 1, Folder 99, Delmore Schwartz Papers, Beinecke Rare Book and Manuscript Library, Yale University Library.

88. Bockris, *Transformer*, 195.

89. Reed, *Between Thought and Expression*, ix.

90. Ibid., 37.

91. Aram Saroyan, *Complete Minimal Poems* (New York: Ugly Duckling Presse, 2007), 127.

92. Bob Perelman, "Speech Effects: The Talk as a Genre," in *Close Listening: Poetry and the Performed Word*, ed. Charles Bernstein (Oxford: Oxford University Press, 1998), 202.

93. Lou Reed et al., *Lou Reed Rock and Roll Heart* (WinStar Home Entertainment, 1998).

94. Delmore Schwartz et al., *In Dreams Begin Responsibilities and Other Stories* (New Directions, 2012), i.

3. Proto-Punk and Poetry on St. Mark's Place

1. Lewis Warsh, interview with the author, February 13, 2013.

2. Ted Berrigan and Anne Waldman, *The Collected Poems of Ted Berrigan* (Berkeley: University of California Press, 2005), 309.

3. Anne Waldman, interview with the author, February 13, 2013.

4. Bill Berkson, e-mail message to the author, August 1, 2013.

5. Waldman, interview with the author.

6. John Ashbery, e-mail message to the author, August 6, 2013.

7. Tony Scherman and David Dalton, *Pop: The Genius of Andy Warhol* (New York: HarperCollins, 2009), 233.

8. Howard Junker, "The Young Poets," *Newsweek* (March 3, 1969): 84.

9. Ibid.

10. Daniel Belgrad, *The Culture of Spontaneity: Improvisation and the Arts in Postwar America* (Chicago: University of Chicago Press, 1998), 256–257.

11. Tom Clark and Lewis Warsh, "To John Ashbery," in *Angel Hair Sleeps with a Boy in My Head: The Angel Hair Anthology*, ed. Anne Waldman et al. (New York City: Granary, 2001), 278.

12. Ibid.

13. James Schuyler, *Collected Poems* (New York: Farrar, Straus & Giroux, 1993), 32.

14. Frank O'Hara, *The Collected Poems of Frank O'Hara*, ed. Donald Allen (Berkeley: University of California Press, 1995), 358.

15. Poets associated with the Language writing phenomenon, spoken-word culture, and younger contemporary American innovative writers have all pointed to the poets and poetry scene of the second generation as especially significant. The contributors' notes to the St. Mark's Poetry Project anthology *Out of This World* are telling in terms of the debts owed to the second-generation scene. Regarding the Poetry Project at St. Mark's Church reading series when *Angel Hair*'s editor Anne Waldman was serving as its director, Charles Bernstein writes that it "provided an important alternative to the low energy, formally inert poetry of official verse culture." Anne Waldman, ed., *Out of This World: An Anthology of the St. Mark's Poetry Project, 1966–1991* (New York: Crown, 1991), 621. Bernstein and Bruce Andrews went on to publish Bernadette Mayer's celebrated "Experiments" list along with essays on or by Mayer, Clark Coolidge, Lorenzo Thomas, and other second-generation affiliated writers in their collaboratively edited *The L=A=N=G=U=A=G=E Book* (Carbondale: Southern Illinois University Press, 1984). Amy Gerstler recalls: "Dennis Cooper . . .

also introduced me to 'New York School' writers, and *St. Mark's Newsletter*, and numerous East Coast small-press magazines and anthologies. Those introductions provided me with what felt at the time like a direction" (*Out of This World*, 642). Showing the influence not just of John Ashbery, Frank O'Hara, James Schuyler, and Kenneth Koch but also of Padgett and Berrigan, David Lehman in his book *The Last Avant-Garde* (New York: Doubleday, 1998) demonstrates how second-generation poets inspired younger writers including Paul Violi, Alice Notley (who was married to Berrigan during this period), Tim Dlugos, and Eileen Myles (359–379). Geoff Ward draws a link between contemporary avant-garde publications and their predecessors: "Imprints such as Burning Deck, Roof, The Figures or Potes & Poets Press are the intrepid contemporary heirs of Corinth Books, Tibor De Nagy Editions, The Poet's Press, C, Angel Hair Books and other small-scale outfits that published the new American poetry of the 1960s." Geoff Ward, *Statutes of Liberty: The New York School of Poets* (New York: St. Martin's Press, 1993), 179.

16. Waldman et al., *Angel Hair Sleeps with a Boy in My Head*, 143–44.

17. Ibid., 151–152.

18. Ibid., 152–153.

19. Ibid., 148–149.

20. Ibid., 163–164.

21. Ibid., 164.

22. Ibid., 162.

23. Ibid., 146.

24. O'Hara, *Collected Poems*, 328.

25. Groups that influenced the second generation in various ways can be differentiated from them by a sociability that is in marked contrast to what I have been describing so far. Previous literary formations that influenced New York–based writers—including imagists, Dadaists, the Black Mountain School, and the Beats—represent a lineage of community-based poetry. Writers within these earlier "schools," however, did not perform such sociability in their poetry as relentlessly as second-generation poets did in their literary work. That is, earlier poetry communities and associated critics acknowledged the importance of writing within a scene primarily via reviews, manifestos, and essays on poetics and through organizing their own public reception in journals and magazines. (We can think of Ezra Pound in 1913 sending some of H.D.'s verse to Harriet Monroe's *Poetry* magazine and appending the signature "H.D., Imagiste"; Louis Zukofsky's "Objectivist" issue of *Poetry* in February 1931 and *An Objectivist Anthology* in 1932; the polemics associated with the Dadaists; or even Frank O'Hara's tongue-in-cheek "Personism" manifesto as primary ways for readers to gain an understanding of the social dynamics and shared aesthetics of those poetry scenes.) On the other hand, second-generation poets exhibited sociability and group affiliation not through developing an independent and carefully theorized poetics but through public poetry readings and within the body of the poems themselves—affiliations and poetic stances were all performed on stage and within the stanzas. No manifesto needed. Similarly, the Black Mountain writers Robert Creeley and Charles Olson certainly designed work that was informed by their collaborative poetics, and many of us link these two within a group whose members include Paul Blackburn and Ed Dorn. Yet at least

through most of the 1950s and 1960s, we rarely find Black Mountain poets dropping one another's names into their poems or writing collaboratively (though multimedia collaborations among dancers, architects, musicians, painters, and poets were part of the social norm at Black Mountain College). Writers affiliated with the Beats, including Jack Kerouac and Allen Ginsberg, while certainly referring to one another in their work, did so obliquely or in such a way as to practically deify one another. Thus we have Kerouac's Japhy Ryder as a stand-in for Gary Snyder and Ginsberg's cries of "Holy Peter holy Allen holy Solomon holy Lucien holy Kerouac" in his "Footnote to Howl." Allen Ginsberg, *Collected Poems, 1947-1980* (New York: Harper & Row, 1984), 134. Such naming tended more toward icon and myth building in opposition to the refreshing and radically quotidian impulses typical of second-generation writers. Additionally, all of the aforementioned groups' "members" consistently threatened or rejected group affiliation or emphasized and challenged positions of "leadership" overtly.

26. D. A. Pennebaker, *Bob Dylan, Don't Look Back* (New York: Ballantine, 1968), 123.

27. Waldman et al., *Angel Hair Sleeps with a Boy in My Head*, xxiv–xxv.

28. Lewis Warsh, "An Interview with Peter Bushyeager," *Poetry Project Newsletter* 187, (February/March 2001): 13.

29. Waldman et al., *Angel Hair Sleeps with a Boy in My Head*, xxvii.

30. Qtd. in Bryan Waterman, *Marquee Moon* (New York: Continuum, 2011), 25–26.

31. Waldman et al., *Angel Hair Sleeps with a Boy in My Head*, 41.

32. Ibid., 42–43.

33. Ibid., 48.

34. Qtd. in Daniel Kane, "Richard Hell, *Genesis: Grasp*, and the Blank Generation: From Poetry to Punk in New York's Lower East Side," *Contemporary Literature* 52, no. 2 (2011): 357–358.

35. Filippo Tommaso Marinetti et al., *Selected Poems and Related Prose* (New Haven, Conn.: Yale University Press, 2002), 114.

36. Richard Hell and the Voidoids, *Blank Generation* (Sire Records, 1977).

37. Linda Russo adds: "Since 1970 women have started over 70 little magazines and small presses devoted to poetic experimentation, almost half of these since 1990 alone." Linda Russo, "Poetics of Adjacency: *0-9* and the Conceptual Writing of Bernadette Mayer and Hannah Weiner," in *Don't Ever Get Famous: Essays on New York Writing After the New York School*, ed. Daniel Kane (Champaign, Ill.: Dalkey Archive, 2006), 119.

38. *How(ever)* was first published in 1983 as an alternative to essentialist feminism and feminist-affiliated poetry.

39. Kathleen Fraser, "The Tradition of Marginality," *Frontiers: A Journal of Women Studies* 10, no. 3 (1989): 24.

40. O'Hara, *Collected Poems*, 325.

41. Waldman et al., *Angel Hair Sleeps with a Boy in My Head*.

42. Ibid., 487.

43. Ibid., 486.

44. Waldman, interview with the author.

45. Ibid.

46. Anne Waldman, *Fast Speaking Woman* (San Francisco: City Lights, 1975), n.p.

47. Ibid., 58.

48. *John Giorno & Anne Waldman: A Kulchur Selection.* (New York: Giorno Poetry Systems Records, 1977).

49. James E. Perone, *The Album: A Guide to Pop Music's Most Provocative, Influential, and Important Creations* (Santa Barbara, Calif.: Praeger, 2012), 37.

50. In Shaw's compelling account, John Cale, the producer for the *Horses* sessions, replaces Wilhelm Reich as Patti takes the place of Peter. See Philip Shaw, *Horses* (New York: Continuum, 2008), 112.

51. Richard Hell, journal entry, February 16, 1971, Series 1A, Box 1, Folder 2, Richard Hell Papers, Fales Library and Special Collections, New York University.

4. Richard Hell, *Genesis: Grasp*, and the Making of the Blank Generation

1. Richard Hell, *Hot and Cold: Richard Hell* (New York: powerHouse, 2001), 24.

2. Bernard Gendron, *Between Montmartre and the Mudd Club: Popular Music and the Avant-Garde* (Chicago: University of Chicago Press, 2002), 252–253.

3. Robert Christgau and Carola Dibbell, "Liner Notes," in *Spurts: The Richard Hell Story* (Los Angeles: Rhino Records, 2005), 6.

4. Richard Hell Papers, Fales Library and Special Collections, New York University.

5. Anna Balakian, *Surrealism: The Road to the Absolute* (Chicago: University of Chicago Press, 1986), 62.

6. See Pete Astor, *Blank Generation* (London: Bloomsbury, 2014), for additional insights on the connections between French symbolist literature and Hell's lyrics and music.

7. Richard Hell, draft of author's bio for *Out of This World*, Richard Hell Papers, Box 7, Folder 529, Fales Library and Special Collections, New York University.

8. Quoted in Matt Thorne, "Hell Freezes Over When Rodent Attacks," *The Independent on Sunday* (April 14, 2002): 16.

9. Richard Hell, *I Dreamed I Was a Very Clean Tramp: An Autobiography* (New York: HarperCollins, 2013), 47. Hell now qualifies his rejection of Thomas by pointing out similarities between Thomas's and Ted Berrigan's sonnets. For a terrific comparative reading of Thomas's "To-day, This Insect" and Berrigan's "Sonnet #1," see ibid., 47–49.

10. Richard Hell, interview with the author, September 25, 2008.

11. Hell, *I Dreamed I Was a Very Clean Tramp*, 48.

12. Ibid., 49.

13. Frank O'Hara, *Standing Still and Walking in New York* (San Francisco: Grey Fox, 1975), 13.

14. Marjorie Perloff, *Frank O'Hara: Poet Among Painters* (Chicago: University of Chicago Press, 1977), 13.

15. Of Allen Ginsberg, for example, Hell (*I Dreamed I Was a Very Clean Tramp*, 52) writes that he never "felt much rapport with Ginsberg from his writings."

16. In his mock-manifesto "Personism," O'Hara insisted gleefully, "Nobody should experience anything they don't need to, if they don't need poetry bully for

them. I like the movies too. And after all, only Whitman and Crane and Williams, of the American poets, are better than the movies." *The Collected Poems of Frank O'Hara*, ed. Donald Allen (Berkeley: University of California Press, 1995), 498.

17. From 1966 to 1975, Hell lived in at least seven different apartments in Manhattan, most if not all of them in the East Village. From 1975 on, Hell made his permanent residence on East Twelfth Street between Avenues A and B, in the same building that poets and musicians including Allen Ginsberg, Simon Pettet, Arthur Russell, Larry Fagin, and John Godfrey called home.

18. Patti Smith, "Television: Escapees from Heaven," *Soho Weekly News* (June 27, 1974). Richard Hell Papers, Series 3, Subseries D, Box 9, Folder 626, Fales Library and Special Collections, New York University.

19. Robert Christgau, "Television's Principles," *Village Voice* (June 19, 1978): 57.

20. Hell, *I Dreamed I Was a Very Clean Tramp*, 155.

21. Ibid., 135.

22. Richard Hell to Bruce Andrews. May 23, 1972, Richard Hell Papers, Box 5, Folder 154. Fales Library and Special Collections, New York University.

23. Hell, interview with the author.

24. Hell, *I Dreamed I Was a Very Clean Tramp*, 67–68.

25. Ibid., 68.

26. Quoted in Daniel Kane, "Richard Hell, *Genesis: Grasp*, and the Blank Generation: From Poetry to Punk in New York's Lower East Side," *Contemporary Literature* 52, no. 2 (2011): 340–341.

27. Richard Hell and Tom Miller (Verlaine), "Manifesto," *Genesis: Grasp* 1, no. 1 (1968): 3.

28. As Pete Astor recognizes, Baudelaire's vision of the dandy "ties together many of the elements of the Hell persona . . . an elegant, perfectly idle libertine . . . the brooding menace of the outsider, never joining in." Pete Astor, *Richard Hell and the Voidoids' Blank Generation* (New York: Bloomsbury, 2014), 63.

29. Charles Baudelaire, "Le Gouffre," trans. Sylvia Townsend Warner, in *Genesis: Grasp* 1, no. 3 (1969): 20.

30. Charles Baudelaire, *The Flowers of Evil / Les fleurs du mal*, trans. William Aggeler, (Fresno, Calif.: Academy Library Guild, 1954).

31. Roy Campbell, *Poems of Baudelaire* (New York: Pantheon, 1952), 44.

32. As Dylan Jones, Lauraine Leblanc, and other historians of punk style have noted, Johnny Rotten purportedly designed his trademark shocked-hair look by copying a photograph of Richard Hell given to him by the Sex Pistols' manager Malcolm McClaren. McClaren himself recalls, "Richard Hell was a definite, 100 percent inspiration, and, in fact, I remember telling the Sex Pistols, 'Write a song like Blank Generation, but write your own bloody version,' and their own version was 'Pretty Vacant' . . . I came back to England determined. I had these images I came back with, it was like Marco Polo or Walter Raleigh. I brought back the image of this distressed, strange thing called Richard Hell. And this phrase, 'the blank generation.'" Qtd. in Legs McNeil and Gillian McCain, *Please Kill Me: The Uncensored Oral History of Punk* (New York: Grove, 1996), 199. "'We wore ripped-up clothes because we wanted our insides to be outside,' said Richard Hell . . . . 'The whole intention was to deliver your core self without any filters. The final idea was, 'I don't care.''" Qtd. in Woody Hochswender, "Patterns; Punk Fashion Revisited," *New York Times* (September 27, 1988),

http://www.nytimes.com/1988/09/27/style/patterns-punk-fashion-revisited.html.

33. Quoted in Lisa Persky, "Suicide," *New York Rocker* 1, no. 3 (May 1976): 33.

34. Lisa Persky, "Are the Ramones, or Is the Ramones?" *New York Rocker* 1, no. 3 (April 1976): 28–29.

35. Considering punk in relationship to glam rock through the lens of Baudelaire's dandy goes a long way in explaining why so many punks looked back on glam as a formative influence in their own self-fashioning. At first glance, the feminized drag glamour and cabaret shenanigans we associate with bands like the New York Dolls or T-Rex might seem worlds apart from the snarling, spit-soaked near-nihilism of punk. See John Holmstrom, Roberta Bayley, and Legs McNeil, "Big Deal, Right?" *Punk* 1 no. 3 (1977): 7–10, for a lively discussion with David Johansen about how mid-1970s punks understood the "punk" significations of glam rock.

36. Charles Baudelaire, *The Painter of Modern Life: And Other Essays*, trans. Jonathan Mayne (London: Phaidon, 1964), 28.

37. Michel Foucault, "What Is Enlightenment," in *The Foucault Reader* (New York: Pantheon, 1984), 41–42.

38. Comte de Lautréamont, *Maldoror (Les chants de Maldoror)*, trans. Guy Wernham (New York: New Directions, 1965), 4.

39. Hell, interview with the author.

40. *Sounds* (October 8, 1977): 25, 26.

41. Lester Bangs, "Richard Hell and the Voidoids," in *Spurts: The Richard Hell Story*, 8–9.

42. Richard Hell, "Hot Ice, Seed Water, Letterfwesh," *Genesis: Grasp* 1, no. 3 (1969): 34.

43. Hell's journals from the period around the composition of "Hot Ice" reveal that Hell was reading Gerard Manley Hopkins and Robert Creeley's book *Pieces* carefully. I would suggest that Hopkins's "sprung rhythm" and Creeley's use of enjambment also inform the overall structure of "Hot Ice."

44. Richard Hell to Clark Coolidge, January 30, 1970, Box 5, Folder 211, Richard Hell Papers, Fales Library and Special Collections, New York University.

45. Ibid., February 11, 1970.

46. An early version of "Love Comes in Spurts" that Hell performed in his and Tom Verlaine's Neon Boys is included in *Spurts: The Richard Hell Story*.

47. Richard Hell, untitled poem, *Genesis: Grasp* 1, no. 3 (1969): 33.

48. Richard Hell, "IT," *Genesis: Grasp* 1, no. 4 (1970): 15.

49. Richard Hell, "Rimbaud Knew," Richard Hell Papers, Box 3, Folder 83, Fales Library and Special Collections, New York University.

50. *Blank Generation.*

51. Hell, interview with the author.

52. Richard Hell to Clark Coolidge, February 11, 1970, Richard Hell Papers, Box 5, Folder 211, Fales Library and Special Collections, New York University.

53. "Juliana Spahr on Bruce Andrews," http://epc.buffalo.edu/authors/andrews/about/spahr.html.

54. Bruce Andrews, "5th Collaboration," *Genesis: Grasp* 1, nos. 5/6 (1971): 15.

55. Richard Hell to Bruce Andrews, February 8, 1971, Box 5, Folder 1, Richard Hell Papers, Fales Library and Special Collections, New York University.

56. Ibid., February 12, 1971.

57. Richard Hell, untitled poem, *Genesis: Grasp* 2, nos. 1/2 (1971): 25.

58. Richard Hell, untitled poem, "Loose Material from Slum Journal and Interview," Box 3, Folder 57, Richard Hell Papers, Fales Library and Special Collections, New York University.

59. Richard Hell, "Another World, Blank Generation, You Gotta Lose" (New York: Ork Records, 1976).

60. Hell to Charles Plymell, August 16, 1972, Box 7, Folder 427, Richard Hell Papers, Fales Library and Special Collections, New York University.

61. Hell to Bruce Andrews, July 17, 1972, Box 5, Folder 154, Richard Hell Papers, Fales Library and Special Collections, New York University.

62. Andrew Wylie, now famous as a literary agent to the stars, was in the 1960s and early 1970s involved in New York School–affiliated poetry publishing and writing. Wylie exhibited suspicions similar to Hell's toward "great works" and revealed a fondness for popular culture and a propensity for violence, however rhetorical. "The general feeling I've received from living is one of extreme violence," Wylie wrote. "I knew that primarily I didn't relate to big powerful works like Howl, The Cantos, or the work of Schonberg or Berg, but to a more tenuous expression, an expression that seemed at the same time both more fragile and more violent. I tried to understand how it was that I could listen to, say, Webern's Six Bagatelles and feel at the same time a deep fragility and an almost intolerably high level of violence.... We can't concentrate on anything for a long time, we flick on and off at an almost unbearable speed, across the face of a blank wall. We pick up a book of poems and look for the shortest poem in the book because we can't read anything extended. I think we sense that nothing extended can really be an expression of what we're experiencing.... Some people say they don't understand 'modern poetry'. I thought—what's this all about? You took a song like LUCY IN THE SKY W/DIAMONDS; no one was concerned with the hidden esoteric qualities of the song. I mean the general feeling was, we can understand this, 'I can dig it.'" Andrew Wylie, *Andrew Wylie Special Issue*, ed. Barbara Casto and Victor Bockris (Philadelphia: Telegraph, 1971), n.p.

63. Bruce Andrews to Richard Hell, 1972, Box 5, Folder 155, Richard Hell Papers, Fales Library and Special Collections, New York University.

64. Ibid., January 14, 1973.

65. The first issue of the journal *New York Rocker* positioned arena rock's penetration into the market as a disaster that essentially wiped out the dissident sensibility of mid-1960s punk one-hit wonders like ? and the Mysterians and the Blues Magoos—a sensibility reinvigorated by the scene then developing at CBGB. In his article on the Ramones, for example, Brock Altane complained: "Supposedly, we're living in the 'liberated' seventies, right?? Well let's take a look at our 'liberated' record charts: Chicago, Olivia Newton John, John Denver, America, Seals and Crofts, Ohio Players, Neil Sedaka, Barry Manilow, K.C. & the Sunshine Band, Glen Campbell, Helen Reddy, and on and on and on." Brock Altane, "The Ramones," *New York Rocker* 1, no. 1 (February 1976): 4.

66. Astor, *Richard Hell and the Voidoids' Blank Generation*, 2.

67. Bob McFadden (Rod McKuen), *Songs Our Mummy Taught Us* (New York: Brunswick, 1960).

68. Bob McFadden (Rod McKuen), *Beatsville* (Hollywood, Calif.: High Fidelity Recordings, 1960).

69. Greil Marcus, *The Dustbin of History* (Cambridge, Mass.: Harvard University Press, 1995), 116.

70. *Blank Generation*.

71. Hell, interview with the author.

72. Ibid.

73. Richard Hell and Tom Miller (Verlaine), *Wanna Go Out?* (New York: Dot, 1973), 14.

74. "The light's too dim in here." Ibid., 25.

75. "A promise that squirts." Ibid., 31.

76. "The stranger and the moon are good buddies." Ibid., 32.

77. Ron Silliman to Richard Meyers (Hell), n.d., Box 7, Folder 488, Richard Hell Papers, Fales Library and Special Collections, New York University.

78. Mary Harron, "Theresa Stern," *Punk* 1, no. 4 (July 1976): 15.

79. Richard Hell, "Journal from Patti Smith," n.d., Box 1, Folder 3, Richard Hell Papers, Fales Library and Special Collections, New York University.

80. Hell, *I Dreamed I Was a Very Clean Tramp*, 259. The benefit gigs ran for three nights and featured musicians including Lou Reed and the Erasers performing and reading alongside writers including John Ashbery, Ron Padgett, and Kathy Acker.

81. Hell is referring here to Berrigan's "Ten Things I Do Every Day," a poem that lists Berrigan's daily routines, including smoking pot and drinking Pepsi.

5. "I Just Got Different Theories": Patti Smith and the New York School of Poetry

1. For example, "[Smith's poetry] performances," the critic Kate Ballen pronounced in 1977, "were sexual bruisings with the spasms of Jagger and the off-key of Dylan." Kate Ballen, "Sexual Bruisings: The Poetry of Patti Smith," *Oxford Literary Review* 2, no. 1 (January 1, 1977): 20.

2. NME, *Patti Smith's My First Gig: Desecrating a Church with Electric Guitar* (2014), https://www.youtube.com/watch?v=tNOuHNlZwEk.

3. Ballen, "Sexual Bruisings," 21.

4. Ballen (ibid.) continued to read Smith's work in poetry as of a piece with the New York School. On Smith's book *Witt* (1973), "the poems tend to be written in longer lines with less rock rhythms [in comparison to *Seventh Heaven*]. The poet's sense of humour is extended to include the reader by using the New York Poet's technique of 'we' instead of 'I.'"

5. Patti Smith, *Early Work, 1970-1979* (New York: Norton, 1995), 52.

6. Frank O'Hara, *The Collected Poems of Frank O'Hara*, ed. Donald Allen (Berkeley: University of California Press, 1995), 108.

7. Ibid.

8. Allen Ginsberg, *Howl and Other Poems: Pocket Poets Number 4* (San Francisco: City Lights, 1956), 11.

9. Patti Smith, *Seventh Heaven* (Philadelphia: Telegraph, 1972), 35.

10. Robert Duncan, "A Little Language," in *Ground Work: Before the War* (New York: New Directions, 1984), 98–99; O'Hara, "In Memory of My Feelings," in *Collected Poems*, 256; Aram Saroyan, *Complete Minimal Poems* (New York: Ugly Duckling Presse, 2007). "Grace" is designed to evoke both the state of grace and O'Hara's close friend Grace Hartigan, the painter.

11. Victor Bockris, *Patti Smith* (London: HarperCollins UK, 2008), 12.

12. Anne Dewey and Libbie Rifkin, eds., *Among Friends: Engendering the Social Site of Poetry* (Iowa City: University of Iowa Press, 2013), 5.

13. NME, *Patti Smith's My First Gig*.

14. Patti Smith, *Just Kids* (New York: Ecco, 2010).

15. Lisa Robinson, "The High Poetess of Rock 'n' Roll," *New Musical Express* (April 12, 1975): 17.

16. Ted Berrigan, *The Collected Poems of Ted Berrigan* (Berkeley: University of California Press, 2005).

17. See Daniel Kane, "*Angel Hair* Magazine, the Second-Generation New York School, and the Poetics of Sociability," *Contemporary Literature* 45, no. 2 (2004): 345–346.

18. As Smith herself notes with gusto in *Just Kids*, Corso often heckled poets in the downtown scene. Sam Kashner's descriptions throughout his memoir *When I Was Cool* of Corso's resistance to being folded into anything resembling a collective designation, "Beat" or otherwise, are also helpful here in further identifying Corso's iconoclasm. Sam Kashner, *When I Was Cool: My Life at the Jack Kerouac School* (New York: HarperCollins, 2005).

19. Anne Waldman, e-mail to the author, February 19, 2012.

20. Smith, *Just Kids*, 182. On the contrary, numerous amplified musical events took place at the church well before Smith's and Kaye's performance in 1975. In April 1969, for example, the Christian rock band Mind Garage performed their "Electric Liturgy" at St. Mark's. See http://www.mindgarage.com/ABC.html.

21. Smith, *Just Kids*, 182.

22. Smith, as Dan Graham insists, "represented a free woman's access to essentially male passion, or teenage romanticized passion—the passion of Jim Morrison via the Symbolist poets via Arthur Rimbaud. She represented herself—as did Rimbaud (but not Morrison)—as androgynous." Dan Graham, *Rock/Music Writings* (New York: Primary Information, 2009), 133.

23. Patti Smith at the Poetry Project, recorded February 10, 1971.

24. Bockris, *Patti Smith*, 3.

25. Smith, *Just Kids*, 214.

26. Robinson, "The High Poetess of Rock 'n' Roll," 35.

27. Robert Hilburn, "New Rock Star: Mick Jagger Look-Alike Also Known as Patti Smith," *Spokesman Review* (February 1, 1976): B2.

28. Daniel Kane, "'Nor Did I Socialise with Their People': Patti Smith, Rock Heroics, and the Poetics of Sociability," *Popular Music* 31, no. 1 (January 2012): 111–112.

29. Lytle Shaw, *Frank O'Hara: The Poetics of Coterie* (Ames: University of Iowa Press, 2006), 21.

30. John Malcolm Brinnin, *Dylan Thomas in America* (London: Prion, 2000), 18.

31. Victor Bockris, "The Poetry of Performance: An Interview with Patti Smith," *Carry Out* (1972): 11.

32. Ibid., 12–13. Smith would repeat variations on the "hero" theme in a number of her interviews. "I've always been hero-oriented," Smith insisted to Penny Green in an interview published in Warhol and Malanga's *Interview* magazine. "I started doing art not because I had creative instincts but because I fell in love with artists. I didn't come to this city to become an artist, but to become an artist's mistress. Art in the beginning for me was never a vehicle for self-expression, it was a way to ally myself with heroes, 'cause I couldn't make contact with God." Penny Green, "Patti Smith," *Interview* (October 1973): 25.

33. Bockris, "The Poetry of Performance," 15–16.

34. Victor Bockris, *Beat Punks: New York's Underground Culture from the Beat Generation to the Punk Explosion* (New York: Da Capo, 2000), 42.

35. See Richard E. Hishmeh, "Marketing Genius: The Friendship of Allen Ginsberg and Bob Dylan," *Journal of American Culture* 29, no. 4 (2006): 395–405, for an account of Ginsberg's and Dylan's friendship as a mutually beneficial transaction.

36. Robinson, "The High Poetess of Rock 'n' Roll," 35.

37. Qtd. in Bockris, *Patti Smith*, 72.

38. Ibid., 70–71.

39. Will Hermes, *Love Goes to Buildings on Fire: Five Years in New York That Changed Music Forever* (New York: Faber and Faber, 2011), 132.

40. Patti Smith, foreword to *An Accidental Autobiography: The Selected Letters of Gregory Corso*, ed. Bill Morgan (New York: New Directions, 2003), xi.

41. Ibid.

42. Smith identified *Seventh Heaven* as a kind of hinge moment marking her move from the page to the stage, telling Victor Bockris that the book "represents me on the tightrope between writing and performing." Bockris, *Patti Smith*, 296–297.

43. Ibid., 80.

44. "Brigid Polk" is the nom de plume of the New York debutante and Andy Warhol confidante Brigid Berlin.

45. "DC's: Brigid Polk's 'Scars,'" http://denniscooper-theweaklings.blogspot.com/2007/10/brigid-polks-scars.html. © Brigid Berlin.

46. Ibid., © Brigid Berlin.

47. *Horses* (New York: Arista, 1975).

48. Qtd. in Kane, "'Nor Did I Socialise with Their People,'" 117–118.

49. "Ginsberg above all . . . [regarded] that [1960s] generation of songwriters as supremely important. In 1981 he praised the 'evolution of rhythm and blues into rock 'n' roll into high art form, as evidenced by the Beatles, Bob Dylan, and other popular musicians influenced in the late 1950s and '60s by beat generation poets' and writers' works.'" Laurence Coupe, *Beat Sound, Beat Vision: The Beat Spirit and Popular Song* (Manchester: Manchester University Press, 2007), 8.

50. Hélène Cixous, *The Newly Born Woman* (Minneapolis: University of Minnesota Press, 1986). Cixous (90–91) argues for a decentered model of female erotic pleasure and power as emanating out of women's libidinal and procreative abilities.

51. Bernadette Mayer, "Experiments," in *The L=A=N=G=U=A=G=E Book*, ed. Bruce Andrews and Charles Bernstein (Carbondale: Southern Illinois University Press, 1984), 80.

52. Smith, *Seventh Heaven*, 44.

53. Bebe Buell, among others, has made an issue out of Smith's breasts. She records how Smith told her "one time, ' . . . I'm not beautiful and blonde, and I look like a boy,' and I said, 'For a boy you have the biggest breasts I've ever seen!' A lot of people didn't know how big her boobs were because of the way she wore them. She would wear a nice baggy T-shirt or a man's shirt with a good flattening bra or no bra which brought them down even flatter. She was very endowed. My god, I almost fainted when she showed them to me!" Bockris, *Patti Smith*, 65.

54. Bockris, "The Poetry of Performance," 9.

55. Tom McCarthy, "Patti: Poet as Macho Woman," *Village Voice* (February 7, 1974): 42.

56. Ibid.

57. Mark Paytress, *Break It Up: Patti Smith's* Horses *and the Remaking of Rock 'n' Roll* (London: Portrait, 2006), 126–127.

58. As Annie Finch contends, in literary and popular criticism "the term 'poetess' [throughout] the twentieth century" was used as "a label of contempt and condescension." Annie Finch, "The Poetess in America," *Able Muse* (Winter 2002), http://www.ablemuse.com/v5/a-finch_poetess.htm.

59. Robinson, "The High Poetess of Rock 'n' Roll," 17.

60. Richard Middleton, *Voicing the Popular: On the Subjects of Popular Music* (London: Routledge, 2007), 98.

61. Mike Daley, "Patti Smith's 'Gloria': Intertextual Play in a Rock Vocal Performance," *Popular Music* 16, no. 3 (1997): 238.

62. Ibid., 238–239.

63. Smith, "Kimberly," *Horses*.

64. Smith, "Land," *Horses*.

65. This recording was included in John Giorno's Dial-A-Poem LP *Sugar, Alcohol, and Meat* (1980) and titled "Parade."

66. http://ubumexico.centro.org.mx/sound/dial_a_poem_poets/sam/Sugar-Alcohol-Meat_14-_Patti_Smith-_Parade.mp3.

67. Ibid.

68. Bockris (*Patti Smith*, 83) reports how Smith's "move from poetry towards rock and roll was cause for celebration but also concern. The poetry community had come to appreciate the attention she had helped bring to it with her increasingly popular readings. Patti was at the top of her form after three years of performances, and many believed (and this debate continues today) that she was at her best and purest as a poet backed by Lenny."

69. Ibid., 163.

70. Ibid., 162.

71. Robinson, "The High Poetess of Rock 'n' Roll," 17.

72. Maybe it is partly because of these performative stances that Smith's influence can be detected more within male "arty" circles of post-punk and indie music (Sonic Youth's Thurston Moore as Parnassian poetry-penning guitar god; R.E.M.'s Michael Stipe as poetic tortured soul) than in the ideologically driven, punk-inflected, and avowedly feminist "riot grrrl" phenomenon of the late 1980s and 1990s, a scene indebted more to the style of British punk bands like the Slits, X-Ray Spex, and the Raincoats than it was to Smith's comparatively baroque efforts.

6. Giorno Poetry Systems

1. Nicholas Zurbrugg and John Giorno, "Poetry, Entertainment, and the Mass Media: An Interview with John Giorno," *Chicago Review* 40, no. 2/3 (1994): 98.

2. Qtd. in Daniel Kane, *All Poets Welcome* (Berkeley: University of California Press, 2003), 267.

3. John Giorno, "I'm Tired of Being Scared," in *An Anthology of New York Poets*, ed. Ron Padgett and David Shapiro (New York: Random House, 1970), 267. Copyright © John Giorno.

4. Zurbrugg and Giorno, "Poetry, Entertainment, and the Mass Media," 87.

5. Ibid., 85.

6. "Went to Alex Katz's party, nobody would speak to me," wrote Giorno to Brion Gysin, adding, "got very paranoid, but forced myself to stay. After a few hours, I found out that MOTHER had come out that day with all the poems I sent them last August. Then dear sweet Frank Lima said in an aside to Frank O'Hara 'I like John Giorno, but I don't like his poetry'. The rest of them, Tony Towle, Kenward Elmslie, etc made believe I wasn't there." John Giorno to Brion Gysin, November 27, 1965, Box 78, Folder 1, William Burroughs Papers, Berg Collection, New York Public Library. Copyright © John Giorno.

7. Ibid.

8. Ibid., December 8, 1965. Copyright © John Giorno.

9. Quoted in Brad Gooch, *City Poet: The Life and Times of Frank O'Hara* (New York: HarperCollins, 2014), 280.

10. John Giorno to Brion Gysin, September 30, 1967, Box 78, Folder 1, William Burroughs Papers, Berg Collection, New York Public Library. Copyright © John Giorno.

11. Quoted in Michael Hennessey, "Poetry by Phone and Phonograph: Tracing the Influence of Giorno Poetry Systems," in *Audiobooks, Literature, and Sound Studies*, ed. Matthew Rubery (London: Routledge, 2011), 77.

12. Giorno, "Pornographic Poem," in *An Anthology of New York Poets*, 255.

13. Ibid.

14. Frank O'Hara, *The Collected Poems of Frank O'Hara*, ed. Donald Allen (Berkeley: University of California Press, 1995), 223–224.

15. Joe LeSueur, *Digressions on Some Poems by Frank O'Hara: A Memoir* (New York: Macmillan, 2004), 112.

16. Allen Ginsberg, *Howl and Other Poems: Pocket Poets Number 4* (San Francisco: City Lights, 1956), 12.

17. Ibid.

18. Ibid., 14.

19. Giorno, "Pornographic Poem," 255.

20. Ibid., 256.

21. Ibid.

22. Simon Frith, "Why Do Songs Have Words?" in *Popular Music: Critical Concepts in Media and Cultural Studies* (London: Routledge, 2004), 200.

23. Hennessey, "Poetry by Phone and Phonograph," 77. Hennessey perhaps underestimates the confrontational force of Giorno's performances. Rather than

assault the audience, Hennessey claims, "Giorno's intricate preparations aim to *cater to* [the audience's] every need, providing a nurturing (albeit overstimulating) environment that privileges a full sensory experience of his poetry" (79–80, my italics). I would argue with Hennessey's claim that Giorno's events were "nurturing." Taking LSD with a hundred or more people at a Giorno poetry event was undoubtedly disorienting for some if not most of those involved, particularly when their drug experience was heightened by fog machines, sirens, flashing lights, and the like.

24. McCandlish Phillips, "Outdoor Poetry Assaults Senses," *New York Times* (September 20, 1968).

25. John Giorno to William Burroughs, December 17, 1967, Box 78, Folder 1, William Burroughs Papers, Berg Collection, New York Public Library. Copyright © John Giorno.

26. Hennessey, "Poetry by Phone and Phonograph," 78.

27. Ibid., 79.

28. Giorno to William Burroughs.

29. Ibid.

30. Robert Palmer, "Pop Jazz; Beat Generation Lives in a Night of Rock and Poetry," *New York Times* (January 15, 1982), http://www.nytimes.com/1982/01/15/books/pop-jazz-beat-generation-lives-in-a-night-of-rock-and-poetry.html.

31. Zurbrugg and Giorno, "Poetry, Entertainment, and the Mass Media," 85.

32. Ibid., 87. Giorno also found that punk audiences "got" poems better than the supposedly more qualified literary audiences hanging out at the Poetry Project and related spaces. Told by an interviewer that "one friend wrote that he saw you and William Burroughs perform in San Francisco where there was a punk audience, and was rather upset because they were laughing at all the wrong places," Giorno replied simply, "No, they were laughing at all the *right* places!" Ibid.

33. Tyler Hoffman, *American Poetry in Performance: From Walt Whitman to Hip Hop* (Ann Arbor: University of Michigan Press, 2011), 83.

34. Ibid.

35. "It would seem that Lindsay's desire to have his voice preserved was an attempt on his part to secure a future for himself and for his poetry, to try to convey something of his vocal presence for posterity, no matter the playback quality. Better a mechanical voice than no voice at all." Ibid., 85.

36. Derek Furr, *Recorded Poetry and Poetic Reception from Edna Millay to the Circle of Robert Lowell* (Basingstoke: Palgrave Macmillan, 2010), 1.

37. Ibid., 2.

38. Ibid.

39. David Meltzer, *Reading Jazz* (San Francisco: Mercury House, 1993), 178.

40. John Giorno et al., *The Dial-a-Poem Poets* (New York: Giorno Poetry Systems, 1972).

41. Inside the gatefold sleeve, for example, Giorno writes: "On this LP of *Dial-A-Poem Poets* are 27 poets. The records are a selection of highlights of poetry that spontaneously grew over 20 years from 1953 to 1972, mostly in America, representing many aspects and different approaches to dealing with words and sound." Ibid.

42. Quoted in Anne Waldman et al., *Nice to See You: Homage to Ted Berrigan* (Minneapolis: Coffee House Press, 1991), 106.

43. Qtd. in Sean Stewart, *On the Ground: An Illustrated Anecdotal History of the Sixties Underground Press in the U.S.* (Oakland, Calif.: PM, 2011), 18.

44. Anne Waldman, *Fast Speaking Woman: Chants and Essays: Pocket Poets Number 33* (San Francisco: City Lights, 1996).

45. Libbie Rifkin, *Career Moves: Olson, Creeley, Zukofsky, Berrigan, and the American Avant-Garde* (Madison: University of Wisconsin Press, 2000), 13.

46. Ibid.

47. *The Dial-a-Poem Poets.*

48. Qtd. in Wolfgang Mieder, *"Making a Way out of No Way": Martin Luther King's Sermonic Proverbial Rhetoric* (Oxford: Peter Lang, 2010), 71.

49. John Sinclair, "The Destruction of America," in *This Is Our Music* (Detroit: Artists' Workshop Press, 1965), 37–38.

50. Imamu Amiri Baraka, *Transbluesency: The Selected Poems of Amiri Baraka/LeRoi Jones (1961–1995)* (Venice: Marsilio, 1995), 142.

51. Miles Davis denigrated Ornette Coleman: "Hell, just listen to what he writes and how he plays. If you're talking psychologically, the man's all screwed up inside." Paul Rinzler, *The Contradictions of Jazz* (Lanham, Md.: Scarecrow, 2008), 63.

52. Iain Anderson identifies Coleman's album as crucial in changing the direction of jazz and emphasizes throughout his book how free jazz polarized opinion. "In the summer of 1960, jazz composer and alto saxophonist Ornette Coleman, trumpeter Don Cherry, bassist Charlie Haden, and drummer Ed Blackwell recorded *This Is Our Music* for Atlantic Records. The album captured an original musical vision that had polarized performers, critics, and fans since the quartet's New York City debut the previous year. Coleman reordered structural principles to afford the members of his group maximum melodic and rhythmic freedom. By allowing each musician to play inside or outside conventional chord, bar, pitch, and tempo guidelines, he pursued an expressive and collective approach to improvisation. . . . [He] changed the entire sound of jazz." Iain Anderson, *This Is Our Music: Free Jazz, the Sixties, and American Culture* (Philadelphia: University of Pennsylvania Press, 2012), 1.

53. Rinzler, *The Contradictions of Jazz*, 62.

54. Charles Hamm, *Putting Popular Music in Its Place* (Cambridge: Cambridge University Press, 1995), 94.

55. Ibid., 124.

56. Lester Bangs, "Free Jazz Punk Rock," http://www.monoculartimes.co.uk /monomusic/freejazzpunkrock_1.shtml.

57. Ibid.

58. Ajay Heble and Rob Wallace, eds., *People Get Ready: The Future of Jazz Is Now!* (Chapel Hill, N.C.: Duke University Press, 2013), 112.

59. Ibid., 117–118.

60. Michael Brownstein, *Strange Days Ahead* (Calais, Vt.: Z, 1975), 14.

61. Ibid., 15.

62. Ibid.

63. Ibid.

64. Ibid., 17.

65. Joe Harvard, *The Velvet Underground and Nico* (New York: Continuum, 2004), 49.

66. Patti Smith, "The Histories of the Universe," in "UbuWeb Sound :: Giorno Poetry Systems—Big Ego," http://ubu.com/sound/big_ego.html.

67. Ibid.

68. As Mapplethorpe's biographer Patricia Morrisroe attested, "if Giorno traveled in Mapplethorpe's circle, or if he knew Mapplethorpe, he would have known about the picture ['Jim and Tom']. Mapplethorpe showed all his latest work to practically everyone who walked into his studio. Back then, 'downtown' was a small world, and everyone knew what everyone else was doing, and Mapplethorpe would have talked up the photo because he liked it a lot. I'm sure Patti Smith saw it." E-mail to the author, April 15, 2014.

69. Kent Brintnall, *Ecce Homo: The Male-Body-in-Pain as Redemptive Figure* (Chicago: University of Chicago Press, 2011), 110.

70. John Giorno, *Grasping at Emptiness* (New York: Kulchur Foundation, 1985), 4. Mapplethorpe "had a lifetime pass to the [S&M leatherbar] the Mineshaft and was there so often he inspired the running joke 'Who did you see out last night *besides* Robert Mapplethorpe?' Yet he rarely participated in any of the public orgies; he spent most of his time roaming the dimly lit passageways that led to rooms where men were being whipped and chained." Patricia Morrisroe, *Mapplethorpe: A Biography* (New York: Random House, 1995), 190.

71. "UbuWeb Sound :: Giorno Poetry Systems—Big Ego."

72. Ibid.

73. Luc Santé, *Kill All Your Darlings: Pieces, 1990–2005* (Portland, Ore.: Yeti, 2011), 273.

74. Steven Heller, "Putting the Punk in DIY: An Interview with John Holmstrom," *AIGA | the Professional Association for Design*, http://www.aiga.org/putting-the-punk-in-diy-an-interview-with-john-holmstrom/.

75. "UbuWeb Sound :: Giorno Poetry Systems—Big Ego."

76. John Giorno, *Sugar, Alcohol, & Meat* (New York: Giorno Poetry Systems, 1980).

77. The way Smith pronounces "stone" in the recorded version of "Gloria" sounds like /o:/, which is a monophthong; that is, it has the same quality throughout (the colon indicates that it is long). It is actually the vowel one finds in words like "stone" in communities in the North East of England such as Newcastle. The extended vowel in Smith's "me" is very elongated, so one would transcribe it as something like /i::/. Kathy Acker's pronunciation of the word "man" is again very elongated. In Southern British English there are two similar vowels. First, /a/ is the vowel in words like "bat." Second, /a:/ is the vowel in words like "bath." They have completely different qualities (the first is a front vowel, as we would find it in words like "bit" or "beet," and the second is a back vowel, as we would find it in words like "boat" or "book"). They are also different in length. What Acker is saying seems to be "/a:/"—this pronunciation has the quality of "bat" but the length of "bath" (or even longer). This vowel is also nasalized, as American vowels tend to be more than British before and after nasal consonants like /n/. The vowel in "you" is normally /u:/, a long monophthong, but on Acker's recording featured in *Big Ego* it sounds more like "/əʊ/," that is, what the vowel in "stone" would normally be. My thanks to Dr. Lynne Cahill for explaining the way vowels work in Smith's and Acker's performances.

78. John Giorno et al., *Better an Old Demon Than a New God* (New York: Giorno Poetry Systems, 1984).

79. Andreas Huyssen, *After the Great Divide* (Bloomington: Indiana University Press, 1986), 216.

7. Eileen Myles and the International Fuck Frank O'Hara Movement

1. Miles Champion, "Insane Podium: A Short History | The Poetry Project," *The Poetry Project*, https://www.poetryproject.org/about/history/.

2. Eileen Myles, interview with the author, February 19, 2013.

3. Laurie Johnston, "St. Mark's Bell Signals Church's Rise from Ashes," *New York Times* (August 19, 1980).

4. Qtd. in Brandon Stosuy, *Up Is Up, but So Is Down: New York's Downtown Literary Scene, 1974–1992* (New York: New York University Press, 2006), 86.

5. Myles, interview with the author. Myles also discussed her participation in the Fire Benefit with Dennis Cooper: "It was a great honor to be a poet reading in it—it was just the dream of being a poet and to be there with all the rock people. Totally seventies. It was very glamorous and great." Qtd. in Stosuy, *Up Is Up, but So Is Down*, 475.

6. Ron Padgett, e-mail message to the author, July 21, 2014.

7. Interview with the author.

8. Elinor Nauen explains, "Issue 4 *was* a T-shirt. Nobody really understood that it was an issue of the magazine—& we sort of called it that just for our own fun." Interview with the author.

9. In 1995, in an effort to challenge what she perceived to be an increasingly tendentious gay political-literary culture, Myles and Liz Kotz edited *The New Fuck You: Adventures in Lesbian Reading*. "We knew that anyone who read our journal, *The New Fuck You*, would get the joke," recalled Myles, adding: "There was something really perverse about that. They'll never know who fucking Larry Fagin is, they'll never know about Ed Sanders . . . there's even a moment in one of Charles Olson's talks when he talks about the *New Fuck You*, which is so funny, one of his talks where he refers to the magazine, and we were thinking about putting one of his photos on the back . . . and I think Ed Sanders was a little weirded out. . . . I thought he would be excited but I heard that he thought it was very strange . . . but it was also a critique, because at that moment in the nineties every mainstream publisher did a gay and lesbian poetry anthology, acknowledging queerness in publishing . . . there was a queer publishing boom in the nineties, but they were not interesting, thematically organized." Myles, interview with the author.

10. Elinor Nauen, e-mail message to the author, September 12, 2014.

11. Maggie Dubris, e-mail message to the author, November 10, 2014.

12. Dubris confirmed in an e-mail message to the author on September 11, 2014: "Ted Arwulf was indeed a person—I vaguely knew him in high school, and he wrote these great poems. So, when we did *Koff* I asked him if we could publish one and he said yes. I haven't talked to him in years—I was at a different school so didn't know

him well at all, but he was always a very cool guy. He is still in Ann Arbor and has some radio show."

13. Ted Arwulf, "SEX LUST AND ORTHOPEDIC SHOES," *Koff* 1, no. 1 (1977): n.p.

14. Walt Whitman, *Leaves of Grass* (New York: New American Library, 2000), 55.

15. "Problems," *Never Mind the Bollocks, Here's the Sex Pistols* (London: Virgin, 1977).

16. Elinor Nauen, Maggie Dubris, and Rachel Walling, "Consumptive Poets League," *Koff* no. 1 (1977): n.p. One wonders if this subscription ad was aimed at Patti Smith. Smith, after all, had chanted "Go Rimbaud" in her song "Land," included in her 1975 debut album *Horses*. Her cri de coeur inspired thousands of fans to wear T-shirts with Picasso's portrait of Rimbaud "covering the chest of the wearer, and at the top of the shirt the words 'GO, RIMBAUD.'" Wallace Fowlie, *Rimbaud and Jim Morrison: The Rebel as Poet, a Memoir* (Durham, N.C.: Duke University Press, 1993, 14. Johnny Rotten was not impressed by such gestures. Performing in London soon after a Patti Smith Group gig at London's Roundhouse, Rotten asked his audience, "Did anybody go to the Roundhouse the other night and see the hippie shaking the tambourines? Horses, *horses*, HORSESHIT." Qtd. in Legs McNeil and Gillian McCain, *Please Kill Me: The Uncensored Oral History of Punk* (New York: Grove, 1996), 244–245.

17. Maria Mancini (Nauen and Dubris), "Men," *Koff* 2 (1978): 42. "Bodies," one of the Sex Pistols' most notorious songs and interpreted widely as an antiabortion tirade, features the refrain "Bodies—I'm not an animal!" Near the end of the song, Rotten gives himself up entirely to the frenzied repetition of "I'm not an animal an animal an animal an animal," to the point where "animal" ends up sounding like "Mancini's" "animo."

18. David Lehman points out: "The hyperactive poetry scene at St. Mark's Church in the Bowery in the 1960s took O'Hara's taste as Gospel. The untranslated works of the French poet Pierre Reverdy were tracked down, read, and translated because O'Hara once ended a poem 'my heart is in my / pocket, it is Poems by Pierre Reverdy.'" David Lehman, *The Last Avant-Garde* (New York: Doubleday, 1998), 73. The poem Lehman refers to is "A Step Away from Them," one of O'Hara's best-known "lunch poems." *The Collected Poems of Frank O'Hara*, ed. Donald Allen (Berkeley: University of California Press, 1995), 258.

19. "Letters to the Editor," *Koff* 2 (1978): 4.

20. O'Hara, *Collected Poems*, 360.

21. Mancini (Dubris and Nauen), "Having a Coke with You," *Koff* 2 (1978): 28.

22. Maggie Dubris and Elinor Nauen, interview with the author, March 25, 2015.

23. Yuki Hartman, Bill Kushner, Bill Duckworth, and Mike Slater, "Bill Kushner," *Koff* 2 (1978).

24. Rachel Walling, "Washing Machine," *Koff* 2 (1978): 20.

25. O'Hara, *Collected Poems*, 499.

26. Dubris, "They Said That He Was Bad," *Koff* 2 (1978): 40.

27. Nauen, e-mail message to the author. The following sarcastic message was printed on the back of the T-shirt: "Because I am an artist, things affect me deeply & I am constantly depressed. Because an artist must be totally honest, I can say without a trace of self-consciousness that my inability to deal with the world proves definitively my superiority to most of the human race, yourself included. It is impossible for you to understand even grossly the nature of my pain. In your dull way,

you can only admire my suffering, as you might admire a computer or a large, shiny car; I suffer for all of you. As you go daily to your draining and repetitive jobs, I feel the futility of your lives. I understand without having to experience. I am the antennae of the race, & for that reason much more fragile than those of you who make up the thick and ugly body."

28. Donald Allen, ed., *The New American Poetry, 1945–1960* (Berkeley: University of California Press, 1999), xi.

29. Qtd. in Stosuy, *Up Is Up, but So Is Down*, 474.

30. Eileen Myles, *Chelsea Girls* (New York: HarperCollins, 2015), 75.

31. Stosuy, *Up Is Up, but So Is Down*, 26.

32. Eileen Myles, interview with the author and Marina Corrêa da Silva de Araujo, February 19, 2013.

33. Ibid.

34. Ibid.

35. Ibid.

36. Ibid. Myles recounts her exchanges with Mapplethorpe in her short story "Robert Mapplethorpe Picture," included in her collection *Chelsea Girls* (228): "We smoked a joint, I drank a ginger ale, said no to beer. I guess we talked about John Giorno who had set this thing up. I said I was a poet. You got a band he said. No. How come he asked. I just write poems. He didn't get it. I felt like I was being lazy."

37. Lisa Zinna, "Aftermath on the Avenues," *East Village Eye* (May 1979): 4.

38. Myles's reading alone "cannot be cited as having jumpstarted Downtown writing [in the 1970s]. Even devoted fans of New York's underground will be hard-pressed to name a watershed literary moment." Stosuy, *Up Is Up, but So Is Down*, 26.

39. Myles, interview with the author.

40. Ibid.

41. Poets participating in the Laundromat series were Rose Lesniak, Joel Chassler (soon to be a founding member of the no-wave band the Avant Squares), Barbara Barg (also in the Avant Squares and who would go on to front the band Homer Erotic with Maggie Dubris), downtown poetry personality Didi Susan Dubleyew (born Susan Waldman), Michael Slater (who edited the magazine *Fresh Paint*), Bob Holman, David Herz, Yuki Hartman (whose early work was published regularly in Richard Hell's *Genesis: Grasp*), Steve Levine, who edited the influential magazine *Mag City* with Greg Masters and Gary Lenhart (also in attendance), poet and Poetry Project secretary Shelly Kraut and her husband Bob Rosenthal, Simon Shuchat, Elinor Nauen, Susie Timmons, and Tom Carey. While watching a videotape of the event, I, Elinor Nauen, and Maggie Dubris noted there was a young woman with curly light hair participating in the reading who we could not recognize, though Nauen suggested she might have been Lesniak's girlfriend at the time.

42. Myles highlights Barg as "another important link between poets and bands. . . . Barbara lived in a loft first in SoHo, then in Chelsea, then in the Lower East Side . . . and she was friends with Nan Goldin and all those people. . . . She bought typesetting equipment, this was before computers and everything . . . the people who did the typesetting were both poets and people in bands, I mean people basically making their heroin money and their band money by typesetting for Barbara . . . and then Barbara also had a van, and so they were driving bands around, and so they

were driving Sonic Youth . . . so Barbara published my second book *A Fresh Young Voice from the Plains*, she published Ed Friedman's book, she was Power Mad Press." Interview with the author.

43. Eileen Myles, Bob Holman, et al., "Laundromat," MSS 128, Box 1, Bob Holman Audio/Video Poetry Collection, Fales Library and Special Collections Library, New York University.

44. Ibid.

45. Charles Olson, *Selected Writings of Charles Olson*, ed. Robert Creeley (New York: New Directions, 1966), 19.

46. Myles, interview with the author.

47. Eileen Myles, *Maxfield Parrish: Early and New Poems* (Santa Rosa, Calif.: Black Sparrow, 1995), 187.

48. "I don't care" is from the Ramones' song "I Don't Care," included in the LP *Rocket to Russia* (New York: Sire, 1977). Hell's "I can take it or leave it each time" is repeated in his song "Blank Generation." The Dead Boys' "I'm so sick of romance" is a line from their song "Ain't Nothin' to Do," included in their LP *Young, Loud, and Snotty* (New York: Sire, 1977).

49. J. H. Prynne, "English Poetry and Emphatical Language," *Proceedings of the British Academy* 74 (1988): 143.

50. Terry Castle, *Boss Ladies, Watch Out! Essays on Women, Sex, and Writing* (New York: Routledge, 2013), 255.

51. "Eileen Myles on James Schuyler," in *Thus Spake the Corpse: An Exquisite Corpse Reader, 1988-1998*, ed. Andrei Codrescu (New York: Godine, 1999), 34.

52. Timothy Gray in his book *Urban Pastoral* (Iowa City: University of Iowa Press, 2010) highlights Schuyler's and related poets' and painters' commitment to the pastoral. He is particularly keen to explore the possibilities of the pastoral mode as it engages with New York City as a material place and as a poetics. My references to Schuyler's urban pastoral are indebted to Gray's work.

53. "Eileen Myles on James Schuyler," 32.

54. Ibid., 31.

55. James Schuyler, *Collected Poems* (New York: Farrar, Straus & Giroux, 1993), 370.

56. Ibid., 360.

57. Ibid., 366.

58. Codrescu, *Thus Spake the Corpse*, 33.

59. Gray, *Urban Pastoral*, 105.

60. Ibid., 106.

61. Ibid., 107.

62. Myles, *Maxfield Parrish*, 142.

63. Schuyler, *Collected Poems*, 24.

64. "Hudson Ferry," in ibid., 49.

65. Myles had a complicated relationship with the Poetry Project, despite serving as its director from 1984 to 1986. Referring to her tenure in a conversation with Dennis Cooper, Myles stated flatly, "I had that job—working at the Poetry Project drove me out of the poetry scene quicker than anything." Qtd. in Stosuy, *Up Is Up, but So Is Down*, 469.

66. Myles, interview with the author.

67. Richard Hell, *I Dreamed I Was a Very Clean Tramp: An Autobiography* (New York: HarperCollins, 2013), 63.

68. Myles, *Maxfield Parrish*, 143.

8. "Sit on My Face!": Dennis Cooper, the First Punk Poet

1. Qtd. in Brandon Stosuy, *Up Is Up, but So Is Down: New York's Downtown Literary Scene, 1974–1992* (New York: New York University Press, 2006), 463.

2. Ibid., 465.

3. Dennis Cooper, "The East Village and Its Gay Ways," *The Advocate* (March 19, 1985): 26.

4. Qtd. in Stosuy, *Up Is Up, but So Is Down*, 463.

5. Diarmuid Hester, "Passionate Creation, Passionate Destruction: Art and Anarchy in the Work of Dennis Cooper," PhD diss., University of Sussex, 2015.

6. Stosuy, *Up Is Up, but So Is Down*, 464.

7. Ibid.

8. See, for example, Elizabeth Young and Graham Caveney, *Shopping in Space: Essays on America's Blank Generation Fiction* (New York: Atlantic Monthly Press, 1992); and James Annesley, *Blank Fiction: Consumerism, Culture, and the Contemporary American Novel* (London: Pluto, 1998).

9. Dennis Cooper, *The Terror of Earrings: Poems* (Arcadia, Calif.: Dennis Cooper, 1973), n.p.

10. Ibid.

11. "Printing—New Again: David Bowie—Interview Magazine," http://www.inter viewmagazine.com/music/new-again-david-bowie/print/.

12. In an interview with Dan Epstein, for example, Cooper was scathing: "The whole idea of gay literature is just ridiculous. I have a basic problem with the way the idea of gay identity has evolved. I have a huge problem with it in general. Most of so-called gay literature has no interest to me at all simply because I don't relate to it. Just because I'm gay and they're gay doesn't mean I feel much commonality with their art, experiences or what they're trying to do. It just doesn't do anything for me. . . . I couldn't relate [to gay culture]. I didn't like disco, I didn't want to go to the gym and I didn't want to grow a mustache back then. I didn't think about going out and scoring every five minutes. I didn't want to hang around in bars. I grew up being into reading books, rock and roll, art and my friends were always really mixed people. I'd go into that world to get laid just like anybody. It still doesn't interest me at all. I'm an anarchist by philosophy so I'm not interested in this collective stuff so it doesn't comfort me to feel like I'm part of some sub-group." "LITERATURE: INTERVIEW WITH DENNIS COOPER," http://www.3ammagazine.com/litarchives /2001_dec/interview_dennis_cooper.html.

13. Dennis Cooper, *Tiger Beat* (Los Angeles: Little Caesar, 1978).

14. Ilana Nash, "Hysterical Scream or Rebel Yell? The Politics of Teen-Idol Fandom," in *Disco Divas: Women and Popular Culture in the 1970s*, ed. Sherrie Inness (Philadelphia: University of Pennsylvania Press, 2003), 144.

15. Dennis Cooper, "Boy Talk," in *Tiger Beat*, n.p.

16. Frank O'Hara, *The Collected Poems of Frank O'Hara*, ed. Donald Allen (Berkeley: University of California Press, 1995), 325.

17. Bill Morgan, *Beat Generation in New York: A Walking Tour of Jack Kerouac's City* (San Francisco: City Lights, 1997), 34.

18. Cooper, "Boy Talk."

19. Dennis Cooper, "Diary 1978–1981," Friday, October 13, 1978, Dennis Cooper Papers, Series 4, Folder 715, Fales Library and Special Collections, New York University.

20. Ibid., Monday, October 23, 1978.

21. Ibid., Tuesday, October 31, 1978.

22. Ibid., Wednesday, November 1, 1978.

23. Ibid., Thursday, November 2, 1978.

24. Rudy Kikel, "A Review by Rudy Kikel," *Gay Community News*, Dennis Cooper Papers, Series 1A, Folder 4.

25. Dennis Cooper Papers, Series 1A, Folder 4.

26. Danny Fields to Dennis Cooper, September 11, 1978, Series 1A, Folder 3, Dennis Cooper Papers.

27. "Cooper's affection for the New York School enabled Little Caesar Press to develop a book list that perhaps indirectly provides an estimate of how thoroughly the New York School by the late 1970s had managed to influence young poets on a national level. Not only did Cooper publish books by poets from Los Angeles such as Amy Gerstler and David Trinidad, who would go on to appear in anthologies edited by Anne Waldman . . . but Cooper also published substantial collections by poets such as Lewis Macadams, Tom Clark, and Peter Schjeldahl as well as Michael Lally, Elaine Equi, Dlugos, and Eileen Myles." "Little Caesar," in Terrence Diggory, ed., *Encyclopedia of the New York School Poets* (New York: Facts on File, 2009), 295.

28. Qtd. in Stosuy, *Up Is Up, but So Is Down*, 467.

29. In an interview with Steve Lafreniere featured in *Vice*, Cooper identified the Poetry Project at St. Mark's Church and a number of New York School–affiliated magazines as crucial to his developing sensibility: "Particularly inspiring to me was a New York one called *A Muzzled Ox* [*sic*—the correct title of this magazine is *Unmuzzled Ox*]. It had pictures, that's what interested me. It had the usual New York crowd publishing in it, but it was just a little bit more multimedia-looking and I liked that. And then Kenward Elmslie had his magazine *Z*, and I was really into that and some of the others like *The World*, and *Angel Hair*. There was also this press in Boston called Telegraph that was really big to me. They did these small books. They did Patti Smith's first book. They did Brigid Polk's *Scars*." "Dennis Cooper on Zine Days (They Were Good) and Transgressive Blogs (There Is Such a Thing)," *Vice*, https://www.vice.com/en_uk/read/dennis-cooper-v14n12.

30. Dennis Cooper and Jim Glaeser, "Introduction," *Little Caesar* 1, no. 1 (1976): 1.

31. Ibid.

32. Ibid. Rexroth was a foundational figure in the San Francisco poetry scene during the 1950s, promoting poetry readings, poetry-jazz events, and the like. Rexroth helped organize the legendary Six Gallery reading on October 7, 1955, at which Ginsberg read his poem "Howl" to great acclaim.

33. The relationship between punk and poetry was heightened all the more in Cooper's Beyond Baroque reading series that took place in Venice Beach during the same period Cooper was editing *Little Caesar*. A flyer for one particular reading, for example, displayed the message "POETRY For PUNKS FREE POETRY READINGS," followed by a list of that evening's participants (Cooper, Glaeser, Mark Watt, and Charles Wasserburg).

34. *Little Caesar* can also be understood as anticipating the combustible queer-core DIY subculture of the mid-1980s and early 1990s that found 'zine publishers like Bruce LaBruce and bands including Tribe 8 and Pansy Division employing a punk style to celebrate a queerness that contested both the homophobia of straight society and the increasingly mainstream gay movement itself.

35. Dennis Cooper, *Little Caesar* 1, no. 3 (1977): n.p.

36. In *Little Caesar* 11, Cooper went on to publish a photo spread of the artist David Wojnarowicz in a Rimbaud mask wandering the streets and subways of New York City.

37. Dennis Cooper, "The Population of Heaven on Earth," *Little Caesar* 1, no. 3 (1977): n.p.

38. Arthur Rimbaud, *A Season in Hell. The Illuminations* (Oxford: Oxford University Press, 1974), 115.

39. While Cooper claimed in his editor's letter in *Little Caesar* 6 that "In the beginning we were going to be a punk poetry zine. That seemed pointless quickly," this and later issues of *Little Caesar* seemed committed precisely to the "punk poetry zine" vision, particularly the poetry of the New York School and related writers. Indeed, given that this issue featured a full-page photo of Billy Idol on the page facing Cooper's letter, it's safe to say we should take Cooper's denial with a grain of salt.

40. Peter Schjeldahl, "On Cocksucking," *Little Caesar* 8 (1979): 63.

41. The Stooges, "T.V. Eye," *Fun House* (New York: Elektra, 1970).

42. Dennis Cooper and Toby Ross, "The Toby Ross Interview," *Little Caesar* 10 (1980): 10.

43. Brad Gooch, "Origami," *Little Caesar* 10 (1980): 11.

44. Lawrence Grossberg, *Dancing in Spite of Myself: Essays on Popular Culture* (Durham, N.C.: Duke University Press, 1997), 4.

45. Though often associated with the Black Mountain poets, New York School writers also appreciated Wieners. He appeared regularly in magazines including John Ashbery and Harry Mathews's *Locus Solus*, Ted Berrigan's *C*, and Lewis Warsh and Anne Waldman's *Angel Hair*. Frank O'Hara dedicated a poem to him entitled, simply, "To John Wieners" (*Collected Poems*, 247).

46. *Little Caesar* 6 included Cooper's passionate obituary for the Quick, who had broken up recently, followed by diary entries by Gerard Malanga. Some pages later, readers were treated to "OUT TO LUNCH: A Portfolio of Silly Visuals by Joe Brainard," work by Ted Berrigan and Tim Dlugos, and Wieners's poems from the mid-1960s.

47. Dick Hebdige, "Style as Homology and Signifying Practice," in *On Record: Rock, Pop, and the Written Word*, ed. Simon Frith and Andrew Goodwin (London: Routledge, 2006), 50.

48. John Wieners, "With You Gone," *Little Caesar* 6 (1978): 24; John Wieners, "An Evocation," *Little Caesar* 6 (1978): 26.

49. "Dennis Cooper on Zine Days."

50. By the late 1970s and early 1980s, many of the New American and New York School poets had been folded into one academic environment or another. In 1975, for example, John Ashbery won the Pulitzer, National Book Critic's Circle Award, and National Book Award for his *Self-Portrait in a Convex Mirror*. James Schuyler received the Pulitzer in 1980 for his *The Morning of the Poem*. Other New York School and Beat Generation poets had found an alternative academic home at the Jack Kerouac School of Disembodied Poetics based at Naropa University, Boulder, Colorado.

51. Jon Savage to Dennis Cooper, February 19, Series 2, Folder 447, Dennis Cooper Papers.

52. Dennis Cooper, *Closer* (New York: Grove, 1990), 28.

53. As Dave Markey's particularly important documentary of Sonic Youth and related bands' 1991 tour through Europe put it, 1991 was "the year punk broke." 1991 was also the year Nirvana's second album *Nevermind* was released—it went on to sell over thirty million copies.

54. Mayer's "Experiments" list concludes with the injunction "work yr ass off to change the language & don't ever get famous." Bruce Andrews and Charles Bernstein, eds., *The L=A=N=G=U=A=G=E Book* (Carbondale: Southern Illinois University Press, 1984), 83.

55. One of Cooper's promotional blurbs for Pavement written to promote the band's 1997 album *Brighten the Corners* asked rhetorically: "Is there a smarter American rock band than Pavement? Hard to imagine. It's been said that literature sacrificed itself back in the 60s so that rock could grow. That's when poetic kids picked up guitars. That's when the rock song turned sneaky, erudite and sublime on occasion, and the novel began overstating the obvious, except in rare instances. From Pavement's earliest four-tracks (see: *Westing [By Musket and Sextant]*) to the phenomenal *Brighten the Corners* (see: enclosed), [the band has] been writing and recording great, picturesque, spooky, wacked out, tear jerking soul music that finesses American experience like nothing else on record, in print, on film, or in art galleries. Take it from an awestruck novelist who's prone to overstating the obvious. Pavement aren't just America's most literate band, they could be its finest living writers, I mean in addition to their songs being wildly catchy and unpretentious and all that." "Pavement at Matastore View," http://store.matadorrecords.com/artists/view/name/pavement.

Afterword: People Who Died

1. Chet Flippo, "A Star Is Borning," *New York* (January 26, 1981): 32.

2. Ibid.

3. Ibid.

4. Ibid.

5. Ibid., 35.

6. Ibid.

7. Ibid. Carroll adds that he was scheduled to perform with Smith on the night of her first reading at St. Mark's. "I was supposed to read with her the first night she

did it with music, with Lenny Kaye playing guitar behind her, but I got busted in Rye, New York, because I was visiting a friend who had some hash. So I was in jail." Ibid.

8. In his blurb for Carroll's *The Basketball Diaries*, Burroughs swooned, "With an eye for detail & ear for narrative, Jim Carroll brings us through a world of youthful crime and streetplay, where drugs are as much a commonplace as sasparilla was when I was a boy. He must be a born writer." As Chris Norris reminds us, "*The Basketball Diaries* won [Carroll's] hero Kerouac's apocryphal but oft-repeated line, 'At 13 years of age, Jim Carroll writes better prose than 89 percent of the novelists working today.'" Chris Norris, "Wild and Free," *NYMag.com*, http://nymag.com/news/intelligencer/59263/.

9. Jim Carroll, *Forced Entries: The Downtown Diaries, 1971-1973* (New York: Penguin, 1987), 29.

10. Flippo, "A Star Is Borning," 35.

11. Carroll, *Forced Entries*, 58–59.

12. Flippo, "A Star Is Borning," 35.

13. Carroll felt strongly about reconciling intellectual and emotional registers in both his poetry and rock lyrics. Near the end of his interview with Flippo, for example, he offered: "Henry Miller's study of Rimbaud, which is really a study of Henry Miller, was the big factor for me going into rock—that was *it*. That whole thing about getting a heart quality out of work rather than just the intellectual quality. A good poet works on both. Miller spoke about the inner register and how a good poet has to affect virtual illiterates as well as affecting people through the intellect, and I figured so many poets are just writing for other poets today. It's all intellectual concrete minimal poetry." Carroll then ended the piece with a dig at the L=A=N=G=U=A=G=E poets: "There's a school of poets in San Francisco called Language Poets. What the fuck does that mean?" Ibid.

14. Ted Berrigan, *The Collected Poems of Ted Berrigan* (Berkeley: University of California Press, 2005), 236.

15. Ibid., 237. Woody Guthrie actually died in October 1967. Neal Cassady actually died in February 1968.

16. Ted Berrigan, *Ted Berrigan Reading*, BBC Radio 3, February 1, 1971, SA: P602, Beats and Friends Collection, British Library.

17. Carroll, *Forced Entries*, 164.

18. Jim Carroll, *The Basketball Diaries* (New York: Penguin, 1987), 37.

19. Dennis Cooper, "King of the Jumble: The Sense and Sensibility of Pavement's Stephen Malkmus," *Spin* (June 1997): 74.

20. My thanks to Andrew Gorin for providing me with the phrase "parodist of poetic rhetoric."

21. For further links between the New York School of poetry and contemporary musicians, see Andrew Epstein, https://newyorkschoolpoets.wordpress.com/category/music/page/2/.

22. "The Compleat Purge," *Kenning Editions*, http://www.kenningeditions.com/shop/the-compleat-purge/.

23. Sean Bonney, "Poems," http://www.onedit.net/issue6/issue6.html.

Index

"Heroin" (Velvet Underground):
  analysis of, 59–63; on drug addiction, 60–63; homosexuality in, 60,
  62; "Howl" (Ginsberg) compared to,
  60–62; Januszczak on, 59; sailor suits
  in, 62–63
heroism, 13–14, 124, 126, 138, 231n43,
  251n32
"Hey Joe" (Smith), 9, 11
"Hip Hip Hustle in New York City"
  (Chatham), 5–6
Holiday, Billie, 204–5
homosexuality: in "At the Old Place,"
  150; Cooper on, 198, 200, 261n12; in
  "Heroin," 60, 62; in "Howl" (Ginsberg), 150; in *Little Caesar*, 209–12;
  *The New Fuck You: Adventures in
  Lesbian Reading* and, 257n9; in
  "Pornographic Poem," 148–52; sailor
  suits and, 62–63, 150, 240nn75–77
Horses (Smith), 122–23, 140–43, 258n16
"Hot Ice, Seed Water, Letterfwesh"
  (Hell), 104–6, 247n43
How(ever), 84, 244n38
"Howl" (Fugs), 12, 35–38, 233n11
"Howl" (Ginsberg), 12, 24, 36, 123,
  233n11; analysis of, 37–38; distribu-
  tion of, 23; "Heroin" compared to,
  60–62; homosexuality in, 150; jazz
  relating to, 46

"I Belong to the Beat Generation"
  (McKuen), 114–15
"I'm Tired of Being Scared" (Giorno),
  146–47
"I'm Waiting for My Man" (Reed),
  239n70
International Fuck Frank O'Hara
  Movement, 181–84
"International Poetry Incarnation"
  (mass reading), 38
"IT" (Hell), 106–7

Januszczak, Waldemar, 59
jazz: Beats on, 46–47; "The Destruction
  of America" and, 158–63; in drug

culture, 25; "Howl" (Ginsberg)
  relating to, 46; influences on,
  162–64, 255nn51–52; poetry and, 25,
  46; popular culture and, 25
"Jim and Tom" (Mapplethorpe), 167–69
Jim Carroll Band, 216–17. *See also*
  Carroll, Jim
Johansen, David, 16
*John Giorno & Anne Waldman: A Kulchur
  Selection*, 88
Jones, LeRoi, 23, 43
Joseph, Brandon, 41
Joyce, James, 104–5
Just Kids (Smith), 125, 128, 250n18

Kaye, Lenny, 4, 10, 14
Kennedy, John, Jr., 209
Kerouac, Jack, 25, 45–46, 243n25
Kikel, Rudy, 206–7
Kiley, Rilo, 225
"Kimberly" (Smith), 141
Kline, Greta, 225
Knowles, Christopher, 169
Koch, Kenneth, 9, 42, 54, 61, 72, 75, 146,
  182–83, 204, 224, 230n35, 236n5,
  237n28, 242n15
Koff: "Bill Kushner" in, 182–83; Interna-
  tional Fuck Frank O'Hara Movement
  and, 181–84; issue 1 of, 178–81, 258n16;
  issue 2 of, 181; issue 3 of, 181–84; issue
  4 of, *184*, 185, 257n8, 258n27; Myles
  and, 176–85; Rotten in, 178–81, *180*
Kotz, Liz, 257n9
Kozak, Roman, 11
Kubernik, Harvey, 7, 229n22
Kupferberg, Tuli, 20, 233n11; avant-
  garde poetry and, 22; Miles and, 27,
  28; solo albums by, 38

Latimer, Tirza, 240n75
Laughner, Peter, 18
Laundromat reading: Myles and,
  188–93; poets involved in, 259n41
Lautréamont, Comte de, 91–92, 102–3
law, 23–24
Lewis, Jeffrey, 19, 20